CORRUPTION, DEVELOPMENT AND UNDERDEVELOPMENT

Also by Robin Theobald and published by Duke University Press

POLITICAL CHANGE AND UNDERDEVELOPMENT: A Critical Introduction to Third World Politics (*with Vicky Randall*)

Corruption, Development and Underdevelopment

Robin Theobald
Senior Lecturer in Sociology
Polytechnic of Central London

Duke University Press   Durham

First published 1990
Published in in the USA by Duke University Press
Durham, North Carolina

Printed in Great Britain
on acid free paper ∞

Library of Congress Cataloging-in-Publication Data
Theobald, Robin.
Corruption, development, and underdevelopment/ Robin Theobald.
p.   cm.
ISBN 0–8223–1027–9.—ISBN 0–8223–1044–9 (pbk.)
1. Corruption (in politics)   2. Corruption (in politics)—
Developing countries.   I. Title.
JF1081.T47   1990
320.9172'4—dc20   89–23393
                                                           CIP

To my mother and to the memory of my father, and to Alma and Arthur

Contents

Preface

At the beginning of 1983 I was sitting shivering in my office at the University of Jos – it was the coldest harmattan season for twenty-five years – when I became conscious of the fact that the lecture rooms opposite, normally in continuous use, were unusually quiet. Looking out of the window I was surprised to discover that they were totally deserted. Some kind of spontaneous strike seemed to be taking place although for what reason I knew not. About an hour later I was to find out for a huge body of students surged by singing repeatedly to the tune of John Lennon's 'Give Peace a Chance': 'All we are saying, Shagari must go!' What prompted this outburst, it transpired, was the news that the Nigerian Telecommunications Building in Lagos – the country's main link with the outside world – had been deliberately set ablaze in an attempt to conceal a multi-million naira fraud involving telephone bills. It is certain that the students' demonstration articulated the profound disgust felt by the overwhelming majority of ordinary Nigerians over an act which displayed a quite appalling degree of irresponsibility and total disregard for public property. Not only had the culprits stolen large amounts of public money, they were prepared to go to the lengths of destroying a crucial national asset in order to escape detection.

For me, however, this was not the most shocking affair in what was a generally atrocious period. Some months later, just before the general election of that year, I read in the newspaper that armed guards had had to be placed on government-owned flats in Lagos in order to stop departing assemblymen stealing the furniture and fittings. Here was one of the most highly-paid and privileged groups in the country apparently stooping to make off with relatively minor items they could easily have afforded to buy. To be fair, however, it is likely that it was probably not the assemblymen themselves who were doing the pilfering but less well-off members of their followings. It is also likely that what had been a few cases had been blown up into a full-scale scandal by anti-government newspapers. None the less even had there been only one case the fact that it could be presented as normal behaviour for politicians is indicative of the contempt in which they were popularly held.

What I found particularly depressing about such incidents was the contrast between the conduct of the politicians and their hangers-on and that of ordinary Nigerians. In my experience not only were the vast majority of market people, traders and even the much-maligned taxi drivers extremely open and above board in their dealings, but I encountered a number of examples of exemplary honesty, ironically usually on the part of people who were obviously poor. Furthermore I had frequently to deal with minor public officials as well as policemen and soldiers at roadblocks, never bribed anyone and was invariably met with courtesy and cooperation. How then was one to explain this awesome contrast between the Nigerian masses and the people who were supposed to represent their interests and administer their society?

With this kind of question in mind I embarked upon a lengthy journey which has taken me, in terms of the literature I have had to cover, well beyond the bounds of Nigeria. Originally I sought an understanding of the roots of corruption in the more developed countries of Tropical Africa. However I soon found my field of study extending beyond that continent to the third world generally and ultimately to developed countries. The more I examined corruption the more it seemed best to treat it as a universal phenomenon which manifests itself in ways that vary with specific social and economic backgrounds. After more than five years of reading books and articles I believe that I have clarified my thinking about corruption, and the related phenomenon of patrimonialism, to a degree which I hope will be of interest not simply to those concerned with corruption, but to that wider academic body which is preoccupied with development and political change generally. I should emphasise that this is not a detailed study of corruption as such in either developed or underdeveloped parts of the world. Many such studies already exist and without them this book could not have been written. Rather this is an attempt to understand the interrelationships between the private appropriation and abuse of public authority on the one hand, and the course of social and economic change on the other.

My greatest debt in writing this book is to my wife Elizabeth and my three sons Wally, Ernie and Dave for their stoicism and good humour in the face of exceptional provocation. I must also thank my colleagues at the PCL – Bob Freedman, Vicky Randall and Len Shackleton – for reading and commenting on various parts of this work. Thanks also to PCL librarian Martin Faulkner, for extending to me over many years the benefit of his encyclopaedic knowledge of social science publications. In addition I am extremely grateful to Alan Doig for reading and supplying many acute observations on an earlier piece, as well as to Luis Roniger for his generous comments on an article I wrote some years ago, as well as for subsequent help. Naturally none of the above bears any responsibility for what follows.

ROBIN THEOBALD

The author and publishers are grateful to André Deutsch for permission to reproduce copyright material from V. S. Napaul's *A Bend in the River*.

1 What is Corruption?

MOSCA: But what, sir if they ask
          After the body?
VOLPONE: Say it was corrupted.
MOSCA: I'll say it stunk, sir; and was fain t'have it
          Coffined up instantly and sent away.

Ben Jonson, *Volpone* Act v, scene 1

It would be very convenient if we could start off with a neat definition of corruption and proceed to spend the rest of the book looking at actual examples in some detail. But corruption, like many other forms of behaviour when placed under the scrutiny of the social science lens, proves to be an elusive and complex phenomenon: in fact the more one examines it the more difficult it becomes to separate corruption from other forms of social exchange. The task of definition is not made easier by the fact that corruption, by its very nature, is inseparable from questions of public morality and morality in general. This has sometimes excited a tendency to condemn which has impeded objective analysis. It is perhaps not surprising, therefore, that some writers whilst dealing with the phenomenon in some detail have deliberately avoided defining it (see, for example, Williams, 1987). My feeling, however, is that an attempt at definition should be made not simply out of the primordial academic need to demarcate, to classify or to pigeon-hole, but because, I suggest, the enterprise itself helps us to tease out the essential characteristics of the phenomenon under discussion.

Where do we start? A suitably uncontroversial beginning is provided by the Oxford English Dictionary which identifies nine meanings of corruption. These nine may be roughly grouped into three with the first referring to the process of physical decay, disintegration and decomposition with associated unwholesomeness and putrefaction. Secondly corruption is used to signify moral deterioration and decay; a loss of innocence or decline from a condition of purity. However, it is the third general meaning of corruption with which we

1

shall primarily be concerned in this book; one that relates specifically to the sphere of government and administration, to the discharge of *public* duties: 'Perversion or destruction of integrity in the discharge of public duties by bribery or favour; the use or existence of corrupt practices, esp. in a state of public corporation'.

The salient characteristic of this *political* variant of corruption is on a *public* sphere, on a realm of public affairs. As it happens not a few academics seeking to define political corruption relate it to this public sphere, to a conception of public office:

> Corruption is behaviour of public officials which deviates from accepted norms in order to serve private ends. (Huntington, 1968, p. 59)

> Corruption is behaviour which deviates from the formal duties of a public role because of private-regarding (Personal, close family, private clique) pecuniary or status gains; or violates rules against the exercise of certain types of private-regarding influence. (Nye, 1978, p. 565)

> Corruption is the misuse of public power for private profit. (Senturia, 1931, vol IV)

> The practice of using the power of office for making private gain in breach of laws and regulations nominally in force. (Andreski, 1968, p. 92)

Such definitions obviously depend upon the existence of a public domain which is recognisably separate from the private sphere. So far as social scientists are concerned any conception of public office is strongly influenced by Max Weber's ideal type of rational-legal bureaucracy. This is a bureaucracy which is run by hierarchically ordered corps of officials who are recruited and promoted according to objective criteria such as educational qualifications and professional experience; who are paid a regular salary which is graded according to rank and qualifications; and who are allocated fixed jurisdictional areas governed by clearly laid down rules and procedures. The core characteristics of this type of bureaucracy are impartiality, impersonality and, above all, the strict separation of incumbent and office. The means of administration are administered on behalf of others, usually the state or a private corporation.

Weber conceived of legal-rational bureaucracy in ideal type form so that empirical examples are never more than an approximation to it. Nonetheless the bureaucratic principle, the tendency for human affairs to be organised more and more along bureaucratic lines, is well advanced in modern industrial societies. Although bureaucratic forms of organisation now exist in all areas of human activity, it is in the state apparatus where this form first emerged. The development of the nation-state in the nineteenth century resulted in the consolidation of modern public administration; the appearance of the career public servant who allegedly makes decisions on the basis of neutral, universalistic criteria and scrupulously segregates public affairs from personal interests. Most discussions of corruption are informed in one way or another by this conception.

However the public office perspective on corruption has not gone unchallenged, having for a number of writers certain important limitations. The most important of these are described below.

The first objection maintains that the notion of public office originally emerged in European societies and is essentially a western concept. In underdeveloped countries (UDCs) public office as an institution and the ethos that goes with it are not well established. In such countries nepotism, patronage and minor forms of bribery embodied in gift-giving, far from attracting opprobrium, are often socially approved. Therefore a definition which is based on the notion of public office imposes on many if not most of the countries in the world a conception and related norms of behaviour which are quite alien to them.

A second objection argues that to make public office central to definitions of corruption requires that we accept the standards of a government which defines the norms and procedures of the public offices within its jurisdiction. This may involve implicitly condoning a regime which is extremely repressive and which regularly abuses the most basic of human liberties. Some governments, for example, have publicly justified the use of torture against 'enemies of the state'. Do we regard, therefore, the action of a policeman who takes a bribe not to torture a suspect or to torture him/her less severely, as an example of corruption? (see Rose-Ackerman, 1978, Chapter 1). The moral and conceptual dilemmas thrown up by such questions, together with the implicit endorsement of obnoxious or unacceptable behaviour, are seen as major shortcomings of the public office conception of corruption.

A third objection submits that the idea of public office which typically underpins definitions is imbued with a spurious precision.

That is to say bureaucratic roles are commonly conceived in terms of sets of rules and procedures which are precisely formulated so that non-compliance is immediately and unequivocally apparent. In fact the vast body of literature on formal organisations, both public and private, clearly demonstrates that the performance of all bureaucratic roles involves an element of discretion or some degree of flexibility in the interpretation of rules and procedures. Indeed many writers have argued that without this area of discretion bureaucracies could not function; rigid adherence to the rules would rapidly bring administration to a standstill. Therefore to base one's conception of corruption on deviations from the norms of public office when such deviations are usual, if not necessary, is to invite confusion.

If the question of deviations from the norms of public office presents difficulties, the situation of elected politicians is even more problematic. And here we come to a fourth limitation of the public office conception. There are no formal qualifications for politicians, neither are there clear-cut rules and procedures as to how they should behave once elected, other than those relating to the rituals of debate as well as the constraints imposed by the need for party discipline. Whereas the behaviour of civil servants, particularly in relation to outside interests and the acceptance of gifts, is usually quite circumscribed, politicians need to endure few restraints. In Britain a member of parliament may accept regular retainers or lavish hospitality from commercial interests, foreign governments or trades unions. An MP may hold company directorships, run a law practice or a firm of consultants. Although there are procedures for the registration and declaration of outside interests, contravention of them does not necessarily lead to censure. Aside from behaviour at elections it is extremely difficult to decide at what point an elected politician may be said to be abusing his office for private gain. For this reason many writers choose to treat administrative corruption separately from electoral and legislative corruption. Weber was in fact thinking of administrators and not elected politicians when he formulated his ideal type. For the time being we note that public office-centred definitions seem to present certain difficulties when applied to the situation of politicians.

Finally, there is the argument that both the idea and the reality of public office are very recent historical developments, that in pre-modern times the all-important distinction between a public and a private sphere did not exist. Mediaeval monarchs, Mogul emperors and the sultans of Sokoto regarded the state as their personal property and patrimony, whose resources were to be disposed of to favourites, supporters, hangers-on and the like entirely at their discretion.

Similarly, these royal 'officials' regarded their offices or positions as their private property making no distinction between the taxes, customs or revenues they collected and their personal wealth. To insist that corruption is irrevocably bound up with the notion of public office is to deny its existence in the pre-modern era. This presents something of a problem because conceptions of corrupt behaviour quite clearly existed in pre-modern times. From Biblical times through the classical period to mediaeval and early modern Europe there are numerous examples of laws against corruption as well as prosecutions of the perpetrators of corrupt actions (see, for example, Venkatappiah, 1968).

PUBLIC INTEREST

In the light of these and other perceived weaknesses of the public office conception of corruption other approaches have been suggested. One of these is to focus on the 'public interest'. Corruption in this view is behaviour which is inimical to the public interest and involves the subversion of the public interest for private ends:

> A *corrupt act* violates responsibility toward at least one system of public or civic order and is in fact incompatible with (destructive of) any such system. A system of public or civic order exalts common interest over special interest; violations of the common interest for special advantage are corrupt. (Rogow and Lasswell, 1963, p. 132)

This definition turns on the meaning of 'responsibility', which is understood by Rogow and Lasswell in terms of the individual citizen striving 'to protect the fundamental institutions and the basic pattern of value distributions within the commonwealth'.

Carl Friedrich also takes a similar line:

> Corruption can be said to exist whenever a power-holder who is charged with doing certain things, i.e. who is a responsible functionary or office-holder, is by monetary or other rewards not legally provided for induced to take actions which favour whoever provides the reward and thereby does damage to the public and its interests. (Friedrich, 1966, p. 74; see also Hurstfield, 1967, p. 19)

The main difficulty with this type of approach centres upon the vagueness of terms like 'public' or 'common' interest. In small scale hunting, gathering or pastoral societies it may be possible to decide upon what constitutes the common interest, but in large, complex societies this task seems to present insuperable problems. Are trades unions in the public interest? Is cigarette smoking? Is a shoot-to-kill policy against alleged terrorists in Ulster in the public interest? The answers to such questions rather depend upon whether one is a trades unionist, employer, right- or left-wing politician, a cigarette smoker, doctor, cigarette manufacturer, member of the Royal Ulster Constabulary, Northern Irish catholic, protestant and so on. In other words, in complex societies there is not just one but a wide range of publics each with its own interests. Under such circumstances 'the' public interest tends to be appropriated by politically dominant groups and used to protect their position. This will often entail restricting the flow of information or the liberties of individuals or groups who are seen to be subverting the 'public' or 'national' interest. History, of course, is replete with examples where the 'national interest' has required the denial of basic rights, repression and even physical extermination of minorities and sometimes majorities (for example South Africa and Burundi).

A second defect in the public interest approach relates to the position of a number of writers (whose arguments we shall consider later) who have maintained that certain forms of corruption can actually have beneficial consequences for a society such as promoting economic growth or fostering political stability. This seems to be suggesting that corruption can be in the public interest which, if true, creates difficulties for a definition which demands that it cannot. In effect Friedrich does recognise that corruption can play a 'positive role' where, for example, a cumbersome administrative system obstructs the implementation of much-needed policies. His interpretation of such a situation is that this is not really a case of corruption but the 'employment of deviant and devious modes for accomplishing what is necessary'. Such a position, however, does not help us surmount the obstacles presented by the imprecision of the term 'public interest'. On the contrary it seems to point to a series of rather arbitrary classifications which are unlikely to be analytically productive. For these reasons it is sometimes argued that 'public opinion' is preferable to 'public interest'.

PUBLIC OPINION

One of the main advantages of relying on 'public opinion' seems to be that it gets us over the problems presented by imposing the western-based public office concept. Corruption then is simply what public opinion in a given society deems to be corrupt. But, again, what is public opinion? Public opinion is not some monolithic entity but a confection of shifting and often conflicting 'opinions'. Under such circumstances the problem of deciding which section of public opinion to focus upon seems to pose serious difficulties. As with 'public interest' there is a danger of fixing upon the opinions of vociferous, dominant or politically powerful groups. This in fact seems to be the line positively advocated by Senturia in his entry 'Corruption, Political' in the *Encyclopaedia of the Social Sciences*: 'Where the best opinion and political morality of the time, examining the intent and setting of an act, judge it to represent a sacrifice of public for private benefit, it must be held corrupt' (Senturia, 1931).

Heidenheimer, however, in an ingenious and complex typology seems to eschew this distinctly elitist slant proposing instead three types of corruption 'white', 'gray' and 'black'. Black corruption designates those actions which a majority consensus of both elite and mass opinion in a given society would condemn and want to see punished. Gray corruption exists when some elements, usually elites, would condemn the action while the masses may be ambiguous. In the case of white corruption neither a majority of mass nor elite opinion would see the action as worthy of punishment, although some elite elements might.

Heidenheimer combines these three categories of corruption with ten types of behaviour exploring the incidence of and reactions to the latter in four basic types of political system (Heidenheimer, 1978, pp. 3–30). His typology is interesting in that it emphasises the variability of societal reaction to various types of behaviour (for example from minor forms of nepotism to outright extortion). Whereas a given action may excite immediate and widespread condemnation in one society, in a second it may be widely tolerated. Despite this one wonders about the applicability of Heidenheimer's typology in concrete situations. Terms such as 'elite', 'elite opinion', 'mass' and 'mass opinion' are rather insubstantial and extremely difficult to identify with any degree of accuracy in specific situations. So despite its apparent sophistication Heidenheimer's approach does not overcome the vagueness and imprecision of terms like public opinion.

Given the difficulties presented by these alternatives might it not be prudent to reconsider the public office approach and ask whether it can meet the criticisms laid against it?

WESTERN BIAS?

With regard to the western bias of the public office conception it is certainly true that the universalism and impersonalism which are typically seen as the core features of modern bureaucracies are unfamiliar, not to say alien, to many if not most of the societies in the world today. The abundant literature on peasant societies leaves no doubt as to the pervasive importance of *personal* forms of exchange (see, for example, Wolf, 1966). The individual peasant is linked through a network of dyadic relationships with members of his immediate family, wider kin and the community at large. Through this network the peasant obtains the 'resources' that are indispensible to his existence: land, labour, water, women, honour, prestige, moral and armed support. In addition to dyadic relationships some peasants may be linked to socially and politically dominant patrons for whom resources such as land, jobs, loans and legal and physical protection may be exchanged for loyalty, deference, information, violence against 'troublemakers' and the like. Whatever the nature of the relationship it is personal, with known individuals and able to endure over time.

This is in marked contrast to the fleeting, anonymous, 'single-stranded' relationships which predominate in industrial societies, especially within the orbit of public administration. Accordingly if the peasant finds himself in a position where he must deal with a 'functionary' to obtain, say, a tax certificate, register his land, find a hospital bed or a school place, then he will look around for someone who is known to him, someone he can trust – a relative, friend, co-religionist – either to deal with his case or put him in contact with someone who will. In the west such behaviour is usually referred to as nepotism and is invariably regarded perjoratively as violating the fundamental principles of public administration. In UDCs such practices are viewed differently, being widely tolerated if not specifically approved. Consequently, whatever his own orientation and however modern his outlook, the civil servant in Africa, Asia or Latin America will come under enormous pressure from relatives and friends to 'do something', to find them a job, a school place, obtain government contracts, import permits or scholarships abroad. The relatives of a cooperative supervisor will be dumbfounded, not to say outraged, at his reluctance to give them preferential access to fertilizer, agricultural credits, the cooperative tractor and so on.

The contrast between modern and traditional values in UDCs is

illuminatingly brought out by Wraith and Simpkins, who counterpose
the rampant dishonesty of government officials of Nigeria in the 1960s
– 'local government has reached the point of being a conspiracy against
the public!' – with the well-attested probity of ethnic unions. These
ethnic unions are urban mutual aid associations based upon a
particular ethnic group, usually a specific town or village. The unions
offer financial and other forms of support to their members helping
them particularly to adjust to the urban context. Wraith and Simpkins
are struck by the honesty with which large sums of money are handled
by the unions and the deeply entrenched taboo surrounding theft. This
is in marked contrasts to the alacrity with which *public* funds are
misappropriated and reflects a very different set of values towards
one's peers on the one hand, and towards the public or the state on the
other (Wraith and Simpkins, 1963, ch. 2). Peter Ekeh, in an ingenious
inversion of modernisation theory (to be considered later), contrasts
the 'primordial public' with the 'civic public'. The primordial public
(the public of the ethnic unions for example) is perceived as a sacred
moral universe of sacrifice and duties. The civic public by contrast is a
profane amoral world based on instrumental relationships premised
on the accumulation of *rights* rather than duties (quoted in Onoge,
1982). This profoundly amoral attitude towards the civic order is
immortalised in President Mobuto Sese Seko's advice to Zairean civil
servants: 'if you want to steal, steal a little in a nice way'. (Sandbrook,
1986, p. 95). If such attitudes and values are widely diffused in Africa
and other UDCs where primordial ties continue to exert a powerful
influence, is there not indeed a strong case for rejecting public office as
the defining component of corruption?

Notwithstanding the undoubted western origins and therefore
western bias of the idea of public office, it is certainly the case that
governments throughout the world have adopted modern forms of
public administration. This means that not only are substantial
resources expended on the selection and training of public servants,
but a considerable degree of effort is directed to establishing,
ideologically and institutionally, a corrupt-free public service. Special
departments are set up to police public administration, committees of
inquiry undertaken, purges of civil sevice personnel conducted.
Corruption in many UDCs is probably the most salient political issue;
governments rise and fall on the strength of what they have done or
failed to do about it. The ending of rampant corruption is the most
frequent justification for military takeovers. Therefore in the light of
the formal acceptance by virtually every government in the world of

the desirability of efficient and honest government it seems difficult to avoid using public office as the yardstick against which corruption is measured. In addition, the apparent readiness to use personal connections or bribery when dealing with the state in UDCs should not permit us to conclude that third world masses are indifferent to the negative consequences of these practices. On the contrary there is widespread resentment at having to use them as well as profound disgust at the depredations of politicians and bureaucrats (see, for example, Waterbury, 1976).

ETHICAL PROBLEMS

With regard to the ethical problems of the public office conception – that using it can involve us in implicitly condoning undesirable policies – does seem to present serious difficulties. This is especially the case in the light of the fact that authoritarian and repressive regimes are not unusual in Africa, Asia and Latin America. In fact there is a view that sees the essence of corruption in the use of the state apparatus by a minority for the oppression and exploitation of the majority. Such a view is cogently argued by O. F. Onoge in his keynote address to the Nigerian Anthropological and Sociological Association's conference on corruption in 1982. Onoge proposes that a notion of *primary corruption* should be included in the general discussion of corruption. Primary corruption is the 'class misappropriation of the surplus value created by the labouring majority'. What Onoge refers to as *secondary corruption*, the everyday abuse of office with which we are concerned in this book, is a derivative of primary corruption. Onoge sees it as highly significant that it is in the ranks of those classes which live off the producers (primary corruption) that we find a large proportion of those who have 'elaborated illegitimate appropriation' (secondary corruption) 'to a fine art'. Onoge is interested primarily in Nigeria under the Second Republic (1979–83) but his arguments have a more general application. It could be maintained that there is no grosser form of corruption than the deliberate use of state terror by a minority to maintain its political and economic ascendancy (Onoge, 1982).

The main problem, however, with this position is that it is too all-embracing since the very existence of a state structure necessarily requires the appropriation by a minority of state incumbents of surplus from a majority of producers. Furthermore there is no case in history in which this minority has assiduously and consistently abstained from using its incumbency to enhance its own material and political position. Therefore the very existence of the state entails exploitation – corruption indeed in the sense of movement from the uncorrupted Rousseau-esque state of nature. Yet as we know there are large variations in the degree of exploitation as between states: Duvalier's Haiti as compared to contemporary Denmark; or more interestingly Shagari's Nigeria as compared to Doe's Liberia.

Similarly there are thought to be significant variations in the volume of corruption. What is the relationship between the two? Do more repressive states exhibit higher levels of corruption? Is there a relationship between inequality or GDP per capita and corruption? Are less developed states indeed more prone to corruption than developed ones? These are questions that will be among the central concerns of this book. To attempt to answer them requires some working definition of corruption and the public office version may be the most practical. But this would not mean that we need be oblivious to broader questions of public policy in the societies we are studying. Indeed a basic theme of this book will emphasise the necessity of relating the phenomenon of corruption not only to political and economic conditions within the society under consideration, but also in the world economy.

PERSONALISM WITHIN MODERN BUREAUCRACIES

We turn now to what is probably the most serious difficulty of the public office approach: the fact that it is based on a spuriously precise conception of the bureaucratic role. The problem arises primarily because much of the discussion of public office is informed too closely by Weber's ideal type of rational-legal bureaucracy. The type proposes a hierarchy of roles each with its carefully defined area of competence within which decisions are taken according to clearly laid down criteria. Every incumbent knows exactly where and when his/her competence begins and ends so that departures and deviations from rules and procedures are readily apparent. In reality, of course, decision-making within bureaucracies is never like this as there are a number of apparently insuperable obstacles to complete rationality. The main ones have been usefully set out by Anthony Downs:

1.   Each decision maker can devote only a limited amount of time to decision making.

2.   Each decision maker can mentally weigh and consider only a limited amount of information at one time.

3.   The functions of most officials require them to become involved in more activities than they can consider simultaneously; hence they must normally focus their attention on only part of their major concerns, while the rest remain latent.

4.   The amount of information initially available to every decision maker about each problem is only a small fraction of all the information potentially available on the subject.

5.   Additional information bearing on any particular problem can usually be procured, but the costs of procurement and utilization may rise rapidly as the amount of information increases.

6.   Important aspects of many problems involve information that cannot be procured at all, especially concerning future events; hence many decisions must be made in the face of some ineradicable uncertainty. (Downs, 1967, pp. 61–73)

Whilst we may accept these perhaps obvious limitations in the decision-making situation it may be objected that we are still a long way from corruption which entails the *conscious* abuse of public office for private ends. However Downs goes on to point out that the bias introduced by this pronounced element of uncertainty is amplified by the tendency of incumbents to use these limitations to further their own interests.

Downs identifies four major biases: firstly the tendency of officials to distort information that is passed upwards, exaggerating data which reflects favourably on themselves and minimising that which reveals their weaknesses. Secondly, each official tends to exhibit biased attitudes towards the policy decisions in which he is involved. Biases result from his prejudices either in favour or against programmes which he perceived either will or will not advance his own interests. Thirdly, each official will vary the degree of compliance with directives from above depending upon whether these directives advance or retard his own interests. Certain directives will be implemented with considerable zeal, others with acceptable efficiency and still others with inconspicuous lethargy. Some directives will be ignored altogether so long as it is expedient or safe to do so. Downs maintains that it is virtually impossible for superiors to avoid this situation. The fourth major bias dealt with by Downs concerns the variability as between officials in the degree to which they are prepared to enlarge the scope of their responsibility. All successful organisations, argues

Downs, depend upon the willingness of some of their employees to take on more responsibility than formally required without exhortations from superiors. The willingness of officials to take initiatives, to take risks, varies with such factors as personality, degree of aggression, ambition, passivity and so on.

Downs very effectively points up the artificiality of the distinction between 'politics' and 'administration', a distinction which continues to influence much of the literature on modern government (for examples see the review of literature on public bureaucracies by Sheriff, 1976). All bureaucratic decisions are political in the sense that they are made by individuals who are located within a context of (invariably hierarchical) authority and power, and whose behaviour cannot but be influenced by interests, ambitions, fears, frustrations, the desire for status, achievement or the need for a quiet life, not to mention the complexities of informal group interaction. Hence the image of the civil servant meticulously working through established rules and procedures to reach an objective decision is, to say the least, simplistic. Decision-making and policy formulation in all organisations is, as Hickson and McCullough have succinctly put it, a process of 'muddling through':

A process of decision-making moves spasmodically within a restricted set of possibilities, priorities, switching from one to another and different aspects being weighed in the balance from one point to the next. It arrives gradually at a compromise that will do for the time being within the bounds of power and practicality. That is it 'muddles through' incrementally to a satisfactory solution. (Hickson and McCullough, 1980, p. 50)

Now it may be objected, doubtless with some impatience at this point, that Weber was formulating an ideal type and that everybody knows that organisations in reality do not and cannot function like the abstraction. Although there may be widespread formal recognition of this it is beyond question that the notions of neutrality and universality, the theme that personalism recedes before a tide of rational-legality, continues to permeate discussions of modern bureaucracies and modernisation generally. Furthermore, such ideas implicitly provide a basis for contrast with Third World bureaucracies which are allegedly riven with favouritism, factionalism and personalism, and are heavily politicised.

To illustrate this tendency let us return to the Heidenheimer model touched on above. Heidenheimer combines his three basic categories of corruption with four types of 'political obligation relationship'. These are, firstly, the traditional 'familist' system where loyalty to the nuclear family is the only loyalty that counts. Next come traditional 'patron–client' systems where protection and support are sought outside the family from politically and economically dominant patrons. Thirdly, we have 'Boss–follower' systems which were the basis of the political machines which dominated American cities during the first half of this century. Lastly, we find 'civic culture' based systems which prevail in 'clean' medium-sized towns or suburbs in America or Britain. Under this last dispensation citizens do not feel the need 'to work through an influential intermediary' to obtain benefits from the political process. 'Sophisticated and respectable' forms of political exchange such as testimonial dinners, lawyers fees and campaign funds have now replaced 'crude political reciprocity' such as bribery (Heidenheimer, 1978, pp. 22, 23).

Apart from the somewhat unfortunate reliance on heavily normative terms such as 'clean', 'respectable' and 'crude', the evolutionary drift (the notion that personal mediation is eventually replaced by impersonal organisational forms) is readily apparent in Heidenheimer's scheme. It is probably unfair to single out Heidenheimer at this juncture as his is but one example of an approach which dominated political science and sociology in the 1950s and 1960s. To these modernisation theories we shall return in Chapter 3. Let us meanwhile get back to our attempt to grapple with the problems of defining corruption.

If personalism is widespread, perhaps even dominant (see for example Dalton, 1959; Perrow, 1972) in modern bureaucracies then the dividing line between everyday organisational behaviour and corrupt (or deviant) behaviour becomes much more difficult to draw. There is no problem about the public servant who employs departmental appropriations to set up his own import/export business, or who uses his position to extort payments from subordinates to keep their jobs. But what about the administrator who colludes with associates to exclude information from a report because it will reflect badly on his department and thwart his career ambitions? (For a chilling example see Vandivier, 1978). Or the university lecturer who at a crucial stage in an examination board intervenes on behalf of a student with whom he is having an affair? Or the policeman who takes particulars from a motorist with regard to illegal parking when the day before he had ignored exactly the same offence because he was about to go off duty? Or the municipal dustmen who are less assiduous about collecting rubbish from people who neglected to give them a Christmas gratuity? What if I use my office telephone to book my holidays and so on and so on? One could think of endless examples of behaviour of public employees which it may seem excessively punctilious to label corrupt, but which clearly deviate from what is in some sense expected from persons in their respective positions. The essential point is that all of the above examples would be encompassed by at least three and possibly all four of the definitions introduced at the beginning of this chapter. All entail a degree of illegitimacy as well as a strong element of self-interest.

One way of dealing with the problems posed by this shading over of normal bureaucratic behaviour into illegitimate activities is to formulate some kind of graduated scale of corruption, from 'petty' to 'serious' for example. Charles Schwartz attempts this when dealing with corruption in the USSR, identifying 'black', 'gray' and 'white' variants. White corruption involves no material gain for participants beyond the normal money bonuses for completing the job in good time. But since completing the job has entailed bending and manipulating rules and procedures the term corruption is judged not inappropriate. Gray corruption leads to 'limited' material gains whilst black corruption involves 'politically dysfunctional methods' which bring 'sizable' material gains for their perpetrators (Schwartz, 1979). Whereas Heidenheimer's colour-variegated corruption is meant to reflect public reaction to specified deeds, Schwartz' is the outcome of his own classification. The problem with such an approach is that it tends to be *ad hoc* and descriptive. It also begs the question as to what corruption actually is. These together with the scheme's dependence on such vague notions as 'limited material gains' and 'dysfunctional political methods' raise doubts as to its analytical value.

A LEGALISTIC DEFINITION?

A possible way out of the cumulative difficulties outlined above is to define corruption as the *illegal* use of public office for private gain. The main advantage of such a definition is that it gets us over the apparent impossibility of fixing the point at which the flexibility inherent in the interpretation of all bureaucratic roles becomes corruption. Such a definition could also encompass the activities of administrators and politicians, using the term 'public office' to signify both. We have seen that the liberty which politicians typically enjoy in the performance of their public role makes it practically impossible to define such corrupt activities that they might engage in other than in legalistic terms. However since legal prescriptions concerning the activities of elected representatives tend to focus upon behaviour at elections then the definition needs to be modified to take account of this: 'Political corruption is the illegal use of public office or the process of selection to public office for private ends'. Some comment on the components of this definition is required.

The term 'illegal' means that there exist laws/statutes governing the conduct of those occupying public office and/or the process of selection to public office. Whether or not such laws are actually enforced, whether contravention of them is systematically prosecuted is a quite separate question altogether. Nonetheless it is a question in which we would be interested as the mode of enforcement or non-enforcement of laws tells us a good deal about attitudes, both official and unofficial, to the behaviour which such laws seek to regulate.

In the study of political corruption we shall be concerned with *public* organisations. That is to say the state apparatus, government at both national and local levels together with the organisations set up by and under the ultimate ownership and control of government. In modern industrial societies this will encompass a large number and wide range of organisations from those dealing with core functions of government such as defence, law and order, fiscal and monetary policy to social services such as health, education and the administration of various state benefits; government owned utilities such as airlines, rail networks, power supply together with other publicly-owned industries; to owning and operating public housing schemes and recreational services, as well as engaging in extensive regulatory activities. The focus on the public sphere is justified by its being a qualitatively different area of human affairs. The illegal use of public in the sense of 'corporate' resources is evident in all areas of social life: from business organisations to tennis clubs, from trades unions to pentecostal churches. However the corporation, tennis club, trades union or pentecostal church administers the resources under its control on behalf of that group of people which has voluntarily chosen to invest in or join the body in question. The organs of the state, or at least the modern state, by contrast, administer resources on behalf of the population at large, adult members of which have no choice but to pay taxes and rates as well as the salaries of the public servants who administer them. The public sector, therefore, has a distinctive character and abuses there touch on the very legitimacy of the state itself. Ultimately pervasive political corruption, as numerous commentators throughout history have observed, undermines the moral fabric of society itself (see for example Dobel, 1978). It should be made clear that our focus on the public sphere does not exclude entirely the extremely important area of corporate deviance. But since this area is so large in itself (see for example Ermann and Lundman, 1978) we will be dealing with the corporate deviance only in so far as it impinges on the state.

Now, the most obvious objection to a legalistic view of corruption is that it is far too narrow in scope, excluding from its purview a wide range of behaviour usually considered to be within its orbit. Nepotism is an obvious example. The practice of according favour to relatives and friends in the disbursement of public resources, whether jobs, import licences or public housing, is usually thought to contravene one of the basic principles of modern public administration: the application of universalistic and objective criteria in decision making. Yet even in modern industrial societies nepotism is seldom illegal, although it may be grounds for censure in the case of politicians or for serious disciplinary measures (perhaps even dismissal) in the case of public servants. Other examples of behaviour which might generally be regarded as being within the orbit of corruption are the bestowal of honours on cronies, sycophants and contributors to party funds, fiddling expenses, abuse of confidential information, string-pulling and subtle forms of extortion. Behaviour which, in short, while not perhaps customarily labelled corrupt is nonetheless considered to be unacceptable in that it clearly falls short of what is expected from people in public life. 'Misconduct' or 'malfeasance' are terms which are often applied to this class of behaviour.

Clearly such behaviour is of major interest to anyone studying the phenomenon of political corruption. Accordingly it should be understood that in proposing a legalistic definition I am not suggesting that more general public misconduct be excluded from our purview. On the contrary the interrelationships between activities which society defines as illegal and those adjacent to it, are of key importance in understanding corruption. The legalistic definition here proposed, then, is not intended as a definitive statement as to what corruption is but is aimed at providing a focus for the subsequent discussion – a kind of benchmark on the basis of which further analysis may proceed.

CONCLUSION

We have seen that in the study of political corruption it is difficult to get away from the notion of public office. Certainly 'public office' has a number of limitations but these, I have attempted to argue, do not present us with insuperable difficulties. Furthermore the alternatives that are usually proposed such as 'public interest' and 'public opinion' seem to pose greater problems in operational terms than 'public office'. Having suggested that our discussion of corruption be based upon the idea of abuse of public office I have opted for a legalistic definition on the grounds that the notion of 'illegitimacy' is too vague and does not allow us to distinguish between, on the one hand, the 'innovation' which is a normal feature of the interpretation of all bureaucratic roles and, on the other, what is considered to be deliberate *abuse*. This does not, I emphasise once more, exclude from the scope of this book the consideration of actions by public officials which are frowned upon but tolerated. Indeed the interrelationship between the two will be a central focus, hence the need to offset the illegal from the barely legitimate.

In striving to formulate a workable conception of political corruption I have chosen to break with what has become something of a convention, which is to treat administrative and political corruption separately. It is obviously the case that administrative roles are more narrowly circumscribed than those of politicians. This means, among other things, that the illegal use of administrative position is much more readily observable than abuse by elected representatives. Nonetheless, as we have seen, all administrative roles have a political dimension. Accordingly I want to argue that the difference between politics and administration is one of degree and not one of kind. Indeed I hope to show that the degree to which administrative roles are politicised is central to our understanding of the phenomenon of corruption. Hence I am treating administrative and political corruption as dimensions of the same phenomenon, as different sides of the same coin.

Finally, we have not yet dealt with what has been seen as one of the major weaknesses of the public office approach: this is that since a clear-cut conception of public office is a very recent historical development, making it central to our definition seems to deny the existence of corruption in pre-modern societies, which is clearly contrary to the facts. However in order to deal adequately with this apparent limitation we need to look in some detail at the emergence of modern public administration, which is discussed in the following chapter.

2 The Emergence of Modern Public Administration

RICHARD: We will ourself in person to this war,
And for our coffers with too great a court
And liberal largesse are grown somewhat light,
We are enforced to farm our royal realm,
The revenue whereof shall furnish us
For our affairs in hand.

William Shakespeare, *Richard II* Act I scene iv

In his excellent short study of the development of public services in western Europe Sir Ernest Barker defines the state as 'a territorial society (generally in our times, a territorial nation) organized as a legal association under and in virtue of a constitution. As such an association it observes a common law, and its members enjoy the rights and perform the duties which are guaranteed in that law' (Barker, 1944, p. 3). But, Barker is quick to point out, this is a particularly modern conception of the state belonging to the twentieth century. If we go back to the pre-modern era, to the seventeenth century for example, the state is not regarded as an impersonal legal entity but as the living embodiment of an inheritance which reached into the dim and distant past.

This pre-modern state has three basic characteristics: firstly, it is an emanation of the Royal household, the Royal family – 'The Family is the true source and origin of every Commonwealth' (Jean Bodin, quoted in Barker, 1944, p. 4). Accordingly the French king governed by a sort of *conseille de famille*. Household staff and government officials were indistinguishable. The expenses of government and the expenses of the household are confused and there is no clear-cut separation between the income of the royal family and the revenues of the state. Secondly the state is viewed as personal property, in the first

19

instance the property of the monarch who may legally own the whole territory or at least a part of it. The notion of personal property ramifies through the whole administration so that the appropriation of office as private property, which can be passed on to one's heirs or sold, is quite normal. Thirdly, the state *is* society in the sense that it is immersed in and buffeted by the interplay of social forces of which society is composed. This is the converse of the liberal notion of the state as an entity set apart, and in some sense above, the complex of shifting interests and alliances which constitute the social order.

PATRIMONIALISM

In outlining these characteristics, Barker was thinking primarily of the European absolutist states of the seventeenth and eighteenth centuries. But there are strong grounds for seeing them as features of pre-modern states generally. Weber in fact formulated an ideal type of *patrimonial domination* which embodied the essentials of the pre-modern state. Patrimonialism is a development out of what for Weber was the most basic form of traditional authority – patriarchalism. Patriarchalism is dominated by the head of the household over its members. This form of domination is based upon the filial respect of members of the family and other dependents for the patriarchal head. Within the household, domination is the personal prerogative of the master, who is designated according to the rules of inheritance and succession (i.e. tradition). In securing compliance the patriarch has no administrative or military machine, being solely dependent upon the authority tradition gives to him augmented by his control over key resources such as land, grazing rights, cattle and women (Weber, 1968, pp. 1006–10).

Patrimonialism appears when patriarchalism must extend its authority to meet the needs of an expanding political community, ultimately a state. The main point about this patrimonial state is that it derives its impetus from the need to provide for the ruling household; to ensure regularity of provisions – food, clothing, furnishings, servants, women, manpower, armaments and so on. As a consequence governmental offices originate in the household administration of the ruler. Herein lies the essential difference between patrimonialism and patriarchalism: patrimonial domination requires an administrative apparatus. However the administrators are initially recruited from among kin, followers, servants and other personal dependents of the ruler. In return for their services they are maintained as part of the ruler's household. But to the extent that the state expands its territorial base this arrangement ceases to be practical.

Weber suggests three ways in which officials may be supported. Firstly, there is the *benefice* which consists of an allowance in the form of moveable property – an allowance of produce from royal granaries for example – or from the accumulated wealth of the ruler. The second alternative is a *fee benefice* under which the administrator is entitled to appropriate for his own use such fees, taxes, dues or 'gifts' as the performance of official functions will yield. Lastly the official may be granted a *landed benefice*, a territorial area the produce of which he may appropriate by whatever means can be deployed.

Enserfment is the characteristic mechanism in such cases and Weber recognises that the landed benefice is close to what western historians usually refer to as feudalism. Nonetheless he strives to maintain a distinction between these two basic forms maintaining that patrimonial government is an extension of the ruler's household in which officials are bound to the ruler by their filial dependence. Feudal government, by contrast, replaces the paternalistic bond with voluntary and contractually fixed allegiance by a formally independent military aristocracy. Whether in reality it is possible to maintain such a distinction is a conceptual minefield which we cannot enter here (see Bendix, 1966, pp. 360–9). The essential point is that patrimonialism signifies a particular type of administration, one that differs very markedly from its more familiar successor, rational-legal bureaucracy.

The essential features of rational-legal bureaucracy – hierarchy of graded authority, fixed jurisdictional areas with clear-cut procedures, salaried officials who are recruited and promoted according to objective qualifications and experience and, above all, the strict separation between incumbent and office, between the private and the public spheres – these are almost entirely absent from patrimonial administration. Under the latter office holders are the personal dependents of the ruler, appointed at his whim on the basis of criteria that are subjective and non-standardised. Patrimonial bureaucrats hold office at the pleasure of the ruler and may be moved or dismissed by him when expedient. Such conditions are replicated at lower levels of the administration as officials may appoint their own functionaries according to similar criteria. But all officials, in theory, hold their positions as servants of the traditional ruler. Throughout the administration there are no clear-cut procedures for taking decisions other than the very general bounds set by tradition. Decision-making tends therefore to have an *ad hoc* character and is beset by a fair degree of latitude.

Given this procedural instability together with the absence of remuneration by regular salary, then some degree of appropriation of office is endemic. Under such a system there is a powerful tendency for governmental authority to become a private possession. A key corollary of this is the propensity of the ruler, to the centre, to lose control over the state apparatus at the periphery. Accordingly the central focus of Weber's wide-ranging comparative studies of pre-modern empires is the complex interplay between centrifugal and centripetal forces and correspondingly the tactics adopted by rulers to prevent governmental authority slipping from their grasp. Whilst the ruler may well be able to assert authority and control over household dependents at the centre, the enlargement of the state, the incorporation of additional territorial units, will present serious problems of integration. This is particularly the case when the patrimonial state brings within its orbit social groups, clans, tribes – sub-societies which lack ties of traditional loyalty to the centre. On the contrary such sub-units typically cohere around strong parochial loyalties, often centred on local notables or potentates. Patrimonial rulers may adopt a variety of stratagems in their attempts to counter the local build-up of power. It is not necessary to detail these in this context but a mention of some of the more usual will help the discussion along.

A policy adopted almost universally in pre-modern empires was the creation of local associations which provided the basis for tax collection, corvée labour and the maintenance of law and order through collective responsibility. Patrimonial administrators were also transferred from one area to another in order to prevent their building up a local following. This was a tactic widely employed in the 'despotic' East under a particularly centralised form of patrimonialism which Weber termed 'sultanism'. But even here the ability of the 'sultan' to exercise direct control over his subordinates was severely constrained by his limited resources. As Weber and other writers have pointed out, ultimately the only reliable form of control the state has over its officials is the payment of a regular salary (see for example Moore 1973, ch. 4). But this is unattainable, at least on a permanent basis, in a pre-modern, largely subsistence economy. Certainly there have been instances of rulers who have succeeded in establishing a corps of salaried administrators. The Mogul emperor Akbar (1542–1605) set up a centralised bureaucracy run by a graded corps of *mansabars* who were paid salaries in cash. However it seems that this system depended heavily on the unique talents and determination of its founder. Akbar's successors found it too arduous to maintain and resorted to the time-honoured method of tax farming; that is assigning to the *mansabars* specific areas of the empire from which taxes could be collected in lieu of salary (Spear, 1973, p. 41).

Poor communications and a predominantly subsistence economy with limited cash transactions severely inhibit the centre's ability to appropriate the revenue needed to establish the equivalent of a centralised salaried administration. Weber repeatedly stresses that under pre-modern conditions the ruler lacked the means to exercise direct control over all administrative, judicial and police functions at the periphery. Some compromise with local magnates or notables was always necessary. The relationship was a bargaining one in which law and order were maintained, taxes collected in return for titles, honours, pensions, rights to land, labour, gifts in kind and so forth.

Notwithstanding a wide range of variation, all pre-modern states, according to Weber, were primarily patrimonial in character: 'The majority of all great continental empires had a fairly strong patrimonial character until and even after the beginning of modern times' (Weber, 1968, p. 1013). The emergence of industrial society, however, leads to the decline of patrimonial forms of administration and their supercession by rational-legal bureaucracy. Weber's sociology of bureaucracy, reflecting his overall perspective on industrial society, proposes an evolutionary transition from patrimonial to rational-legal forms of government. The bureaucratisation not only of government but of social life generally, the cumulative subjection of human organisations to rational principles, is for Weber the fundamental trend in human history.

If Weber's claim as to the ubiquity of patrimonial features in pre-modern societies is substantiated then this raises important questions about the nature of corruption in the pre-modern era. If conditions were such as to make any clear separation between incumbent and office difficult if not impossible; if the state apparatus was permeated by personalism and the appropriation of office for private ends was normal, in what sense would it be meaningful to talk about the illegal use of public office for private gain? Would it be meaningful to talk about public office at all? If a conception of *public* office did not exist, under what circumstances did it emerge? Since the answers to such questions are crucial to the understanding of the phenomenon of corruption, we now move to consider them beginning with a closer look at the patrimonial nature of the pre-modern European state.

FROM PATRIMONIALISM TO RATIONAL-LEGAL ADMINISTRATION

Firstly, if we look at English society in the late Middle Ages the patrimonial element, the origins of the state in the Royal Household, is readily apparent. In the thirteenth and fourteenth centuries the king's household comprised a small army of precisely-ranked followers and servants. These included royal officers with titles like 'Keeper of the Great Wardrobe', 'Keeper of the Signet Seal' and 'Master of the Jewels'. Henry VII maintained the rather primitive system of the 'kings coffers', a private treasury whose contents he disbursed in person and for which no proper accounts were kept. Offices, sinecures and pensions were bestowed on supporters, favourites, sycophants as well as being used to co-opt powerful potential opponents.

Right up to the modern era the granting of favours permeated the whole society. G. R. Elton notes that the king was a 'fountain of privilege' from whom the powerful and not so powerful expected their reward for services rendered. Offices, manors, wardships, distinctions, titles, church livings, help in lawsuits, keeperships of parks, castles, offices in the Household, the Exchequer and so forth – men sought such favours not only for themselves but for their families, dependents, retainers and servants. 'This network of service and patronage extended through the whole society, the situation between king and suitor being repeated at every level down the scale (Elton, 1977a, p. 24). Similarly Lawrence Stone agrees that a vast network of patronage was the cement that held sixteenth-century English society together. This was a society run by a 'patrimonial bureaucracy' in which offices, favours and perquisites were disbursed, not on the basis of merit, but according to particularistic criteria. These criteria reflected a system of values in which personal loyalty took precedence over everything, including the precepts of law and religion (Stone, 1982).

As the business of government became more complex formal departments began to differentiate themselves from the Household. Royal servants no longer accompanied the monarch on his wanderings around the kingdom, but settled at Westminster having become separated from the Court. Throughout the Middle Ages it is possible to identify two systems of government: those areas of administration that had left the retinue and become separate departments of state and, behind these, the Household, continuing to operate according to traditional practices but exerting influence, where possible, over the departments. The relationship between the two areas of government varied with the character and determination of the ruler. Under strong kings or queens the Household would predominate, while under weak, the departments (Hill, 1976, ch.1).

The emergence of separate departments of state, especially after the Tudor 'revolution' in government (see Elton, 1977b) does not mean, however, that they operated according to radically different principles to those that underpinned the Household. Patronage and personal influence continued to be the norm well into the early industrial period. Government patronage was only its most obvious manifestation – 'the visible lopgrowth', Harold Perkin tells us, 'of a plant whose roots and branches ramified throughout society, the political aspect of a personal system of recruitment which operated at every level and served to articulate the rigidities of a structure based on property' (Perkin, 1969, p. 44). Church-livings, salaried county, borough and parish offices, chaplains, tutors and governesses – all were disposed of through a system of personal influence and selection. When a man of rank and property was to make or have a hand in making an appointment he looked first among kinsmen and friends. Far from being considered reprehensible such behaviour was expected and a matter of principle and honour. Thus the eminently respectable Edward Gibbon quite naturally assumed that the principal motive for entering parliament was 'to acquire a title, the most glorious of any in a free country, and to employ the weight and consideration it gives in the service of one's friends' (Perkin, 1969, pp. 44, 45).

Patronage also played a pivotal role in the executive's control over parliament, especially after the Restoration. In an age when political programmes were virtually non-existent, where there were no continuous parties nor organised opposition, parliament left to its own devices would soon have degenerated into an anarchy of selfish interests. The Household and the appropriations under the Civil List prevented this or rather coupled selfish interests to the Crown's need for a parliamentary majority. Those who supported the Government were given pensions or sinecures such as 'Master of the King's Tennis Court' or 'Taster of the King's Wines in Dublin'. Government contracts were also handed out as well as cash payments for votes: in 1762 Prime Minister Lord Bute solicited members' votes for the Treaty of Utrecht by opening a shop at the Pay Office 'wither the Members flocked, and received the wages of venality in bank bills even to so low a sum as £200, for their votes of the Treaty' (Horace Walpole, quoted in Wraith and Simpkins, 1963, p. 82). Further down the line public positions were doled out to constituents it being understood that recipients would vote for the government of the day (see Finer, 1978; Plumb, 1966, ch. 6).

The outcome of centuries of personalised government was a state apparatus composed of a bewildering array of offices, titles and departments whose duties overlapped, were non-existent or had been forgotten. By 1780 its structures resembled, according to S. E. Finer, a 'coral reef . . . made up of the skeletons of innumerable offices and functionaries which had served their turn; but inside this dead structure new creatures burrowed, made their home, and turned the detritus of ages into some kind of working instrument' (Finer, 1978, p. 107). The century following 1780 saw the major reforms out of which were forged the basic structure of the modern capitalist state. It is not necessary in this context to deal with these in detail. In the light of the preceding discussion, however, it is worth mentioning that a highly significant step was taken in 1782 when expenses chargeable against the King's account were brought under control and gradually came to be confined to the actual expenses of the Household. It now became possible to draw a clear distinction between the personal account of the King and the general account of the State. By the accession of Victoria in 1837 the modern arrangement under which expenditure of the Royal Household derives from a parliamentary grant was well entrenched.

The importance of the separation of Household and State cannot be overstated, as it cleared the way for the thoroughgoing regulation of *national* expenditure. In 1787 Pitt replaced the plurality of funds into which customs and excise revenues were paid by a single Consolidated Fund. Henceforth specific appropriations could be drawn from the single fund, instead of from several in a somewhat haphazard way. The gradual introduction of modern systems of accounting obviated the need for physical transfers of money between the chests kept at the Exchequer as well as the dependence on the extremely archaic system of tally sticks (carefully notched and inscribed in Latin) for recording receipts and payments.

By the beginning of the Victorian era it was possible for the Chancellor of the Exchequer to open a true budget for the following year and for the Comptroller and Auditor General (introduced in 1834) to make a survey of past expenditure in his annual audit. The fact that government expenditure could now be presented much more clearly and unambiguously permitted a much greater degree of parliamentary scrutiny and control.

Amid the growing preoccupation with cheap and efficient government it is not surprising that the first decades of the nineteenth century saw many of its more archaic features abolished. By 1834 sinecures had been eliminated and legislation introduced against the sale of offices or their use as inducements at elections. The introduction of salaries for public servants after 1816 and a pension scheme in 1859 were major steps in the transformation of a semi-private bureaucracy into a modern public service. The fact that eligibility for pensions was conditional upon certification at the time of entry, complemented by the total abolition of patronage in the public service after 1870 and its replacement by competitive examinations, seemed to complete the transition to rational-legal administration. Significantly the decline of administrative 'corruption' was accompanied by a succession of acts directed at cleaning up elections and the whole system of representation. The Corrupt Practices Act of 1854 attempted to limit bribery at elections by preventing candidates from making payments through authorised agents. The introduction of a secret ballot in 1872 weakened the system of bribery since the briber could no longer be sure of a return on his investment. The Corrupt Practices Act of 1883 further assisted the decline by limiting election expenses and increasing the penalties proposed in the 1854 Act (see Wraith and Simpkins, 1963, ch. 2; King, 1978). But probably the most important contributor to the eventual obsolescence of electoral bribery was the emergence of a mass electorate the sheer size of which demanded other forms of electioneering.

Whilst in a general sense the development of the British state seems to illustrate the idea of a transition from patrimonial to rational-legal government, it would be simplistic to see this as a smooth evolutionary transition under which an administration based upon patronage and the private appropriation of office is progressively replaced by a modern public service run by salaried professionals. Throughout British and European political development other principles and other modes of acquisition and recruitment to office articulated with patrimonialism. One of the most important and widespread of these was the sale of offices.

SALE OF OFFICES

The sale of offices existed in antiquity and was common in most areas of pre-modern Europe, although its prevalence varied from country to country. The sale of offices was also normal in the 'oriental despotisms' of the East, although whereas offices once sold in Europe acquired the character of private property, in the Ottoman, Mogul, Qajar and Manchu empires they could be revoked at the whim of the ruler or his deputies. In Europe the sale of offices was probably most widespread in France where it penetrated more areas of government than anywhere else. With its origins in the Middle Ages the practice reached its peak during the Age of Absolutism. At the beginning of the seventeenth century the government in France battened on to the already-existing practice under which an incumbent resigned his office in favour of a buyer or a relative. In 1604 a tax on offices, the *paulette*, was introduced which effectively made them a private property. It was probably inevitable that as the needs of the state for revenue grew the temptation to sell more and more offices, especially to members of an increasingly wealthy bourgeoisie, could not be resisted (Fischer and Lundgreen, 1975, pp. 496–8).

As Swart has pointed out, the growth in the sale of offices is associated with the expansion of trade and commerce. The greater the volume of monetary transactions in an economy the greater the opportunities for the state to tap and siphon off wealth through taxes, customs dues, excises and the like. In agreement with Weber and others, Swart observes that at certain levels of economic development the costs of checking up on officials are so prohibitive that it is economically rational to concede to them a degree of autonomy (Swart, 1978, p. 83). Offices are therefore auctioned off to the highest bidder, thereby raising revenue for the state/Household. The purchaser aims to make a profit through the fees he is able to exact for the performance of official duties or from the taxes he is empowered to collect. Sale of offices is typically associated with tax farming: the sale of the right to collect taxes in a certain geographical area or specific sphere of economic activity. Whereas in Britain tax farming was curtailed in the second half of the seventeenth century, the farmers replaced by government functionaries (Hill, 1972, pp. 191–3) in France the system persisted until the Revolution. Pre-Revolutionary France, according to Fernand Braudel, had no public finances at all in the sense of a centralised system which made control and forecasting possible. The collection of revenue depended upon a host of inter-mediaries: the towns, the provincial estates and the tax farmers. The monopolistic *Ferme Générale*, which reached its full development in the first half of the eighteenth century, was run by about 40 farmers who deposited huge sums of money as advanced payments on the taxes to be collected; taxes on salt, tobacco, corn, imports and exports. But these deposits represented only a proportion of the actual taxes collected so that vast profits were made and 'a fantastic share of the nation's wealth remained in the hands of the tax farmers' (Braudel, 1983, pp. 540–2).

In his extremely penetrating study of European absolutism Perry Anderson sees the upsurge in the sale of offices as a transitional stage between, on the one hand, patrimonialism (or what he terms the 'jungle of particularistic dependencies of the high Middle Ages') and rational-legal bureaucracy on the other (Anderson, 1979, pp. 33–35). The growth in the sale of offices was one of the most striking by-products of the increased monetarisation of early modern capitalism and the rise within it of a mercantile bourgeoisie. Through the purchase of office the bourgeoisie not only gained access to the state but could hope to ascend into the ranks of the nobility.

Absolutism and the sale of offices which helped to sustain it certainly represented a distinct stage in the development of the European state. However Anderson's note about its constituting a transitional stage in the evolution of modern public administration, whilst in essence valid, nonetheless needs to be treated with caution. To assume from this that the cash nexus was progressively replacing personalistic criteria would be inaccurate. Not only were the offices hereditary but the whole system of appointments and sub-contracting was permeated by kinship, affinal and other personal connections. The *Ferme Générale*, Braudel tells us, was like a vast clan held together by patronage, bribery, back-scratching and intermarriage (Braudel, 1983, p. 542; Fischer and Lundgreen, 1975, p. 497).

In another way personalistic criteria intervened to check or attenuate the thrust of the cash nexus. In the 1750s the French aristocracy, chafing at bourgeois penetration of the state and the scramble for revenue which the astonishing proliferation of offices had unleashed, sought to restrict high office in the army, church and administration to those of noble birth. By the time of Louis XV the state comprised a bewildering array of offices with thousands of sinecures being sold off to raise revenue (Fischer and Lundgreen, p. 495). Ultimately the vast edifice rested on the backs of the peasantry, who were subjected to a double line of taxation from both the aristocracy and state. Not surprisingly peasant upheavals through out France were one vital source of the torrent that swept away the Bourbon dynasty.

Yet again the structure of the pre-revolutionary French state was even more complicated than has been suggested. Imposed upon this web of venality and patronage and articulating with it was a centralised bureaucracy run by the *intendants*. These were permanent administrators, usually lawyers, selected on the basis of their judicial and administrative experience and who, by 1670, had become entrenched in every *generalité* of France. The role of the *intendant* was to oversee the implementation and operation of Royal edicts in virtually every area of social and economic life. The main function of the *intendant* was to channel back information to the King, but in some areas he took executive initiatives himself. This required that he set up a local bureaucracy quite independent of that of the *officiers* on whose actions he was reporting. Having acquired a staff the *intendants* often built up their own administrative method and routine. There is evidence to suggest that this could by highly systemised. In his comparison of the *intendant* system with its *gubernator* counterpart in Imperial Russia, John Armstrong maintains that the former was characterised by regularity and speed of communications, obedience to the spirit of regulations as well as a tradition of service (Armstrong, J., 1972, pp. 26, 27).

TRAINING

The above example suggests that it would be wrong to assume that training and some degree of professionalism were wholly absent from bureaucracies based upon patronage and/or the sale of office. On the contrary the formal training of public servants was well-established in some areas of Europe more than a century before the industrial revolution. These were generally the large sprawling states of the East where a strong and efficient administration was needed to counter pronounced centrifugal tendencies.

The most obvious example is Prussia where under four succesive Hohenzollern rulers (1640–1786) a highly bureaucratised state apparatus was forged to meet the needs of military expansion. The Great Elector's (1640–88) decision to maintain a standing army is deemed crucial here, since it could only be paid for out of taxes and this required an efficient revenue-gathering apparatus. The importance given to the needs of the Prussian state, especially the need to build up a class of public servants devoted to it and to their profession, brought about an emphasis of merit on recruitment. Accordingly in 1727 Frederick William I established chairs of 'cameral' studies (a combination of applied economics, statistics and some natural sciences) at the universities of Halle and Frankfurt. Frederick II extended the system by making promotion dependent upon examinations whilst his successor Frederick-William II (1786–97) introduced a form of pre-selection under which applicants had to pass certain tests before being admitted to such courses (Rudé, 1972, pp. 104–6). However it is important to note that merit alone was not sufficient to gain entry into the top layers of public service. Family background and political attitudes were of major significance and in fact it seems that by the second half of the eighteenth century these factors were assuming even greater importance (Fischer and Lundgreen, 1975, pp. 525–6). As in France during the same period, this represented a reaction by the aristocracy to bourgeois penetration of the state.

In contrast to Prussia, England's state apparatus assumes much more of an amateur character with little apparent formal training and the predominance of patronage in recruitment. Yet this did not necessarily betoken a situation of general incompetence and inefficiency. It may have been the case that 'the idle, the useless, the fool of the family, the consumptive, the hypochondriac, those who have a tendency to insanity 'were provided for' by public office (Trevelyan, quoted in Briggs, 1967, p. 117). But it was also the case that most recruits to senior positions had had some form of training either at university or the Inns of Court. This was followed by training on the job in the sense of the cultivation of specialist skills, particularly those required in the drafting of legal documents. Even ordinary clerks needed to develop some expertise in letter writing and elementary book-keeping. Evidence would suggest that as far back as the mediaeval period some reasonable level of competence was achieved in routine administration. The pervasiveness of patronage did not exclude the competent. On the contrary, when a statesman or senior official was seeking an assistant or substitute among relatives and friends he would be sensible to choose someone who was capable. Since office meant power, status and, with sound management, not inconsiderable wealth, there was a clear incentive to exploit it efficiently:

A clever tailor's son like Samuel Pepys or a merchant's son like Thomas Cromwell with a good general education, a bright mind and personal ambition, promised to be a more useful manager of an admiral or bishop's affairs than a dull relative (Fischer and Lundgreen, 1975, p. 490).

Thus we can see that prior to the modern era elements of modern public administration, especially division of labour inherent in departmentalisation, hierarchy and training, articulated with patrimonial principles. But despite a degree of incipient professionalism pre-modern administration was manifestly corrupt by contemporary standards. Governmental authority was inextricably bound up with family connections and the institution of private property. Salaries, where they existed, were insufficient, inducing a necessary dependence on fees, perquisites and bribes. The continued confusion of public and private spheres was the major impediment to the emergence of modern public administration. However, during the nineteenth and twentieth centuries, state bureaucracies throughout Europe underwent a fundamental change: governmental apparatuses riddled with patronage, favouritism, the appropriation of office, overlapping and obsolete jurisdictions and a good deal of administrative confusion, were gradually transformed into modern administrations run by salaried public servants. The pace at which this happened varied considerably from country to country, with Prussia undoubtedly in the forefront and Russia, Italy and Spain lagging behind by perhaps half a century. Our task is not to chart the route taken by respective European states, rather it is to identify the basic conditions which made this transformation possible.

MONETISATION

A necessary pre-condition for the establishment of modern public administration was the expansion of trade and the progressive monetisation of European economies. Obviously this did not happen suddenly in the nineteenth century, but had been a continual development from the decline of feudalism and the emergence of a world economy in the sixteenth. It is generally agreed that the expansion of trade, the growth of cities and industrial production and the commercialisation of agriculture, in increasing the volume of cash transactions in European economies greatly enhanced the state's capacity to cream off revenue which could then be directed to strengthening the administration. Conversely in an economy dominated by subsistence agriculture, with limited cash transactions and where wealth is held in forms (such as land) which make it difficult to quantify, the centre faces formidable obstacles in the appropriation of any surplus that is produced (see Rudé, 1972, ch. 7; Tilly, 1975, pp. 72, 73).

Weber himself was quite clear that a rational-legal type bureaucracy could only develop in a money economy with a stable system of taxation (Weber, 1968, vol. 2, pp. 963–4). Only in such an economy could the centre appropriate the necessary resources to pay its servants a regular salary and generally institutionalise public service as a career. Regular and secure remuneration from the centre is a necessary precondition for the kind of discipline which is a vital component of professional public service (see Moore, 1973, ch. IV). But as Weber was quick to point out the monetisation which accompanied the diffusion of capitalism, although necessary, was by no means a sufficient condition for the development of modern administration. Whilst the increased wealth generated in Europe by trade and industry was undoubtedly appropriated by absolute monarchs and used to strengthen the state apparatus, this was still an apparatus in which, as we have seen, patrimonial principles predominated. What other factors, therefore, were required to make possible the transition?

1   The drive for efficient government

In the second half of the eighteenth century rulers and governments became increasingly preoccupied with the question of national efficiency. This preoccupation had a number of sources, one of the most important of which was the Enlightenment. This great advance in scientific and philosophical thinking not only had a profound influence on the intellectual life of Europe, but also on the world of practical affairs including government. As George Rudé has pointed out, before the French Revolution the works of the *philosophes* were generally received sympathetically not least by a number of European rulers. Joseph II of Austria, whilst opposed to their attacks on religion, used the ideas of Montesquieu and Rousseau in his experiments with 'scientific' government. Catherine the Great was an admirer of Voltaire and Diderot, was a student of Montesquieu and drew upon the ideas of Rousseau and Locke in formulating her educational reforms of the 1760s. In Prussia Frederick II not only welcomed Voltaire to Potsdam but made the French mathematician Pierre Maupertuis president of his new academy in Berlin (Rudé, 1972, pp. 162, 3). Jean d'Alembert, co-editor with Diderot of the *Encyclopédie*, was to become Frederick's adviser on scientific affairs. In addition to continuing the reforms of the Prussian bureaucracy and improving systems of recruitment and promotion by merit, Frederick was also thought to favour the disengagement of the public realm from the Ruler and his Household. At least the Prussian Legal Code of 1794, drafted when Frederick was still alive, subjects the monarch to binding rules in relation to administrative matters, places him under the law and generally depersonalises government. The Code also gave administrators, now transformed from Royal servants into servants of the state, a qualified legal right of permanent tenure, as well as the unqualified right to resort to law with regard to questions of conduct (Krygier, 1979, pp. 6–8).

Ironically, in embracing Enlightenment ideas, progressive European rulers were promoting their own obsolescence or, at least for the monarchies that survived, their eventual confinement to a purely decorative role. Modern, that is 'scientific', government demands regularity and consistency and this for the reform-minded statesmen of this era meant freedom from arbitrary personal interference by autocratic rulers. Furthermore, the complexity of government and the proliferation of departments, boards and ministries had reached a stage which was well beyond the purview and control of a single individual. This brings us to the second major factor behind the drive for greater efficiency: the expansion of the scope of government.

During the period 1800–1900 the population of continental Europe increased from 187 million to 401 million. The size of the population of England and Wales at the beginning of the eighteenth century was between 5.5 and 6 million. By 1801 this had increased to 9 million and by the end of that century to 32.5 million. Not only was the population rising rapidly, but more and more people were living in urban areas. In 1800 only a small minority of the people of England and Wales was living in cities of any size. A century later somewhere near 40 per cent were living in cities of 100 000 or more, with 60 per cent in cities of 20 000 plus. In 1800 1.7 per cent of the world's population was living in cities of 100 000 or more. By 1900 this had become 5.5 per cent. Overall growth of population in the first instance increased the demand for officials performing the traditional functions of government: revenue collection, the administration of justice and the maintenance of law and order.

In addition to these traditional functions governments, as we move through the nineteenth century, were increasingly constrained to address themselves to the new tasks and problems that had been thrown up by the industrial revolution. This meant, in some cases, providing or improving basic infrastructure such as roads, canals, ports, bridges and railways. Trade and industry were further encouraged through the standardisation of currencies, weights and measures and the strengthening of commercial law. In addition the social problems produced by rapid urbanisation had to be dealt with: poverty, disease, poor sanitation as well as the crucial problem of public order. European governments, accordingly, were increasingly drawn into the provision of public amenities and municipal services from hospitals to street-lighting, from schools to public parks and swimming baths. The excesses of market capitalism had to be contained through a range of legislation running from regulations over factory conditions and the adulteration of funds, to the administration of corporate finances. The enormous expansion in the scope of government and the consequent proliferation of departments at both national and local levels placed a premium on co-ordination, clear lines of communication and authority, the efficient collection and disbursement of revenues, effective accounting and, above all, administrative professionalism.

A third major factor behind the drive for national efficiency was international rivalry between European states. The struggle between European nations during the mercantilist era, primarily a struggle for access to raw materials and markets, increased in intensity as we approach the industrial age. Since the outcome of the struggle depended ultimately on military capability, enormous significance was attached not only to military machines in the sense of fighting units, but equally to their administrative back-up. If we look at the eighteenth and nineteenth centuries it is no accident that major administrative reforms came in the wake of military defeat or disaster. Pitt's reforms, which led to the separation of Household from 'public' expenditure together with the centralisation of the administration of revenue, came after the loss of the American colonies. In Prussia a major rationalisation of government departments, the gradual clearing away of a jungle of overlapping jurisdictions, followed the disastrous defeat by Napoleon in 1806. And, a major stage in the modernisation of the English civil service, the abolition of patronage, followed the Crimean debacle during which a British administration 'contrived through sheer incompetence to let a magnificent army freeze and rot to death . . . only nine miles from its base' (Kitson-Clark, 1977, p. 220).

2 Bourgeois revolution

Reforming autocrats such as Joseph II and Frederick II embraced those aspects of the Enlightenment that would make their rule more efficient and effective. There was, of course, a more radical side to the Enlightenment, a side which emphasised human happiness and liberty, liberty especially in the sense of freedom from arbitrary interference in the conduct of one's affairs and the disposal of property. Such themes had an obvious appeal to Europe's increasingly prosperous bourgeoisie chafing under the arbitrary exactions of the absolutist state, the maze of petty restrictions on trade and industry and the proliferation of taxes and officials collecting them. Nowhere was resentment more apparent than in France, where under Louis XV the flagrant display of wealth and privilege by a narrow circle at Court could not but offend the sensibilities of the class on whose endeavours such opulence very largely depended. Despite attempts to reform the system by Louis XVI and his ministers, France was to become the *locus classicus* of the bourgeois revolution. There can be little doubt that the bourgeoisie were to be among the principal beneficiaries of the radical transformations of the 'decade of revolution' and the Napoleonic era that succeeded it. Not the least of these benefits was new-found access to posts in the bureaucracy and army. The triumph, during the Revolution, of the notion of popular sovereignty and the idea that the will of the people and it alone is the source of all authority, was a vital step in the disengagement of the state from the person of the ruler. Henceforth the nation and not the King was *l'Etat*. Officials after the Revolution became public servants answerable to the state, that is to the nation through its elected representatives. Since the Declaration of Rights of 1791 stated that no 'other distinction than that of their virtues of their talents' should determine admission to public office, it was inevitable that merit as manifested in education should replace the patronage and venality of the *ancien regime*. After the collapse of experiments in local self-government during the Revolutionary Decade, Napoleon radically re-organised, re-central-ised and rationalised the administrative structure of France, providing the essentials of central and local government as it exists today.

In Britain the rise of the bourgeoisie was considerably less dramatic (unless like Engels we see the Civil War period as England's bourgeois revolution) (see Stone, 1973, pp. 39, 40). However, throughout the nineteenth century pressure built up from the middle classes for the opening up of the state. Whilst the 1832 Reform Act and the abolition of the Corn Laws went some way towards meeting middle-class demands, there can be little doubt that the landed classes retained a firm grip on the apparatus of government well into the second half of the nineteenth century. In 1859 Bagehot was complaining that the

British electoral system was too biased towards the landed interest with the gentry dominating not only the cabinet and shires but also the smaller boroughs (Kitson-Clark, 1977, p. 209). Twenty years later Matthew Arnold could still claim that government in England is composed of 'a string of aristocratic personages, with one or two men from professional class who are engaged with them' (Perkin, 1969, p. 313). However legislation in the 1880s considerably loosened the grip of aristocracy and gentry on the state apparatus. In 1883 the Corrupt Practices Act made old methods of electioneering impossible. The 1884 Reform Act gave the vote to the farm labourer and divided the whole country into equal electoral districts resulting in the disappearance of small patronage-dominated boroughs. In 1888 the County Councils Act transferred virtually all administrative powers from the justices of the peace to elected county councils. These changes, together with the adoption after 1870 of entry into the Home Civil Service through competitive examination, were of crucial significance in the rise to dominance of industrial over landed interests.

It has been argued that such reforms were conceded by an enlightened aristocracy preoccupied with its very survival. Mindful of events across the channel in 1789 and 1848, the aristocracy opened the doors of the state to the bourgeoisie, or rather to the sons of the bourgeoisie pouring out of the newer public schools onto the job market. In the face of over-crowded professions the public service, currently monopolised by aristocracy and gentry, constituted an obvious goal for the rising middle classes. It is noteworthy that Sir Charles Trevelyan, co-author of the famous Northcote–Trevelyan Report on the civil service, admitted that the revolutions of 1848 'gave us a shake and created a disposition to put our house in order' (Hart, 1972, p. 67).

As against this position there are those who would emphasise the primacy of ideological factors, particularly the triumph of the 'entrepreneurial ideal'. This perspective would see the nineteenth century reforms as the outcome, not of middle class pressure from outside the state but the conversion of prominent men within it. Leading statesmen such as Grey and Russell came to embrace a bourgeois view of property, that is to say a view which held that passive property in land should enjoy no automatic political supremacy over active capital in industry and commerce (Perkin, 1969, pp. 315–6). More generally a bourgeois ethos encapsulating an evangelical zeal for efficiency and probity in public life, implacably hostile to aristocratic place-seeking and dissipation, is held to have captured the hearts and minds of the politically powerful (Perkin, 1969, ch. VIII; Hart, 1972). Our task, however, is not to arbitrate between these views, rather to note the connection between a burgeoning entrepreneurial class and the transformation of the state.

3 The development of mass democracy

The opening up of the state to the industrial bourgeoisie was eventually followed by the incorporation of the industrial masses. This entailed not simply the extension of the franchise but also the underwriting of a minimal standard of living by the state through the extension of welfare and social services. The extension of the franchise had two major consequences which were to change fundamentally the character of politics. Firstly the need physically to win the working-class vote required the establishment of nation-wide party organisations. As a result what had been little more than factions within the legislature were gradually transformed into mass parties the leadership of which were, to varying degrees, accountable for policies and conduct to a mass membership. The second major consequence of the development of universal suffrage was that parties across the political spectrum had to evolve policies which would appeal to the masses. Since the overwhelming preoccupation of the working class was that of meeting basic material needs and avoiding the slide into pauperism, it was inevitable that party policies focused on the standard of living issue. The primary incentive to transform electoral promises into the reality of reforms was provided by the goal of national efficiency. The upsurge of European rivalry, particularly during the end-of-century 'age of imperialism', led governments to be increasingly preoccupied with harnessing the energies of the masses to the drive for economic development and world domination. The emergence of mass warfare at the beginning of this century pointed up the negative consequences of a physically debilitated nation (see for example Hall, S., 1984). The consolidation of 'welfare capitalism' after the Second World War, expressing the willingness of European governments of all shades to accept responsibility for the general well being of its 'citizens', cemented public confidence in the state as a responsible and, in theory, impartial entity. Furthermore the development of mass democracy in promoting competition for office encouraged contending parties not only to scrutinise each other but the way in which public resources generally were employed. Public scrutiny was enhanced by the emergence of specialised interest groups and the development of the independent media of mass communication, all of which imposed constraints on the behaviour of those in public office.

4 The development of mass culture

In addition to the granting of 'civil', 'political' and 'social' rights (see Marshall, 1964), allegiance to the centre and identification with a national culture was further promoted by an increase in geographical and social mobility, the expansion of mass education and the development of mass markets and the mass media. These processes combined to produce both a standardised culture comprising common ideals and norms, idioms, modes of expression and styles of life, as well as to intensify the involvement of the people with this common culture. A crucial concommitant of the rise of mass culture is the decline of parochial community-based cultures and with it the gradual attenuation of primordial attachments. This obviously assists national integration by making centrifugal tendencies more unlikely and – particularly germane to our theme – enhances public confidence in the impartiality of the state. This is because the consolidation and dissemination of mass culture considerably reduces the possibility of the 'public interest' being subverted or being perceived to have been subverted by primordial interests.

5 Psychological correlates

It has been noted by a number of writers that conditions of scarcity and instability, of sudden and rapid changes in fortune, tend to be associated with psychological insecurity and emotional instability. The latter manifest themselves in certain attitudes and behaviour patterns – most notably attitudes of suspicion, envy and acute mistrust – which in turn engender a climate of almost pathological opportunism or panic, a frantic scramble for what is available before it disappears for good. In a well-known study of a southern Italian village in the 1950s, E. C. Banfield develops the notion of 'amoral familism' in order to explain the social behaviour of the inhabitants of Montegrano (and, by implication, other peasant communities). Amoral familism denotes the alleged acceptance by the villagers that social behaviour is and always will be governed by the following principle: pursue the immediate short-term gains of the nuclear family and assume that everyone else is doing the same. Consequently claims that a given line of action represents a 'favour' or is done 'for the good of the community' are always disbelieved. They are simply devices which conceal some, as yet undisclosed interest (Banfield, 1958; see also Bailey, 1971).

Banfield's argument has been subjected to a good deal of criticism and he has been particularly taken to task for proposing what seems to be a cultural explanation of underdevelopment. Despite this there is fairly widespread agreement that attitudes of suspicion, mistrust and envy are particularly evident in peasant communities (see especially Foster, 1967) and in UDCs (Underdeveloped Countries) generally (see Feit, 1973), and even in certain developed countries (see Peters, 1978, pp. 57–62). The view now, however, would be that such a behaviour pattern is a consequence of underdevelopment in the sense of poverty and exploitation, rather than its cause. Notwithstanding these arguments, where scarcity and insecurity are the salient features of existence, they tend to encourage frequent resort to illegitimate political influence (for example bribery and nepotism) as well as a reliance upon dependent personal relations (such as clientelism). Conversely, to the extent that development and modernisation reduce scarcity and eliminate insecurity, such tendencies are held to decline. Put simply the citizens of developed societies have little disposition to bribe or use personal intermediaries when dealing with the state because they generally have confidence in the impartiality and competence of the public order (see Lemarchand and Legg, 1972, especially pp. 168–70).

CORRUPTION IN PRE-MODERN STATES?

In objective terms we have seen that the use of office for private gain was not only widespread in the pre-modern era but entirely normal. Many of the transactions habitually engaged in by public officials would now be considered illegal. Pre-modern administration was therefore deeply corrupt by contemporary standards. But was it corrupt by pre-modern standards? This is an extremely difficult question to deal with. However, it does seem that despite the absence of a clear-cut division between public and private interests some notion of corrupt behaviour, of an illegitimate use of public office, has existed in all states throughout history. In ancient Egypt problems of bribery and nepotism were clearly recognised. In classical Athens complex constitutional measures were adopted to safeguard against bribery. Under the Roman Republic the Senate established courts to try governors of provinces outside Rome together with army generals for flagrant abuse of the power entrusted to them. Under the Empire the opportunities for self-enrichment in the administration were so attractive that public offices sold for a high price. Attempts by successive emperors to curtail both the sale of offices and the practice of extortion by incumbents largely failed (see for example Senturia 1931; Venkatappiah, 1968).

Turning to mediaeval and early modern Europe we do not need to look very far to find complaints about corruption and attempts to use the law or other methods to do something about it. The institution of the papacy, for example, furnishes numerous examples of the spectacular abuse of ecclesatical authority: simony, the sale of votes by cardinals, the sale of spiritual dignitaries and favours; even the establishment by Innocent VII of an office for the sale of secular favours where pardons for murder and manslaughter were sold for large sums of money. The English word 'nepotism' derives from the practice of popes of awarding to their *nipoti* or 'nephews' (usually illegitimate sons). Nepotism under Innocent's predecessor, Sixtus IV, threatened to destroy the papacy altogether because of the distrust and suspicion it created; the desperate need to eliminate rivals and replace existing *nipoti* with one's own (Burckhardt, 1965, pp. 64–79).

In mediaeval England laws existed which clearly reflected public concern about the dishonesty of those who occupied public positions. Legislation enacted in 1275 required that the office of coroner should be filled by honest and wise men who should not 'demand nor take any Thing of any Man to do his office'. In 1346 all judges were ordered to dispense justice impartially without taking 'gift or reward' and were empowered to investigate and punish cases where office-holders had accepted gratuities to carry out their duties. An Act of 1552 warned officers and ministers that the acceptance of gifts or inducements could result in loss of position. Such legislation seems to have had little impact for some 30 years later Secretary of State Sir Francis Walsingham referred to his era in a letter to William Cecil as 'this corrupted age' (Hurstfield, 1967; Doig, 1984, ch. 2).

One could quote numerous examples of similar complaints and attempts to control behaviour in public office. In relation to England they are particularly evident in the late sixteenth and late eighteenth centuries – periods, it is worthwhile noting, of rapid commercial expansion and social change. The point is, however, that attempts at reform always ran up against the dominant patrimonial ethos which made any objective and systematic application of rules and laws impossible. Under what circumstances, then, were charges of corruption made and against whom? When everyone considered it his duty to use public office for his own and his dependents' advantage, why were some individuals singled out as transgressors?

In attempting to answer this question it is helpful to look at the interrelationship between politics and levels of economic development, and at the style or character of politics in an underdeveloped economy. In pre-modern societies where resources are scarce and opportunities, especially commercial opportunities, extremely limited, office-holding assumes pivotal significance. Indeed office-holding is likely to be the principle or, for some, the only route to wealth, status and power. In such a context 'politics' consists primarily of a struggle between dominant groups for access to the spoils of office, to the stream of patronage that flows from the Household. The struggle will be highly factionalised; fought out between loose groupings of the powerful constantly manoeuvring and re-aligning. The object of the factional struggle is to keep abreast of the front-runners and through frequent shifts and re-alignments to prevent other groupings becoming too strong. Should a particular faction be seen to be getting too powerful, to be intent on monopolising resources, then it is likely that other factions will coalesce against it. This could involve violence, whether direct or through the official violence of the state deployed through the manipulation of the law against the 'enemy'.

In 1387 five Lords Appellant charged five of Richard II's close companions with 'treason'. The accused were held to have had too much influence over the King and to have embezzled and squandered Household funds. The charges in fact reflected the resentment of certain powerful magnates with huge retinues to satisfy at Richard's channeling his favours too narrowly among a small coterie of cronies. In the early seventeenth century the mediaeval practice of impeachment was revived and used by the powerful to strike at the foes. Lord Chancellor Francis Bácon was impeached by the Commons for corruption in 1621 primarily because Cranfield, Earl of Middlesex and the Duke of Buckingham conspired to get rid of him. Middlesex himself was subsequently impeached, the outcome of a deal done between Buckingham and certain elements in parliament who were hostile to Middlesex' attempts to curtail royal expenditure. But Buckingham's own turn came in 1624 when he became the object of an impeachment charge orchestrated by the Earl of Pembroke. Buckingham was accused, *inter alia*, of abuse of office and self-enrichment. This did not, however, mean that Pembroke and his supporters had never used office to *their* advantage, or had used it in this way less assiduously than Buckingham, but that the latter had become so powerful as to excite the enmity of former allies such as Pembroke.

Similarly the leading proponents, over 150 years later, of the impeachment in 1787 of Warren Hastings, Governor-General of India, were not necessarily less adept than he at using office to amass a personal fortune. In fact Hastings' implacable enemy, former East India Company employee Philip Francis, who played a major behind-the-scenes role in fomenting public hostility against Hastings, was almost certainly more corrupt than the acccused (see Reilly, 1979, ch. xiii). Hastings was impeached for a variety of complex reasons: partly the settling of old scores within the Company itself, but mainly because he was at the centre of a struggle between certain factions in parliament and the company. This struggle crystallised around the attempts of leading parliamentarians such as Burke, Fox and Sheridan to use the issue to embarrass the government. Hastings, in short, had become a political issue. (At the end of a trial which, incredibly, dragged on for seven years, he was honourably acquitted of all charges.)

These few examples (see also Braudel, pp. 538, 9) serve to illustrate the point that accusations of corruption during the pre-modern era were heavily politicised – an extremely useful and often used tactic in the rhetorical mud-slinging of factional politics. As a political device its use has tended to decline for the reasons outlined below. The eventual emergence throughout Europe of a professional civil service, with its emphasis on merit and training, to a considerable extent isolated the administration from the depredations of ambitious politicians. The introduction of systems of payment for elected representatives reduced their dependency on the perquisites of office. The expansion of opportunities afforded by the industrial economy alleviated direct personal pressure on politicians from followings for jobs, sinecures, pensions and the like. The emergence of mass politics with its disciplined political parties, whilst not entirely eliminating factionalism, did at least re-direct attention from short-term self-interest to the longer-term goal of staying in power by pursuing electorally popular policies. Lastly, the coalescence of a capitalist political class or faction led to the emergence of a consensus which cut across political parties. One important aspect of this consensus is that accusations of impropriety or corruption are normally ruled out of the political game as undesirable and unproductive. Why this should be the case will be one of the questions we consider in the next chapter.

CONCLUSION

From the foregoing it will be apparent that some kind of notion of public office has existed in pre-modern states throughout history which, in testimony, is littered with complaints about abuses as well as attempts to eliminate them. Such attempts, however, were doomed to fail until the material advance made possible by the commercial and industrial revolutions, combined with a number of other factors, permitted the full development of modern public administration founded upon a professional civil service, allegedly –

> a corps of specially trained examined and appointed men [sic], independent from the political conjuncture, impartial in discharging their services, fully salaried and pensioned by the state and fully employed by it, subject to a hierarchical order in which they move upward according to seniority or merit or a mixture of both. (Fischer and Lundgren, 1975, p. 459).

The above represents something of an ideal type as we shall see. However, for the time being let us note that the conventions that supposedly governed administration ramified through the political arena generally. That is to say, whilst elected representatives may not be subject to, possibly because they have successfully eluded, the constraints that are imposed on bureaucrats, as public figures they are nonetheless expected to maintain standards that are in some general sense compatible with the public good. As a former President of the USA has put it: 'Public office is a public trust' (Grover Cleveland, quoted in Brogan, 1987, p. 419). That such standards are not always adhered to by politicians or administrators in industrialised societies will be the focus of the next chapter. However before moving on it is of crucial importance that we note the quite different pattern in the development of modern government in the USA. Indeed the USA represents something of a reversal of the European pattern: from a pinnacle of unbending public probity during the Federalist era, we witness a gradual descent under Jefferson to be followed under Jackson by a precipitous fall into the chasm of venality which many believe came to characterise American public life after the Civil War (see especially Finer, 1978).

When the US Congress set up the Federal administration between 1789 and 1792 it was able to do so in a context which was unencumbered by a centuries-old legacy of personal dependencies of the kind which faced European reformers. Accordingly the architects of American government could establish an administrative system which in most respects conformed closely to the ideal type of rational-legal bureaucracy which Weber was to formulate more than a century later. Indeed Washington's successor John Adams's insistence that the public authority entrusted to him should never be made subservient to his own interests or those of family and friends provided a model of conduct in public office which seems to have been followed until the turn of the century. However when Thomas Jefferson was inaugurated in 1801 he found himself surrounded by Federalist party office-holders who had been appointed by Washington and Adams. Jefferson therefore replaced enough of the Federalists with Democratic–Republicans to ensure a more even distribution of power between the two parties. In doing so Jackson initiated the 'spoils' system under which newly-elected representatives, from the President to city councillors, have arrogated to themselves the right to appoint their nominees to public office. By the Jackson era (1829–37) the practice had become so well-entrenched and extensive that one of the President's critics could claim that over 100 000 appointees were on the Federal government payroll (*The Washington Lobby*, 1982). The establishment of the spoils tradition in a wider context of social and cultural fluidity accompanied by spectacular economic growth made the emergence of an essentially opportunistic view of public office virtually inevitable. Throughout the nineteenth century politicians, from the most senior to the least significant, quite unashamedly used public authority to extort a range of material and other privileges from the business world. Such was their reputation that the inclusion of a chapter entitled 'The Best Men Do Not Go into Politics' in a classic work on American society provoked neither surprise nor outraged protest (James Bryce, *The American Commonwealth*, 1888, quoted in Brogan, 1987, p. 419). Despite numerous attempts at reform, the spoils system with its associated graft together with links with organised crime persisted, especially at city level, well into the second half of this century. According to some writers it is still by no means dead and may even be in the process of reviving (see for example Toinet and Glenn, 1982). For these and other reasons the USA is normally held to endure much higher levels of political corruption than most western European societies (see for example Andreski, 1966; Benson, 1978).

3 Corruption in Developed Societies

'We don't think much of our profession but at least when contrasted with respectability it is comparatively honest.'

The Pirate King in W. S. Gilbert and Arthur Sullivan, *The Pirates of Penzance*

In the wake of the Irangate hearings in June 1987 a senior *Washington Post* journalist, David Ignatius, bemoaned the 'Lebanization' of American foreign policy. Ignatius was referring to the 'tawdry Third World' character of Lt. Colonel Oliver North's covert operations to supply arms to the Contra rebels in Nicaragua. One important indicator of this tawdriness was the apparent inability of North's 'slapstick militiamen' to distinguish between public and private funds (Ignatius, 1987). It is a little surprising that one of the world's top journalists writing for a newspaper that played a central role in exposing the Watergate scandal should blithely attribute the well-attested and longstanding low level of public morality in the USA to some third world contagion. Reading Ignatius' hypothesis one cannot help recalling Yankee zealot Elizabeth H. Tilton's phobia about 'protestant America' being overwhelmed by the 'Big City Tammany Masses'; or the widespread W.A.S.P conviction that the 'newer races' are the chief carriers of corruption (see Handy, 1971; Wilson, 1978).

But perhaps social scientists should not be so ready to cast stones at journalists when our own field of academic behaviour was until relatively recently dominated by a more subtle version of this thesis and is by no means free of its influence today. With the massive upsurge of interest in the third world after the Second World War there emerged a body of theories of social change promoted by political scientists and sociologists, usually referred to as 'modernisation' theories. These modernisation theories have been the subject of a vast amount of critical discussion and it is not necessary to review the various arguments here (but see Randall and Theobald, 1985). Suffice

46

it to say that a basic theme underlying the modernisation hypothesis was that of a transition from 'tradition' to 'modernity', a transition which had already been completed by the developed world and one which third world countries were in the process of making. A full catalogue of the trappings of tradition and modernity again need not concern us here. However, pertinent to our central theme of the abuse of public office is that so far as the state apparatus is concerned the transition entailed a shift from an administration permeated by personalism, authoritarianism and bureaucratic confusion to a highly differentiated governmental structure which approximated closely to the rational-legal model and which is accountable for its actions to a mass electorate. Hence Ward and Rustow include the following among their characteristics of a modern polity:

1. A highly differentiated and functionally specific system of governmental organisation;
2. A high degree of integration within this governmental structure;
3. The prevalence of rational and secular procedures for the making of political decisions;
4. The large volume, wide range, and high efficacy of its political and administrative decisions . . . Ward and Rustow, 1964, pp. 6, 7)

The basic point about this type of approach is that DCs have arrived at this happy condition or, rather, end-state of modernity. The state apparatuses of western Europe and the USA allegedly operate according to rational procedures and universalistic principles in which there is no place for personalism, cronyism and, most of all, the confusion of public with private interests. Why precisely this should be the case is not too clear from the modernisation literature, which tends to be light on explanations amounting at times to little more than a descriptive exercise in 'comparative statistics' (see A. Smith, 1973). It is possible to locate, however, in the first wave of criticism of modernisation theories – dubbed 'modernisation revisionism' by Huntington (Huntington, 1971) – the basis of an explanation. The core of this explanation lies in the voluminous on patron-client relations and their decline.

CLIENTAGE IN DECLINE

Alex Weingrod has pointed out that when political scientists talk about patronage they might have one of two rather different patterns of behaviour in mind. For some considerable time political scientists have been interested in the process whereby politicians distribute public jobs and other favours in return for electoral support. The idea of the 'political machine' has long been familiar to those dealing with urban politics in the USA. However when it became apparent in the late 1960s that Nuffield-type psephology was of limited use in understanding politics in the third world, attention turned to a second variant of the phenomenon: patron-client relations at the periphery, that is at the level of the peasant village (Weingrod, 1968).

Because of the primitive techniques they are forced to rely on, the peasant lives at the margin of subsistence. Not infrequently he and his family are driven below this margin by the vicissitudes of their existence: flood, drought, disease, illness, death, exploitation, intimidation and violence on the part of outsiders (the landed class, their agents or the state). The peasant is therefore powerless before the uncontrollable forces that hold sway over his daily life. Nonetheless some form of assistance may come from two sources: first there are members of his kinship group, neighbours and the wider community to whom he is bound by ties of reciprocity and mutual aid. Secondly there are powerful and influential persons who are outside the community, socially if not geographically, who may be prevailed upon to help out during times of crisis. It is with such individuals, usually large landowners, that peasant cultivators may attempt to develop patronage relationships. The peasant approaches the landowner to ask for a favour – a loan, the use of a piece of land, a job for his son or protection against someone who is threatening him. Alternatively the landowner knowing that a problem exists might take the initiative with an offer of help. If the favour is granted or the offer accepted the relationship is established and in fact endures over time. The peasant, for his part, reciprocates by showing deference to his patron, lauding his generosity in public, giving him useful snippets of information especially about troublemakers, voting as instructed and, in some situations even giving his patron armed support (see especially Powell, 1970; Weingrod, 1968). J. D. Powell has suggested that at the core of this type of patron–client relationship lie three basic factors: firstly, the relationship develops between persons of unequal status, wealth and power. (In the light of this Powell believes Julian Pitt-Rivers' 'lop-sided friendship' appropriately describes the relationship. See Pitt-Rivers, 1954.) Secondly, the formation and maintenance of the relationship depends upon reciprocity in the exchange of goods and services.

Thirdly, the development and maintenance of the relationship depends upon regular face-to-face contact between the two parties; the type of contact which is habitually found in pre-industrial communities.

According to this view, then, clientage in peasant societies emerges out of the attempts of peasant cultivators to alleviate their critical situation by attaching themselves, where possible, to wealthy and powerful individuals. This type of relationship arises, as Weingrod has pointed out, in societies where the state is underdeveloped, where state institutions are virtually non-existent at the village level so that there is a manifest gap between centre and periphery. If this is the case then to the extent that this gap is closed then we would expect patron-client ties to attenuate.

The decline of patron-client relations is an extraordinarily complex process which has received a good deal of attention (see Guasti, 1981; Theobald, 1983). Generally speaking this decline is thought to be closely related to increased prosperity, urbanisation, the spread of literacy, mass education and the emergence of mass politics. The process is well illustrated in Jeremy Boissevain's account of the decline of patronage in Malta. Forty years ago patrons, usually wealthy landowners, dominated village life. These were the people who disposed of local housing, credit facilities and jobs and had access to government decision-makers. Patrons were jealous of the power they exercised and were frequently ruthless in protecting their interests. However, economic development since the early 1960s has transformed Maltese society. The need to diversify the economy, making it less dependent on the defence establishment, led to the development of manufacturing and tourism. The expansion of these areas of the economy together with the revenue from the renting of defence facilities to NATO has led to rising prosperity, increased mobility and has permitted the expansion of education and the spread of literacy. As a result social relationships have undergone a radical change with authoritarian–deferential patterns in retreat. Patrons seldom fulfil their traditional role, indeed are looked upon with disfavour as the masses have learnt to articulate their interests through modern forms of organisation such as trades unions, professional associations and the like. In short patronage is no longer needed (Boissevain, 1977).

Interestingly this type of explanation is virtually identical to those which have sought to account for the waning of the American political machines. The machines have their origins in the advent of Jacksonian democracy in the 1830s and the need to mobilise large blocks of newly enfranchised and relatively unsophisticated electors. Two main factors lie behind their ascendance: firstly, the bewildering character of city administration with its multiplicity of authorities and jurisdictions. This inevitably resulted in the emergence of informal systems of bargaining based on patronage and the exchange of favours such as contracts and franchises. Secondly, the rise of the machines was set against the context of a rapidly expanding urban population, an increasing proportion of which, as we draw towards the end of the nineteenth century, was made up of immigrants, many of them from the peasant societies of eastern and southern Europe. Totally at sea in the alien and threatening environment of New York or Chicago the immigrant welcomed the hand of friendship from his local precinct captain who knew of someone who might get him a job, a room, his kids into school, who in short spoke a language which literally and metaphorically the immigrant could understand. In return the immigrant would vote – often several times at the same election – according to instructions and persuade family and friends to do the same.

The precinct captain's job was to build up a detailed knowledge of his area and the people in it. He and his aides had to be able to identify and be on good terms with strategically placed individuals such as employers and rooming house owners who might be able to deliver a bank of votes in return for favours – contracts, building permits, information or simply freedom from interference from inquisitive policemen or city hall officials. 'The loyalty of the rooming house owner to the Democrat Party was not a matter of ideology: the owner who did not cooperate with the precinct captain could expect a visit from the city building inspector the next day' (Meyerson and Banfield, 1969, p. 177). Cooperation often entailed supplying the captain with lists of registered guests who had died or were too ill to vote so that arrangements could be made for vagrants and destitutes to be brought in to replace them at the poll. The captain had to ensure that these impersonators did not stray out of the ward on the day of the election and that they were paid for their services – 'A dollar for a negro, a dollar and a half for a dago, and two dollars for an American' (Speed, 1978, p. 424).

If elected the party machine would distribute the 'gravy' to workers, financial backers and key supporters. The gravy might be contracts, information about potentially profitable land sales, non-enforcement of building regulations or legal restrictions relating to drinking, gambling and prostitution. But most important the successful party was able to distribute a considerable number and wide range of jobs – from street-cleaners to senior positions in the bureaucracy – to friends and followers. In the 1950s Chicago boss William J. Connors disposed of between 350 and 400 jobs. In the 'boss' tradition Connors looked after his people supplying them with loans, helping them out when in trouble with the law and generally taking an interest in their family affairs. The relationship between the boss and his supporters and, in turn, between local party workers and their constituents was a *personal* relationship in which the machine 'helped' in a very tangible way those who supported it. Seldom if ever did 'politics' in the form of political discussion, the distribution of leaflets or the holding of meetings, intrude. The relationship between an agent and his ward residents was, as one agent put it in the 1950s, one of 'personal friendship between me and my neighbours' (Meyerson and Banfield, 1969, p. 176).

The machines, although the instruments of the two major US political parties, differed radically from the mass parties of Europe held together by class ties and common programmes. The machines were non-ideological, preoccupied hardly at all with issues of political principle, and directed fundamentally to securing and holding on to political office in order to distribute resources to those who run it and work for it. The machine relies upon what it accomplishes for its supporters in a very concrete way and not on what it stands for. It has been likened to a business in which all supporters are shareholders, and whose dividends are paid in accordance with what one has invested in terms of funds or effort (see Scott, 1969).

The decline of the machine has been attributed to two factors or rather two sets of factors: firstly various administrative reforms which have effectively centralised many of the jurisdictions and programmes which for decades had been virtually local fiefdoms. Centralisation was accompanied by increased bureaucratic control over the distribution of public resources including jobs, thereby reducing considerably the potential for informal bargaining at the city level. But more important from the point of view of our theme is the second set of factors which are encapsulated in the idea of the acquisition of civic competence or citizenship by the American masses. The machines flourished in a context of poverty and insecurity: the poorly educated and possibly illiterate immigrant struggling to remain above the poverty line is particularly susceptible to the material blandishments and paternalism of the machine politician. The development of full employment, the spread of mass education and the increase in social mobility have transformed the 'Tammany masses', or at least their children, into American citizens, now capable of articulating their needs and interests through 'legitimate' channels such as trades unions, civic associations and other interest groups. Material prosperity has, furthermore, not only diminished the value of the benefits formerly disbursed by the machines, but the provision of pension, health and welfare benefits by trades unions and other organisations has further promoted their obsolescence (see Scott, 1969; Gottfried, 1968). Thus we have an exact parallel of Boissevain's explanation of the decline of patronage: affluence, material security and the acquisition of civic competence have radically reduced the demand for the personal services once provided by the patron and the precinct captain.

THE REDISCOVERY OF PATRIMONIALISM

This type of perspective is still widespread in the literature on developed polities. It is one which proposes the supercession of archaic personal modes of political influence by more sophisticated and more 'respectable' forms (see Heidenheimer, 1978, pp. 22, 23). These more sophisticated forms are bureaucratic in character; whether we are talking about the state apparatus, or the range of organisations – parties, trades unions, interest groups – which in advanced societies constitute the media of political influence and communication. The assumption, whether implicit or explicit, is that these bureaucracies conform fairly closely to Weber's ideal type, which is to say that they operate according to objective, universalistic principles. They are, in short, free of irrational bias, of favouritism and cronyism; they are depoliticised, sanitised, 'clean' (see Heidenheimer, ibid).

An apolitical bureaucracy, an easily taxable populace, a *rechtstaat* (a state governed by the impersonal rule of law), freedom of associational activity, and a market economy – these conditions are all characteristics of the modern democratic state. It is not surprising therefore that a political science which has devoted most of its attention to the study of modern western democracies should have found little reason to interest itself in dyadic structures. As other societies achieve similar conditions, we may expect this to the the case there as well. (Landé, 1973, p. 127)

By 'dyadic structures' Landé means the personalistic patron–client-type transactions which predominate in pre-modern states and which, following the logic of his last sentence, may be expected to decline as these states acquire the trappings of modernity listed at the beginning of the quotation.

However Landé has to concede that dyadic structures are not entirely absent from certain levels of modern democratic systems. While the political activity of the American masses is confined to membership of voluntary associations and periodic voting, those who aspire to high political office must, it seems, attach themselves 'dyadically' to someone with political potential (ibid., p. 127). Similarly Lemarchand and Legg in an influential conceptual analysis of clientelism, whilst affirming that there is theoretically no place in industrial societies for 'personalised, affective bargaining relationships', agree in the following sentence that industrial politics do not conform very closely to this ' "ideal" model' (Lemarchand and Legg, 1972, p. 168). This is because modernisation is 'discontinuous', which apparently means that institutional modes of an earlier period survive into the industrial age. Hence in the USA vestiges of the political machine are still visible. In other industrial polities 'personalised affective bargaining relationships' are readily observable among economic and political elites. In Britain the interlocking network of business, family and friendship connections which make up the 'establishment' are well documented. Likewise in Japan and Italy the importance of family and other affective ties within business elites and between them and top politicians and civil servants has been clearly established. Similarly, in socialist industrial states personal ties are known to play an important role in policy-making and political recruitment. Whether these examples of personalism, like the remnants of the city machines, are survivals which can be expected to decline, is not clear from Lemarchand and Legg's argument.

Lemarchand and Legg here touch on an extremely important area of study which warns us to treat with scepticism the evolutionary models of the modernisation theorists. By the mid-1960s writers on social change and modernisation were having to take account of a growing number of studies of industrial societies which demonstrated that recruitment to élite positions were nothing like as meritocratic as modernisation theories implied. The idea of an open contest in which all-comers could compete for top positions on the basis of objective qualifications was seriously questioned by the findings of a variety of surveys carried out in a range of industrial capitalist societies. These surveys demonstrated that the middle and upper classes were disproportionately represented in business and administrative elites, in the judiciary, the military as well as in the upper layers of other dominant areas such as the church and the media. (For a summary of the data see Miliband, 1969, ch. 1.) However this was not just a question of the predominance of middle and upper classes but of the pervasive influence of certain prestigious educational institutions such as the Ivy League universities in the USA, the public schools and Oxbridge in the United Kingdom, and the Ecole National d'Administration and the Ecole Polytechnique in France. Because of this a number of writers have emphasised, in the study of elite recruitment, the importance of a common set of values, predispositions as well as a network of personal contacts rather than simply class background. Whether these values and contacts are formed within these distinguished schools and universities or exist prior to entry is a matter of some debate.

Some writers have devoted a good deal of effort to charting extensive kinship and friendship connections which underpin the dominant elites or 'ruling classes' of capitalist societies. This has been particularly the case with the United Kingdom where the notion of a cohesive and self-perpetuating elite embodied in the term 'establishment' has proved attractive both to social scientists and journalists, not least because a fair amount of evidence supports its existence (see especially Aaronovitch, 1961; Urry and Wakeford, 1973). However, whether we are dealing with a single establishment or a number of competing establishments (see Sampson, 1962, p. 624), with a 'ruling class', 'power elite' or plurality of competing elites, there is broad agreement that patronage plays a major role in recruitment to and in the cohesion of dominant political and economic elites in industrial societies.

The United States

The US with its 'spoils' system is usually seen as the classic example of a polity thoroughly permeated by patronage. Despite numerous attempts at reform since the Pendleton Act first established the principle of merit in civil service appointments in 1883, the right to assign public office to relatives, friends and supporters remains an apparently irremovable feature of the American political scene. The President, for example, disposes of an unknown number of posts estimated to run into thousands. Whereas in 1929 President Hoover made do with one secretary and two assistants, half a century later White House staff ran to 600 with the Executive Office covering a further 5000 posts. In recent years there has been a tendency for Presidents to counteract the contraction in patronage posts due to civil service and other reforms by creating federal agencies some of whose staff are appointed directly from the Oval Office. In 1974 of the 68 members of the federal boards of economic regulation alone, 61 had been nominated by President Nixon (Toinet and Glenn, 1982). In addition to formal rights of appointment American presidents are noted for surrounding themselves with coteries of hand-picked followers – the Kennedy 'clan' for example – who are usually rewarded with sundry privileges such as lavish hospitality, trips on Air Force One and opportunities for various forms of self-aggrandisement.

In 1983 a public stir was created by the activities of a group of Reagan associates known as the 'Colorado Crazies'. At the centre of the group was Denver brewery owner Joseph Coors, a right-wing Republican, big financial backer of Mr Reagan and member of his unofficial kitchen cabinet. Mr Coors not only brewed beer but manufactured the cans in which it is sold. This left him with the problem of disposing of large quantities of hazardous waste. Fortunately, the President appointed several members of the Coors clan to the Federal Environmental Protection Agency (EPA) which conveniently lifted restrictions on the dumping of toxic waste in Colorado. After a public outcry restrictions were re-imposed and the head of the EPA, Reagan nominee Mrs Anne Burford, resigned, it is said, after reassurances that no legal action would be taken against her (Jackson, 1983). This example suggests that we are dealing not simply with the exchange of jobs for material or moral support, but with a much more complex system of exchange of favours which underpins the political centre in the USA. In an extraordinarily well-informed study of the Washington 'power game' Hedrick Smith supplies us with a few nice examples of the minutiae of doing and soliciting favours and, in the process, making and keeping influential friends:

> It (i.e. one-to-one lobbying) is Bob Strauss's note to Treasury Secretary Jim Baker to help a friend seek appointment to the World Bank. It is Howard Baker's contact with an old Senate colleague to see that some client gets a break on the "transition rules" of a tax bill. It is Bob Gray's phone call to the White House to ask the president to address some convention or wangle an invitation to a state dinner for an industrial bigshot. It is breakfast with a

committee staff director who is drafting intricate legislation. It is little favours such as tickets to a Washington Redskins football game or helping Ed Meese's wife get a job. It is knowing which buttons to push. (H. Smith, 1988, p. 232)

Moving on to state and city levels it is difficult to obtain an overall picture of the volume of patronage which survives. Toinet and Glenn estimate from fragmentary evidence that a governor of New York will have 40 000 posts to dispose of whilst the figure for Illinois is around 14 000. Despite the alleged decline of the machines it seems that doling out city jobs is still a popular way of paying off one's backers and maintaining influence. In 1975 the Chicago City Council decided to abolish the City's Civil Service Commission, thereby relinquishing over 40 000 jobs to the then mayor, Richard T. Daley. Daley's powers of patronage already ran to 30 000 posts, not including jobs in the private sector which city politicians are often able to extract from business in return for favours. Although the Chicago example may not be typical of American cities in the 1970s Daley being one of the last of the old-style bosses (he died in 1976 to be succeeded by reforming mayor Harold Washington), it nonetheless seems apparent that the volume of local level patronage in the USA is still prodigiously high. One estimate claims that about half of the 8 million local government employees are appointed on a patronage basis (see Toinet and Glenn, 1982). The pool, however, is held to be shrinking primarily because of a combination of administrative reform, Supreme Court decisions relating to the hiring and firing of public sector personnel for political reasons and, probably most important, the increasing centralisation of the American political system. The latter, evident in the expanding share of federal expenditure as a proportion of total expenditure, places additional forms of patronage in the president's hands. That is to say substantial federal aid such as the award of government contracts to local industry, the siting of military bases or public utilities such as airports and dams, will be granted to states to which the president owes a political debt. Nelson Polsby maintains that the president can use this power 'to reward and punish congressional friends and foes quite vigorously . . . Small Business Administration and Area Development Administration loans to certain areas may get more and more difficult to obtain as applications fail to qualify. Pilot programmes and demonstration projects may be funneled here rather than there. Defense contracts and public works may be accelerated in some areas, retarded in others' (quoted in *The Washington Lobby*, 1982, p. 18).

We should note, however, that this form of patronage, in that it is channeled through formal organisations, differs qualitatively from the *personal* exchanges with which we have hitherto been concerned. We shall return to the extremely important question of the differences and interrelationships between personal patronage on the one hand, and organisational patronage on the other.

Great Britain

In contrast to the USA with its unashamedly entrepreneurial political culture, Britain, after the Northcote–Trevelyan reforms, became the exemplar of professional and impartial public administration. The apparent absence in Britain of a spoils bureaucracy along American lines lies at the heart of her reputation for honest government and the general consensus within the country that corruption is not a problem. But like much else in Britain the situation when examined more closely is much more complex than appearances would suggest. In fact the scale of political patronage in Britain is far from negligible.

First of all the British prime minister dispenses patronage in a variety of forms: he/she appoints government personnel – that is to say members of the cabinet, ministers and secretaries of state. Since these posts are usually filled by members of parliament and members of parliament are invariably keen to advance their careers, this places considerable powers of patronage in the hands of the prime minister. (It is noteworthy that the Australian Labour Party attempts to avoid this situation by decreeing that members of a Labour Cabinet be *elected* by a Parliamentary caucus. The prime minister is then left to allocate specific portfolios to the ministers that have been elected) (see Richards, 1963, p. 249). In addition to the cabinet there has been a tendency for British prime ministers in recent years to choose or appoint an inner circle of advisers who are then used to promote the government/prime ministerial line especially to top officials in the civil service. Harold Wilson's 'kitchen cabinet' allegedly presided over by his political secretary, Marcia Williams, excited critical comment in the press, as well as upsetting many members of the Party because of its undue influence. Similarly Mrs Thatcher has surrounded herself with special advisers rather as 'a sixteenth or seventeenth century court' surrounded by the sovereign (Riddell, 1985, pp. 52, 53) Mrs Thatcher has also intervened to ensure the rapid promotion of civil servants who have particularly impressed her during briefings. This has led to charges of the over-politicisation of the civil service (Riddell, pp. 53, 54).

As well as appointing bishops in the Church of England and certain judicial posts the prime minister also bestows honours such as peerages, knighthoods and various titles on selected members of the British people. Although technically speaking the honours come from the sovereign, it is the prime minister and his/her advisers who choose the recipients. With the development of mass politics in the last decades of the nineteenth century the practice evolved of exchanging honours for contributions by members of the emerging plutocracy to the campaign funds of the main Conservative and Liberal parties. However the blatant venality of the system embodied in the award of the nation's most prestigious titles to those who were merely rich enough to pay for them, brought it into disrepute. Matters came to a head in 1922 when the King's Birthday Honours list, compiled by the prime minister Lloyd George, included a crook, a tax avoider, a wartime profiteer and a technical traitor (see Doig, 1984, p. 103). As a consequence a royal commission was set up leading to the Honours (Prevention of Abuse) Act of 1925. The Act made it illegal to sell an honour and established a Political Honours Scrutiny Committee as a watchdog. Whilst honours can no longer be employed directly to solicit party contributions and are supposed to be awarded for public service (but see especially Doig, p. 230), they nonetheless remain a useful device for drumming up political support as well as cementing ties with the business world and other centres of power.

Latterly British prime ministers have used the honours system to court popularity with the masses with awards to prominent personalities in the worlds of entertainment and sport. Conversely peerages, knighthoods, CBEs and the like are eagerly sought by ambitious businessmen and those seeking to make their way in public life as they are often a passport to power and influence: a seat on a comany board, an invitation to sit on one of numerous public bodies or even on a royal commission. The 1925 Act has not, however, eliminated controversy. Harold Wilson's 1976 resignation list provoked derision in the press and consternation in his own party not only because of its unabashed cronyism but also because it included certain individuals of extremely dubious reputation in the world of business. (One was subsequently convicted for theft and false accounting and a second property mogul, under threat of investigation by the Department of Trade and Industry, committed suicide.)

But the creation of personal networks within government and the distribution of honours by no means exhaust prime ministerial powers of patronage. He/she and other ministers enjoy extensive powers of personal nomination to the enormous range of public bodies that has been a consequence of the expansion of state involvement in all aspects of social and economic life. These public bodies range from *quasi-governmental bodies* such as the Monopolies and Mergers Commission and the Office of Fair Trading, to *quasi non-governmental organisations* or *quangos* such as the BBC, the IBA or the consumer boards of the nationalised industries. Whereas *quasi-non govern-mental organisations* are concerned with implementing government policy and may therefore be seen as an extension of the executive, *quangos* occupy the administratively grey areas between government and the private sector. A 1980 White Paper listed 489 *quangos* with executive (decision-making) powers – the health authorities and the Arts Council for example – and a further 1661 with advisory powers only. Their chairmen are appointed by the minister responsible for their establishment, although the prime minister has personal patronage of some (Beardshaw and Palfreman, 1985, pp. 437–8). Whilst many of the thousands of staff on these bodies are recruited on the basis of objective qualifications, it is certain that patronage plays a major role in the compositions of their boards:

> we looked around. I sometimes go to Barbados, and since Dick Ross (a member of the CPRS) told me he knew a very good man on one of these sugar boards called Hector Hawkins, I made it my business to have a rum punch with him – perhaps two – and I thought Hector was very nice and very good . . . Well, then Peter Bowcock was recommended to me by Lord Jellicoe. Kate Mortimer I knew because she was a contemporary of my daughter Emma's at Oxford . . . I think I got hold of William Plowden because his father's rather a friend of mine and I asked his father if he might like it. (Lord Rothschild on the recruitment of members of the Central Policy Review Staff, quoted in Martin, 1977, p. 147)

Whilst some of the positions on these boards carry little in the way of direct material reward, they do confer status as well as opening up opportunities for extending networks and further patronage. By the mid-1970s the extent of ministerial patronage in Britain was on a scale that, according to former Labour MP Maurice Edelman's investigations into the number of offices of profit that were within ministers' gift but which were not filled according to normal civil service criteria. One minister (Barbara Castle) told the author that she had '3100 such appointments with a total value of £1¾ million'. Another (Mr Michael

Foot) had '650 salaried and fee-paid appointments worth £600 000'. The Home Secretary was able to select the chairmen and 96 members of nine boards varying from the Race Relations Board to the Horserace Betting Levy Board. During the same period other writers were emphasising the increasing politicisation of such appointments, the trend towards replacing one's opponents' nominees with one's own; a trend which has distinct parallels with the American spoils system (see especially Butt, 1978). If we add to the patronage that emanates from central government to that which operates locally including the appointment of justices of the peace, then the following denunciation by a former leader of the Liberal Party may be taken as more than political hyperbole:

> The first thing we want is to bust open the patronage and privilege by which both Tories and Socialists manipulate our politics and maintain their rigid out-of-date party structure . . . Far too many prizes in the law, the Church, commerce and social life go to those whom the ruling clique find agreeable. (Jo Grimond, quoted in Richards, 1963, p. 247)

The scope that networks of patronage give for unacceptable levels of covert influence has periodically aroused comment from elsewhere. In the 1960s MP Francis Noel-Baker wrote an article on the problems of the business affiliations of members of parliament. These connections, Noel-Baker suggested, gave scope for new forms of corruption under which members might acquire profitable financial spoils – a regular retainer, a seat on a company board, hospitality, holidays – in return for promoting the interests of businesses at Westminster (see Pinto-Duschinsky, 1977). Such links attracted a good deal of publicity as a result of the revelations in the early 1970s relating to the intricate web of contacts with government that had been carefully built up over several years by architects John Poulson. Among Poulson's many 'friends' were three MPs – Reginald Maudling, John Cordle and Alfred Roberts. At the time when the Poulson scandal broke in 1972 Maudling was Home Secretary. He had also been the chairman of one of Poulson's companies, Construction Promotions Ltd., and held directorships in two others. Maudling's family had substantial shares in one of these, International Technical and Construction Services, for which his son worked as an office manager. It subsequently transpired that in the mid-1960s Maudling as an MP and prominent figure in the world of business had personally intervened with the Maltese government to promote the interests of Poulson and ICTS in relation to a hospital contract on the island of Gozo. Likewise Roberts, who was on a retainer from Poulson for liaison work, had queried the Crown Agent's list of approved architects. Why was Poulson not on it? He also strongly recommended Poulson to the Maltese Minister of Works for the Gozo project. Cordle was also receiving a retainer from Poulson for 'consultancy' work. Unfortunately for him a letter was discovered in Poulson's files in which the MP asked for payment from the architect for making a speech in the House which would allegedly further Poulson's interests. In the speech Cordle had pressed for government construction contracts in West Africa to be awarded to British firms (see Doig, 1984, ch. 5).

Whilst it would not be unreasonable to conclude that these three 'honourable gentlemen' had accepted payment to use their public position to promote private interests, they had done nothing illegal under British law. Unlike civil servants they could not be prosecuted for taking bribes (as a number involved with Poulson were). Nonetheless public unease was such as to prompt the prime minister, after some hesitation, to refer the MP's conduct to the Parliamentary Committee of Privileges. In its report the Committee censured all three: Cordle for breaching the standards of the House by raising an issue there with a view to financial gain; and Maudling and Roberts for not declaring their connection with the architect either in speeches or when they intervened personally with government departments. Cordle resigned his seat complaining of unfair treatment, whilst Maudling and Roberts, protesting their innocence, stood firm. A motion that they be suspended from the House for six months was rejected in favour of one merely 'taking note' of the report (Doig, p. 155). This case would seem to suggest that although there may be formal constraints on the behaviour of MPs they do not seem to present much of a deterrent. Furthermore such constraints cannot take account of the fact that a significant degree of influence is deployed outside the debating chamber and takes the form of informal lobbying – a telephone call, a note, a brief word over dinner or in the bar and so on.

Reservations about the behaviour of these holding public office has not, however, been confined to elected representatives. Even Britain's much-praised civil servants have not escaped criticism. This has been particularly noticeable in relation to post-retirement jobs. Existing regulations state that senior civil servants and army officers must obtain the permission of the government before accepting employment with certain businesses within two years of employment. However as Pinto-Duschinsky has pointed out, such permission is not often refused and anyway the rules do not cover consultancies and other forms of payment which do not constitute full-time employment. Accordingly Anthony Sampson has referred to a 'scramble' by senior civil servants for post-retirement jobs often in areas of former employment. Fears have been expressed that the possibility of this type of movement may render top civil servants and army officers susceptible to manipulation by sectional interests. Lord Balogh has even gone so far as to talk about this brand of 'English corruption' which, he believes, is much more effective than the crude passing of money since it can mean that a senior civil servant can spend a fair proportion of his career 'pandering to industrialists' in the hope of a post-retirement job (see Sampson, 1983, pp. 204, 205).

This form of what some would regard as 'indirect bribery' (see Key, 1978) depends upon the possession of key resources, mainly important contacts and/or information. It therefore tends to be restricted to the upper layers of the civil service, the military and the police (senior police officers frequently move across to posts in private security firms. See Pinto-Duschinsky, 1977). However further down the hierarchy and especially in the area of local government disquiet has periodically been expressed about the extent of nepotism in the allocation of jobs and public housing as well as irregularities over the awarding of public works contracts (for numerous examples see Doig, 1984). Britain's police have also failed to live up to the 'Dixon of Dock Green' image. Between 1956 and 1960 disciplinary action or legal proceedings were taken against the chief constables of three forces. The Metropolitan Police and the Criminal Investigation Department within it was the target of such public criticism that when Sir Robert Mark took over as commissioner in 1972 he set up a special department, A10, to investigate irregularities within the 'Met'. Whilst A10 unearthed a considerable number of cases of abuse by Metropolitan officers – accepting or extorting bribes, doctoring evidence as well as actually participating in crimes – the practice developed of pressuring offenders to resign rather than initiating legal proceedings against them. During Sir Robert's term of office around 100 officers a year were leaving the Met under 'unnatural' circumstances (see Pinto-Duschinsky, 1977; Doig, 1984, ch. 8). Controversy over the extent of corruption within London's police and the ability of the force to block attempts to expose it has continued into the 1980s.

The Soviet Union

It is not possible in this context to examine the extent of patrimonialism within the state apparatuses of every industrial country. However, before leaving this stage of the argument, it will be useful to look briefly at the USSR, which is of especial interest for two reasons at least: the Soviet Union lacks the traditional ruling classes and long-established elite educational institutions to which has been attributed such importance in the distribution of power and patronage in capitalist societies. Secondly, the Soviet Union is committed to the attainment of 'rational' political goals by means of rational bureaucratic processes (i.e. comprehensive planning). For these reasons one would expect meritocratic principles to assume much greater significance than in more manifestly class-based societies. To be sure, hard work, commitment, organisational and managerial skills together with political expertise are indispensible for elevation to the top ranks of the Party. But possession of these attributes alone seldom guarantee entry into the exclusive circle of the *nomenklatura*. The term refers to leading positions in the Communist Party and government as well as in the trade union, military and cultural establishments. The *nomenklatura* comprises two lists: the first, the *osnovnaya*, is the list of jobs in key political, economic and managerial positions throughout the country to which the Party has a monopoly of appointment. The *osnovnaya* are thought to compromise around 600 000 posts at the commanding heights of the Soviet system. The second *uchotnaya* list contains about one million names of people who have been judged suitable to fill *nomenklatura* posts as they become vacant (Walker, 1986). Needless to say the *nomenklatura* carry special privileges in addition to money income. These include foreign currency payments for the purchase of goods in special shops, access to shops and restaurants reserved for higher officials, quality housing, holidays, medical facilities and so forth (see Lane, 1985, ch. 5).

Ascent to the summit of the Party hierarchy requires that the clever and ambitious worker be noticed or in some sense be taken up by one of the established *nomenklatura* (see Frank, 1969). Because of the intense rivalry both within and between the various *apparats* which make up the Soviet state, top officials are always on the look-out for politically able and reliable young men who can be incorporated into their following. Nikita Krushchev took his personal network from Moscow to the Ukraine and back. When Leonid Brezhnev succeeded him in 1966 he managed to enlarge the Central Committee to bring in old friends form the Ukrainian Dnepropetrovsk region where he was born and began his career (see Roth, 1968). The extent of the Brezhnev network and the scale of abuse by its members caused something of a stir in 1988 when his son-in-law Yuri Churbanov, was brought to trial for corruption. Churbanov was deputy to the Minister of the Interior, General Nikolai Shchlolokov. Whilst in office Shcholokov used ministry appropriations to purchase Mercedes cars for the personal use of himself, his son, his daughter and daughter-in-law. His wife had a BMW. Shcholokov kept private apartments in different parts of Moscow, one for his personal tailor, his personal dentist as well as for other members of his family and friends. He had his own photographer, architect, masseur, cook, biographer, all of them on the public payroll and even had a film made about himself at a cost to the state of £446 000. Shcholokov's vast apartment was stuffed with antiques which had been seized from black marketeers and should have gone to the Kremlin museum had they not been appropriated for the minister's own use. Churbanov was at the centre of a huge and complex fraud which is estimated to have cost the Soviet state up to 3 billion roubles in payments for non-existent cotton crops (see Cornwell, 1988). The personal networks which make such abuses possible have been referred to as 'clientilistic' (see for example Eisenstadt and Roniger, 1984; and Ionescu, 1977) and even as 'lord-vassal' relationships (Heller and Nekrich, 1986, p. 608). Martin Walker, the *Guardian's* sometime Moscow correspondent, sees the *nomenklatura* as a vast system of patronage similar to the disbursement of church livings by members of the English aristocracy (Walker, 1986).

PATRIMONIALISM AND CORRUPTION IN DEVELOPED COUNTRIES

This brief survey suggests that patrimonialism, in the sense of the distribution of public resources according to personalistic criteria and/or the appropriation of public resources for private ends, appears to be normal among dominant groups in industrial societies, both capitalist and socialist. Is this tantamount to saying that *corruption* is normal? This is an extremely difficult question to answer primarily because of the virtual impossibility of distinguishing between public and private ends; of identifying the point at which the delicate balance between the performance of public duties and the derivation of private advantage shifts decisively in favour of the latter. To help us out of what seems to be something of an impasse I want to suggest that we regard corruption as a sub-category of patrimonialism. That is to say that of the vast body of reciprocities and transactions which are an everyday feature of behaviour in public office, a small minority are selected out, deemed unacceptable and subjected to some form of public examination and perhaps legal prosecution. It is important, however, to look closely at this process under which supposedly 'deviant' cases are selected for special treatment. Seldom it seems does the state itself initiate proceedings. On the contrary, if we look at some of the more prominent cases of serious irregularity in public life in developed countries since the Second World War, most of them seem to have been subject to an official reaction only *after* they have been exposed to public gaze, either by accident or the activities of journalists, or a combination of both. Let us look at a few examples.

In 1968 *The Times* advertised and found an ex-burglar who was wanted to assist with an article on house protection. A year later the ex-burglar introduced to *The Times* reporters a distressed friend who feared that he was in danger of being framed by the police. The reporters went on to record secretly the friend's conversations with three detectives who were attempting to involve him in criminal activities. During the conversations one of the detectives made the following claim about a 'firm within a firm', subsequently to lie at the heart of the issue of corruption within the Metropolitan Police:

> I know people everywhere because I'm a little firm in a firm. Don't matter where anywhere in London, I can get on the phone to someone I know I can trust, that talks the same as me . . . (quoted by Davies, 1982).

The revelations in *The Times* triggered off an inquiry headed by the then Inspector of Constabulary, Frank Williamson, into corruption in the Metropolitan Police force.

In 1972 a highly successful British architect, John Poulson, went bankrupt. In the 1950s and 1960s Poulson had built up a large international practice and had been particularly adept at winning contracts from city and county councils, nationalised industries and other public bodies. During bankruptcy hearings in June of that year it transpired that Poulson had made payments or gifts in kind to a large number of local councillors, local government officers, employees of nationalised industries, senior civil servants and some members of parliament. Some of these payments or gifts were undoubtedly bribes placed in order to secure the award of contracts to Poulson's or his associates' companies. Although Poulson's activities had come under the scrutiny of the provincial and fringe press more than a year before the bankruptcy hearings, established national newspapers did not take up the case until after they had got under way (despite the fact that Poulson's dubious connections with prominent politicians had been well known to Fleet Street journalists for some considerable time. See Doig, 1984, pp. 133, 134). As well as legal proceedings against the principals in the case the Poulson affair spawned two official enquiries: the Committee on Local Government Rules and Conduct under Lord Redcliffe-Maud, reporting in 1974; and a Royal Commission on Standards of Conduct in Public Life, chaired by Lord Salmon and reporting in 1976.

Shortly after the Poulson scandal reverberated through Britain a squad of 'plumbers' hired by the White House to stop 'leaks' of embarrassing information by President Nixon's opponents, broke into the Watergate building in Washington DC. Their aim was to bug the telephones in the offices of the Democratic National Committee. Unfortunately they were disturbed by a nightwatchman who sent for the police with the result that the plumbers soon found themselves in custody. Initially they pleaded guilty only to burglary, but under pressure from a judge suspecting a cover-up and as a result of energetic enquiries by two extremely able *Washington Post* journalists, the plumbers one by one began to 'pull the plug'. The Senate set up a special Committee to investigate Watergate and after fighting a long rearguard action Nixon was eventually forced to resign the presidency in order to avoid impeachment for perverting the course of justice.

In 1983 tax investigators in West Germany looking into alleged tax evasions on gifts to political parties decided to make a routine check on the Flick Concern, the country's largest investment company and a known source of donations. Flick's files revealed a startling list of names of leading politicians and civil servanats who had received gifts not infrequently, it later came out, in the form of buff envelopes containing thousand mark notes. The list contained some of the best known names in Germany including former and current chancellors Willy Brandt and Helmut Kohl. With a good deal of help from rival news magazines *Der Spiegel* and *Stern*, public attention began to focus on Economics Minister Count Otto Lambsdorff, and the decision to waive Flick's tax liability of DM 450 million (£150 million) on its profit from the sale of its 29 per cent holding in Daimler-Benz. The Minister was subsequently charged with accepting bribes totalling £33 750. Although found not guilty on this charge he was in 1987 convicted for tax evasion on party funds and fined £60 000. Throughout the whole affair the Count protested his innocence, remained a member of the Bundestag and his party's spokesman on economic policy. On the death of Franz-Joseph Strauss in the autumn of 1988 Count Otto Lambsdorff was elected leader of the Free Democratic Party (*Guardian Weekly*, 18 November 1984 and 16 October 1988).

On 3 November 1986 a Lebanese newspaper, *Al-shiraa*, revealed that the former US National Security adviser Robert McFarlane had carried out a secret mission to Tehran which concerned the supply of military parts to the Iranian government. The following day the visit was confirmed by the speaker of the Iranian parliament Hojatolislam Rafsanjani. This revelation was extraordinarily embarrassing for the Reagan administration as it had repeatedly denounced Iran as a terrorist state. The President ordered an internal White House review of the affair which resulted in Attorney General Edwin Meese admitting two weeks later that between $10 million and $30 million from the arms sales had been transferred to the Nicaraguan Contras via Swiss bank accounts. The deal, Meese claimed, had been set up with the full knowledge of National security adviser Vice-Admiral John M. Poindexter but without the knowledge of President Reagan or other members of the National Security Council. The day after Meese's announcement Poindexter resigned and Lt. Colonel Oliver L. North, who had personally directed the operation, was dismissed. The Iran–Contra affair or 'Irangate' was firmly in the public domain.

From these few examples we can see that a pattern of behaviour which is often not abnormal in terms of the sub-culture from which it springs, but which conflicts with what is conventionally thought to be proper, is exposed to public gaze (see especially Chibnall and Saunders, 1977). That is awareness of the behaviour becomes part of popular discourse. In this process the media will usually play a pivotal role and will often take the initiative in bringing irregularities in the state sector to public attention. Once this has happened some form of official reaction is needed not least because the legitimacy of public authority has been called into question. One obvious solution is to attempt to re-conceal the offending behaviour by either discrediting and, if possible, suppressing the source of the offending information. Thus complaints by 'whistle-blowers' in the USSR about favouritism, corruption and illegal activities in state enterprises are usually passed for investigation to the local branch of the Party. However, it seems that in most cases local *apparatchiks* connive with management, including the original target of the criticism, to discredit the complainant by, for example, concocting charges of indiscipline, character assassination, scandal-mongering or even counter-accusations of corruption. In the cases of 47 whistleblowers examined by Lampert only a third (16) suffered no penalty at all; 18 were dismissed (six of these without getting their jobs back); 12 incurred some penalty such as demotion, transfer to less well-paid jobs or harassment, and one left voluntarily (Lampert, 1983).

In the USA too it seems that whistle-blowers are often subjected to some form of harassment by the government departments whose irregularities they strive to uncover. In 1988 a psychologist Dr Don Soeken, claimed that he was employed to declare mentally unfit American civil servants who had uncovered fraud, corruption and other iniquities in the State Department, the Defence Department and other areas of the federal government. Their superiors were trying to get rid of them by having them declared insane. Soeken became a whistle-blower himself by exposing Washington's 'secret gulag' to a committee of Congress which fortunately seems to have shielded him from persecution. In a study of 232 whistle-blowers subsequently carried out by Soeken and his wife it came out that 90 per cent had lost their jobs or were demoted, 27 per cent faced lawsuits, 26 per cent faced psychiatric and medical referral, 25 per cent admitted to alcohol abuse, 17 per cent lost their homes, 15 per cent divorced after the aftermath, 10 per cent attempted suicide and 8 per cent went bankrupt (Erlichman, 1988).

However the suppression or containment of potentially embarrassing or threatening revelations does not necessarily require the dismissal, medical referrment of prosecution of those who have exposed them. More mundane forms of obstruction can achieve the desired outcome and, in so far as they are buried within administrative processes, are often more effective. For example Frank Williamson, who was detailed to look into corruption in the Metropolitan Police, resigned in frustration after ten months. Williamson felt that he had been impeded in a number of ways by Scotland Yard: information he needed was not made available, records he was interested in simply disappeared, he experienced difficulty reaching officers he wanted to interview and confidential details of the enquiry were common knowledge not least among officers who were to be investigated. Before resigning Williamson presented his preliminary findings in a 30 page report which he sent to the Home Secretary, Reginald Maudling. The report was returned without comment within the hour.

In 1972 a three-man squad from Thames Valley Police produced a 400 page report on corruption at the Yard naming 30 officers. The

Director of Public Prosecutions maintained that since the principal witness in the affair was a criminal there was little chance of securing any convictions. No charges were brought against the named officers. Also in 1972 the Assistant Chief Constable of Lancashire led an inquiry into the activities of the Yard's Drug Squad. He complained that witnesses frequently reneged on statements that they had made and the Yard was generally unhelpful. One of the witnesses claimed that he had been threatened with a false convicton unless he retracted a statement he had made to the inquiry (see Davies, 1982).

In 1978, after allegations in the press subsequently made to the police about extensive collaboration between Metropolitan officers and criminals, Operation Countryman, the largest enquiry into corruption in the 'Met' began. By June 1979 Countryman had discovered 62 officers against whom there was evidence of corruption. But again the Countryman investigators (senior police officers from other forces) found themselves obstructed in a variety of ways and at all levels. They were castigated by senior Metropolitan officers for relying too much on the evidence of convicted men. Other officers failed to disclose potential evidence, connived to fabricate charges against informants or put pressure on them not to testify or warned colleagues who were to be investigated and generally strove to discredit the Countryman squad. More disturbing was the behaviour of the office of the Director of Public Prosecutions, which took an inordinate time to deal with reports relating to suspected officers as well as in discussions over the immunity to be offered to informants.

The crunch came when the officer in charge of Countryman, Arthur Hambleton, complained to the DPP about the dropping of charges against a City detective who was being held outside London to stop him interfering with witnesses. Hambleton then had a meeting with the Director of Public Prosecutions and the Deputy Commissioner of the Metropolitan Police after which a joint statement appeared insisting that Countryman was *not* being obstructed. However Hambleton later stated on the ITV programme 'World in Action' that he had made the statement under duress in order to save the operation. 'Frankly Countryman was obstructed', he claimed on the programme (Doig, 1984, p. 251). In 1981 Operation Countryman was closed down with the Metropolitan Deputy Commissioner Patrick Kavanagh arguing that most of the cases it produced would have come to light anyway through the normal procedures of the Met's own Investigations Branch, and insisting that there was no evidence that Metropolitan Police officers were involved in organised crime.

Despite the Commissioner's claim there remained the feeling that Countryman had only begun to scratch the surface of corruption within London's police force. After the trial in 1982 of two City detectives who were sent to prison for illegally fixing bail and watering down evidence in relation to two London robberies, an article in the *Guardian* claimed that the 'firm within a firm' still existed and was flourishing. On the authority of sources close to Countryman the article claimed that the 'firm' involved hundreds of officers including many in senior positions. Detectives, it was alleged, had for many years been involved in organising and actually carrying out robberies and burglaries, illicitly taking cuts from rewards and insurance pay-outs, as well as extorting money from criminals for arranging bail, doctoring evidence and generally providing useful information (Doig, 1984, p. 250).

An additional dimension of police as well as judicial corruption in Britain – one that should be mentioned but cannot be explored here – is the role of Freemasonry: 'The insidious effect of Freemasonry among the police has to be experienced to be believed'. Statements such as this, made by a former head of Monmouthshire Criminal Investigation Department (see Knight, 1985, p. 49) have given rise to a good deal of public concern and suspicion that Masons within the police force assiduously promote the careers of their Brothers, shield them from disciplinary action as well as from investigations such as Countryman or the Stalker inquiry into the existence of a shoot-to-kill policy within the Royal Ulster Constabulary (see Stalker, 1988). It is very difficult to evaluate such claims primarily because of the dearth of reliable evidence. Secret societies by their very nature do not readily yield the kind of data which allows social scientists to make balanced judgements. Nonetheless it is generally accepted that Freemasonry – a special variant of patrimonialism – is fairly pervasive in Britain's police forces, the legal and medical professions, the Church of England and certain areas of government (see Knight, 1985; on Freemasonry in Italy and the 'P2' affair see Sassoon, 1986).

We must be careful, though, to avoid concluding from these examples that the exposure of serious irregularities in public life is always met with elaborate attempts to conceal. Criminal proceedings are undertaken against perpetrators and they are sometimes fined or sent to prison. Poulson and a number of the public figures who were part of his network did go to prison as did some policemen whose illegal activities came to light as a result of investigations mentioned above. Nonetheless it is the case that the individuals who are actually proceeded against and punished are invariably only a tiny minority of all those who have come under suspicion. In explaining this we should not rule out the difficulties of obtaining evidence in such cases. This is not only because of the reluctance of witnesses to come forward – but also because of the uncertain nature of the crime itself and the difficulty of drawing a line between legal and illegal behaviour. Furthermore the amount of resources that can be devoted by law enforcement agencies to investigate corruption is always constrained by the incidence of other forms of crime, many variants of which will command greater attention because of their high visibility. So when the British Home Secretary announced in July 1976 that the Poulson file was now closed and that there would be no further prosecutions, this was not necessarily a conspiracy to protect certain big names who were about to be fingered.

The above constraints apply even more so to official inquiries, tribunals, royal commissions and the like. Such bodies can only sit for a limited period; their principals can usually devote only a part of their professional working time to the affair in hand; they are often inadequately staffed; and they may lack the legal powers to subpoena witnesses which means that they must depend upon official spokesmen with all that that entails in terms of presenting an acceptable view of the area under investigation (see Pinto-Duschinsky, 1977). But perhaps the most significant and most subtle constraint is encapsulated within the overall orientation of the enquiry which is usually that basically the state sector is sound so that serious misdemeanours result from the actions of a small minority of unprincipled deviants: ' "rotten apples" in what are basically good barrels' (Riley, 1983, p. 193).

This was certainly the case with the Lynskey Tribunal, set up by British prime minister Clement Attlee in 1948 to enquire into allegations of bribery of ministers and top civil servants at the Board of Trade. The Tribunal found that a Parliamentary Secretary at the Board, John Belcher, had accepted gifts from a Glasgow whisky distiller on whose behalf he had intervened to issue a licence for the importation of casks. The Tribunal also uncovered connections between not only Belcher but a number of prominent public figures and the extremely dubious middleman and fixer, liar and con-man of theatrical proportions Sidney Stanley. But despite all this, together with a somewhat sensational beginning with stories in the press of Mayfair orgies, the affair moved to a tranquil dénouement. The principals in the case, Belcher and George Gibson (a director both of the Bank of England and the North Western Electricity Board) far from being big-time operators were represented as rather colourless boobies who had been duped by an unscrupulous alien (Stanley). Overall less than five hundred pounds had changed hands, and the integrity of public servants generally had been completely vindicated. Attorney-General Sir Hartley Shawcross insisted that the standards in British public life were of the very highest and hoped that the Report of the Tribunal would finally put an end to the 'mean innuendos and reckless gossip' that had recently been common currency (Gross, 1964, p. 280). Sir Hartley's hopes seemed to have been fulfilled for in the press comment on the outcome there was a distinct air of self-congratulation about the standards of conduct in British public life (Gross, p. 285).

Along similar lines the Redcliffe-Maud Report and the Report of the Salmon Commission, which were set up in the wake of the Poulson affair, were both informed by the view that government in Britain is essentially honest and that corrupt activities are isolated occurrences whose significance is invariably distorted by the press:

> It is my belief and accords with my experience . . . that corruption is not widespread in public life. (Attorney-General to the Salmon Commission)

> The TUC and unions representing public service employees firmly believe that there is no evidence to suggest that, except in a few isolated cases, their probity is not of the highest. (Trades Union Congress to Salmon Commission. Both quotes in Doig, 1984, p. 149. See also Pinto-Duschinsky, 1977)

However, such assumptions may be peculiar to Britain with its relatively closed political culture and exaggerated confidence in public morality – a confidence which, incidentally, is shared by many commentators outside Britain (see especially Benson, 1978, p. 3). In the USA where political corruption has been very much to the forefront of public discussion since the 1830s, public enquiries tend to probe deeply and are generally less inhibited about exposing defects in the system of government. Furthermore it is not unusual in the USA for elected representatives as opposed to public servants to be indicted and sent to prison for corruption whereas in Britain this happens very infrequently. But despite all this, despite the fact that the USA is the land of the railway scandals, the unhibited venality of the 'gilded age', Jim Fisk, George Washington Plunkitt's 'honest graft', Tammany

Hall, Watergate and Irangate, the myth of 'the good society' continues to be accepted even, as we saw at the beginning of this chapter, by its more critical citizens. This is primarily because no state can concede publicly that its institutions are deeply and irrevocably flawed. If it does or if such a belief, despite government efforts, becomes widely held then the fabric of social life is well on the way to disintegration. For this reason all investigations into corruption tend to be exercises in damage limitation and a re-affirmation of public confidence in the state.

CONCLUSION

On the basis of the discussion in this chapter it seems that there is a tendency (often implicit) in social science literature to over-state the strength of rational-legal principles in government organisations in developed societies. To be sure, so far as the sphere of routine administration is concerned it does seem that universalitic criteria are institutionalised to a considerable degree and that the boundary between public and private interests is adequately staked out. Exceptions to this rule relate to those areas of activity where the dividing line between legitimate and illicit enterprise is unclear - for example gambling, the sale and consumption of alcohol, prostitution, the sale of pornography and semi-criminal endeavours generally. Here the opportunities for bribe-taking and extortion on the part of public officials are enhanced by the degree of discretion which they typically exercise, complemented by the marginality of the practitioners – the fact that they do not generally enjoy the same rights as 'respectable' citizens. These areas aside, the personalism which undoubtedly persists at lower levels of public administration is insignificant enough in its consequences, is sufficiently constrained by rational-legal principles, as to present no serious challenge to commonly-held expectations about behaviour in public office.

However, if we turn our attention to the apex of the state apparatus it seems that patrimonialism is widespread. That is to say public office, access to public office or public resources such as honours, seats on public boards, commissions and so forth, are normally used for self-aggrandisement whether in a direct material sense, or in terms of status enhancement, the deployment of subtle forms of influence, network-building and the like. Whilst the persistence of patrimonialism or 'industrial clientage' (Lemarchand and Legg, 1972) in developed countries is widely recognised, the reasons for its survival have not always been clearly explained. I suggest that the following are among the most important:

(1)   The higher we ascend bureaucratic hierarchies the greater the degree of discretion enjoyed by incumbents in interpreting organisational roles. The greater the flexibility in role performance the less easy it is to draw a line between legitimate behaviour on the one hand, and illegitimate or illegal behaviour on the other.

(2)   Since the demand for elite positions vastly exceeds supply the intervention of subjective criteria in selection is much more likely. This tendency is intensified by the fact that many of the qualities allegedly needed by incumbents of such positions (e.g. leadership, entrepreneurship, troubleshooting) are not easily codified in objective terms.

(3)   Elite political positions dispose of valuable resources in the forms of finances, jobs, contracts, information and the like. Decisions relating to the allocation of these resources, because of their serious consequences, will come under close scrutiny by peers, superiors, opponents, possibly the media and the public in general. Incumbents of dominant political positions therefore feel themselves politically vulnerable and exposed. In such a situation the natural tendency is to surround oneself with supporters – 'friends' who can be trusted rather than 'experts' who merely have the right objective qualifications.

(4)   The loyalty of one's 'trusties' is, in part, retained through the dispensing of favours – entertainment, cars, official accommodation, expense accounts, trips overseas, knighthoods, seats on company boards and so forth. Because these resources are distributed according to subjective patronage-type criteria which conflict with the universalist, meritocratic ethos of DCs, it is important that recruits to elite networks are the right type, are discreet and will not 'rock the boat'. Hence the further reinforcement of subjective criteria in selection.

Periodically the nature and extent of such exchanges are projected into the public arena either because they have reached a scale where concealment is no longer possible (somebody *is* rocking the boat), or because certain practitioners have been targeted for political reasons (see Doig, 1984, ch. 9, on Britain's right-wing press and Labour governments). Exposure may require some form of official reaction such as court proceedings, an inquiry or commission. The main point is that from the luxuriant undergrowth of personal exchanges which invades the state apparatuses of all industrial countries, only a very small proportion are singled out for 'lopping' and these, furthermore, are not necessarily the most 'overgrown'. In other words there is still a certain amount of arbitrariness about the way in which even developed states single out and process perceived infringements of public trust. However it has to be conceded that underlying this arbitrariness may be a subtle economic logic.

One more point needs to be made before we move on to look at abuse of office in UDCs. This is that a significant proportion, probably a majority of 'public' irregularities in DCs, take place in the private sector. For example in my file of newspaper clippings on illicit self-aggrandisement in Britain and the USA, embezzlement, fraud, insider dealing and the like in the *private* sector outnumber misdemeanours in the public sphere by at least four to one. We merely note, at this point, that the very existence of a large private business sector in developed countries provides a major avenue for personal advancement (both legitimate and illegitimate) outside the state.

4 Corruption in Underdeveloped Societies

'Once, I remember, we came upon a man-of-war anchored off the coast. There wasn't even a shed there, and she was shelling the bush. It appears that the French had one of their wars going on thereabouts . . . In the empty immensity of earth, sky and water, there she was, incomprehensible, firing into a continent.'

Joseph Conrad, *Heart of Darkness*

We saw at the beginning of the previous chapter that under the influence of modernisation theory a number of writers assumed that the governmental structures of the industrialised nations conformed closely to the rational-legal model. We saw, furthermore, that this model became the goal towards which developing countries were supposed to be moving. Along with western-style democracy, 'clean' public administration was the destination that lay at the end of the road to modernity. As Huntington has pointed out, these modernisation theories were characterised by the kind of evolutionary optimism that informed the works of their precursors, sociologists such as Comte and Spencer (Huntington, 1971).

Unhappily the unfolding of events during the first development decade of the 1960s, particularly in newly-independent Africa, gave little encouragement to those who had envisaged a smooth transition to modernity. The Congo debacle in 1960 followed by a series of military coups in West Africa proved to be a harbinger of the internecine violence and blood-letting that reached its zenith in the Nigerian Civil War of 1967–70. Military coups and political repression elsewhere in the third world forced social scientists to abandon their optimism in favour of a more realistic, not to say pessimistic, approach. Not 'modernisation' but 'breakdowns in modernisation', not 'political development' but 'political decay' had become the principal foci of discussion by the second half of the 1960s.

76

In an extremely influential essay Huntington argued that economic development, far from promoting social stability and the gradual emergence of democracy, would rather undermine the public order as social inequalities were exacerbated and newly-aroused aspirations disappointed. Increased social mobilisation, Huntington maintained, would lead to mounting pressure on the state to meet mass demands: demands for jobs, hospitals, schools, roads, electricity and the like. But since governmental structures are inflexible or insufficiently institutionalised most of these demands cannot be accommodated. Political instability is the inevitable outcome. Political modernisation (that is mobilisation) leads to political decay (Huntington, 1968).

A similar point had been made two years previously (in an astringent style that might have offended liberal sensibilities) in S. Andreski's under-rated *Parasitism and Subversion: The Case of Latin America* (1966). However, Andreski did not see under-institutionalisation of the political system as the principal problem for countries of Latin America, rather the siphoning-off of large quantities of wealth produced by *parasitical* groups and institutions. Large landowners, the military, the system of taxation and inflated bureaucracies are leading examples of parasitism. But added to these must be the all-pervading graft with which Latin American societies are riddled, from presidents to the lowliest functionary, and whose ubiquitous and persistent condition is rendered in Andreski's memorable expression 'kleptocracy' (Andreski, 1966, Ch. 3).

Latin American presidents usually amass large fortunes whilst in office. The president, his relatives and friends will take a percentage of all government contracts. Land belonging to the state is sold off to powerful allies or to those who can offer large bribes. Land needed for government installations is bought at grossly inflated prices in order that large sums can be creamed off by a powerful group of insiders. Vast amounts of money are borrowed by the privileged from state banks and never repaid. But the crudest and most audacious form of graft consists simply in transferring huge sums from public funds into the private bank accounts of members of the ruling oligarchy. Péron of Argentina and Jimenez of Venezuela are believed to have accumulated $700 million and $400 million respectively in foreign banks. They, however, are left well behind in the competition for the world's champion embezzler, according to Andreski, by former Dominican president Trujillo. The 'Benefactor of the Fatherland' (Trujillo's official title) brazenly transferred most of his country's foreign reserves into overseas accounts building up a fortune thought to be in the region of $1000 million (At 1930s prices this compares very favourably with Zairean presidential monarch Mobutu Sese Seko's reputed personal fortune of $500 million.) When the 'Benefactor' died nearly all the large estates, factories, banks and commercial enterprises in Dominica belonged to him or members of his family (Andreski, 1966, pp. 65, 66).

With such uninhibited plundering at the top it is not surprising that the public sector is permeated by graft down to its lowest levels. Petty bureaucrats extort payments for doing what they are supposed to do anyway; customs officials deliberately damage or steal the goods of those who have refused to hand over the appropriate bribe; and policemen – 'uniformed bandits' Andreski calls them – impose fines for trumped-up offences on hapless motorists. Corruption on this scale, Andreksi believes, paralyses all development efforts, no matter how sincere, and ultimately undermines the social order. Policy decisions are taken with a view to the interests of the few rather than the needs of society. A public administration saturated by venality cannot respond to direction, so that even the reforms of enlightened politicians are subverted in execution. Worst of all public confidence in the state is virtually non-existent, so that all government decisions are met with hostility and suspicion. Accordingly such societies hover on the edge of ungovernability (Andreski, 1966, pp. 67, 68).

Two years later Andreski turned his critical gaze on Tropical Africa where, he claims, not long after independence most top politicians had built up personal fortunes which exceeded their official salaries many hundreds of times. As with the Latin American dictators, this rapid self-enrichment had sometimes been achieved by transferring public funds into private accounts. More usually the practice was for politicians from those at the top to municipal councillors to rake off ten per cent from all government contracts or to extract payment for publically administered resources such as trading licences, the allocation of market stalls, taxi licences and the like. As in Latin America graft is all-pervasive at every level: tax collectors take bribes for low assessments or alternatively assess non-bribers at ruinously high levels. Policemen extort payments from truck drivers. Customs officials demand their dues for clearing goods as well as helping themselves liberally to goods in transit. Hospital doctors will examine only those patients who can pay them and nurses will not bring the bedpan without cash. Dispensary workers steal drugs which are then sold in local markets. Driving licences and educational qualifications are also sold whilst secondary school headmasters help themselves from the appropriations which are supposed to pay for the board and lodging of their students. This type of behaviour, Andreski is careful to point out, arises not because its perpetrators are unfeeling rapacious ghouls, but because they themselves are under numerous pressures: grossly overworked, utterly unable to satisfy the demands made upon them because of shortages of staff, drugs, everything; paid badly and irregularly; often themselves subject to extortion from their superiors to keep their jobs, or having had to bribe heavily in the first place to get them (Andreski, 1968, ch. 7).

Writing in the mid-1960s Andreski believed that a form of inverted racism has led a number of European scholars to maintain a conspiracy of silence on the extent of corruption in Tropical Africa. Whilst it is true that the problem of corruption in Africa and elsewhere had not attracted a great deal of attention until then (for exceptions see Leys, 1965; McMullan 1961; Wraith and Simpkins, 1963), this probably had more to do with the models European social scientists brought with them to the study of African politics than with excessively liberal sensitivities. The overwhelming concentration on *formal* political arrangements, constitutions, parties, voting behaviour and the like, was ill-equipped to bring within its purview the substratum of *informal* influence. At any rate, by the beginning of the 1970s corruption and the related theme of patrimonialism had moved to the forefront of the analysis of politics in the third world. Furthermore the consensus was that both phenomena, though by no means absent from developed countries, were much more pervasive in the societies of Africa, Asia and Latin America. The following observation made by Gunnar Myrdal in his influential *Asian Drama* (1968) was not and would not now be considered as particularly contentious: 'Concerning the general level of corruption it is unquestionably much higher than in Western countries (even including the US) or in the Communist countries' (Myrdal, 1968, p. 942).

Yet Myrdal and virtually everyone else who has written on corruption has had to concede that there are no reliable indications of the level of corruption in any one society. There are no statistics on corruption, therefore statements about its incidence are necessarily impressionistic, heavily influenced by its public profile in a given country or to the extent to which it is discussed in the press and is also a topic of everyday conversation. This, however, raises the problem that more open societies, societies where there is a free press and political opposition is tolerated, may appear to be more corrupt than more authoritarian regimes. This Myrdal recognises noting that whereas the

Philippines press is (on American lines) quite outspoken about corruption, its counterparts in Burma, Pakistan and Thailand are much more reticent (Myrdal, 1968, p. 942). Nigeria during the Second Republic (1979–83) for example, was widely held to have been one of the most, if not the most, corrupt country in Tropical Africa. Mention to anyone that you lived in Nigeria during this period and the conversation rapidly moves to the subject of corruption. Yet, as I usually point out, I frequently had to deal with tax officials, immigration officers and other bureaucrats and drove through hundreds of police checkpoints, yet never bribed anybody. On the other hand one was very much aware of corruption being regaled almost daily by stories in the newspapers of millions of naira going missing because contractors had absconded, usually with the connivance of politicians whose private jets, fleets of cars and extensive properties also featured regularly. However this may say more about the openness of Nigerian society and the competitiveness of politics at that time than about the actual level of corruption. I doubt very much whether one would have read a great deal about the corruption of politicians in neighbouring Niger, Togo, Cameroon or Benin unless, of course, certain individuals had fallen from grace and were being targeted by the ruling oligarchy. It is also worth mentioning that with a population and GDP many times larger than most of its neighbours put together, the actual incidence of corrupt acts must almost inevitably be greater in a country like Nigeria (see Williams, 1987, p. 67).

But instead of speculating endlessly on the basis of personal experiences, press reports, hunches and so on, a more productive approach would be to ask why UDCs might be more prone to the abuse of public office. What factors, if any, inherent in their social and economic structures might make corruption more likely?

Generally speaking explanations of corruption in UDCs have tended to be socio-cultural in character. That is to say the alleged high incidence of corruption is understood mainly in terms of the survival of traditional patterns of behaviour – familism, communalism, clientelism, friendship, gift-giving and the like – into the era of modern politics and administration. The bureaucrat in Brazil, India or the Ivory Coast is forced to bend the rules over the issue of import licences, scholarships, the assessment of tax liability and so forth in order to accommodate kinsmen, co-religionists or friends. If he does not then he not only loses face but, even more threatening, he runs the risk of losing the right to expect succour from peers should he need it in the future. In an overall situation of scarcity and insecurity, of chronic inflation and sudden shortages, such obligations are not to be taken lightly.

From the perspective of the client the practice of gift-giving is long established in traditional cultures, especially when dealing with authority. When approaching his village head, sheikh or priest with a request to perform some official function, the peasant opened up the transaction with the offer of a bowl of fruit, a basket of eggs or a chicken and so on (see McMullan, 1961). Inevitably the practice has survived into the era of modern bureaucracy and is a convenient way of softening what is often an anonymous and therefore to the peasant, threatening exchange (see Bailey, 1971). So why should the public servant not accept the 'present' even if it now takes the more sordid form of cash. And if acceptance shades over into extortion then this is understandable, for the lowly-paid official in the third world, unlike his counterpart in the West, labours under the burdensome demands of kin and friends; demands to feed, clothe, house and pay school and college fees for 'brothers' and 'sisters'. Even the not so meagerly paid top administrators, commissioners and permanent secretaries are slaves to the cult of the 'big man' and so must display their achievements ostentatiously as well as meet the escalating demands of large followings on their generosity.

I do not wish to discount the significance of these kinds of pressures. Two years residence in Nigeria taught me that they are very real and can be a millstone around the necks of individuals in all walks of life but especially in the public sector. However it might be useful to locate such practices within a broader economic and political perspective. Bearing in mind the relationship, explored in Chapter 2, between economic development and political change on the one hand and the emergence of modern public administration on the other, it would seem reasonable now to examine the links between economic *under* development and the character of the state in UDCs.

UNDERDEVELOPMENT AND THE STATE

The terms 'underdeveloped' or 'less developed' are habitually applied to a wide range of countries, the differences between which are often as great as those between the developed and the underdeveloped worlds generally. Brazil and Malaysia are so different from Mali and Nepal that to lump them together in the same category seems quite unsatisfactory. For this reason recent classifications usually distinguish between really poor countries – what some writers have termed the *fourth* world (see for example Wolf-Phillips 1987) – and the relatively more prosperous 'middle-income' countries (*World Development Report*, 1986). But despite these differences it is important to note that even those third world countries with a strong industrial base, such as Brazil and Malaysia, are significantly less able to provide goods and services to their populations than the industrial economies of the north. On average the GNP per capita of these middle-income countries is around one fifth of that of the developed countries. In the fourth world – the world of Bangladesh, Ethiopia and Zaire – it is between one thirtieth and one fortieth (*World Development Report*, 1986). In terms of day-to-day living this means that not only must a large proportion, in many cases a majority of the population, of these countries survive on extremely low incomes, but that scarcity is the keynote of social existence: scarcity of jobs, material goods, hospital beds, school places, housing, land, skills, spare parts, potable water – in fact scarcity of everything.

Furthermore the extremely limited supply of resources generally is subject to marked fluctuations. The reasons for these fluctuations are complex but at the core of them lies the typically dependent nature of underdeveloped economies. In so far as such economies tend to be over-reliant on the export of one or two basic commodities they are highly susceptible to movements in world markets: high prices followed by low and in some cases, for instance tin in 1986, complete collapse. This susceptibility bears directly on the ability of the UDC to import capital and manufactured goods, raw materials for its manu-facturing sector as well as, of growing significance in many parts of of the third world, basic foodstuffs to feed its rapidly expanding urban population. The ability to import is further eroded by the increasing indebtedness of many UDCs and the way in which debt servicing eats into export earnings. Overall, then, we are talking not just about a low level of supply of 'goods' but a supply which fluctuates significantly. In concrete terms this means that enterprises must periodically close down for want of spare parts or raw materials; household necessities disappear from the markets because they can't be imported or produced locally; jobs generally disappear but especially jobs in the public sector as the latter's already weak material base is particularly sensitive to the vicissitudes of economic life.

This last point needs elaborating as it bears very directly on our theme of corruption. We saw in Chapter 2 that the ability of the centre to cream off revenue played a crucial role in the building up of modern administrative structures in European societies. We saw, furthermore that this 'creaming-off' was given an enormous thrust by the dissemination of capitalism and the progressive monetisation of European economies. We also recall from Chapter 2 Weber's assertion that modern bureaucracy requires a developed money economy and a stable system of taxation. Now, not only do underdeveloped economies yield less in the way of a taxable surplus, but their very structure severely inhibits the appropriation of this surplus by the centre.

Most obviously underdeveloped economies have a high proportion of the labour force in agriculture, over 80 per cent in some of the countries of Asia and Tropical Africa and less than 40 per cent in the more developed states of Latin America. Of this rural labour force a significant proportion is made up of peasant farmers working small family holdings oriented primarily to production for subsistence. The collection of taxes from subsistence farmers is almost impossibly difficult precisely because their cash income, in so far as it can be assessed, is often negligible. Problems of assessment also pose serious limitations on the taxation of the commercial sector, which tends to be dominated by small businesses and petty traders for whom systematic book-keeping and accounting are alien and mysterious pursuits. Such a situation is even more apparent in the informal sector where the bulk of urban economic activity often takes place. This leaves the wealthy – landowners and big businessmen, the wage-earning sector, taxes on imports and exports and indirect taxes. So far as the wealthy are concerned their political power and influence usually enables them to minimise their tax liabilities. In fact it is not at all unusual for the most affluent classes in the third world to pay no tax at all (see Andreski, 1966, ch. 3). The burden of direct taxation falls heavily therefore on the wage-earning sector. This, however, is invariably small and contains a large proportion of public employees anyway which means that the state must derive a not insignificant slice of its revenue from taxing salaries it is itself paying out. Taxes on imports and exports seem to offer the greatest promise as the number of points of entry and exit are, in theory, limited. However the volume of imports is severely limited by the straitened economic circumstances in which UDCs typically find themselves, and a sizeable proportion of exports is usually generated by foreign-owned corporations. Even if these have not been offered tax concessions for investing in the country concerned, they are invariably able to minimise local tax obligations through a range of accounting devices the best known being 'transfer pricing'. Lastly indirect taxes on locally produced goods and services are subject to the constraints of limited monetisation (see Kaldor, 1963; Todaro, 1977).

All in all the structure of less developed economies presents serious impediments to the accumulation of wealth by the state. Third world states thus tend to be caught in a vicious circle of underdevelopment: their ability to appropriate resources is severely hampered by administrative weaknesses; but these weaknesses are, in turn, perpetuated by their restricted ability to appropriate resources:

> Even in poor countries where the industry that exists may be nationalized, the greatest share of GDP usually comes from the agricultural sector. Perhaps a quarter or more of total GDP is in the subsistence agricultural sector. Weak administrative structures find it hard to tax and control rural incomes . . . Thus these administrations find it difficult to build themselves up in a systematic fashion by appropriating national resources which could be used for further development of administration. (Bienen, 1970, p. 59; see also Wallerstein, 1971)

Obviously one would expect administrative weakness to be greater in the poorer countries of Tropical Africa (to which this quotation is referring) than in much more developed Brazil and Chile. The question of variations within the third world I shall return to. For the time being it seems reasonable to accept that there is a relationship between economic underdevelopment and administrative underdevelopment.

Now it is a major irony that the very economies that find it difficult to support modern administrative structures are typically endowed with a state apparatus which is much larger in terms of size and scope than its counterparts in the industrial world. Most commentators agree that third world countries tend to have an over-expanded or 'over-developed' state sector (see for example Alavi, 1972). There appear to be three basic reasons for this: firstly, those countries recently emerged from European rule inherited at independence an extensive administrative apparatus that had been set up by colonisers with the purpose of subordinating economy and society to the needs of the metropolitan country. That is to say the primary goal of this apparatus was precisely to *administer* the colony, to structure its economy and co-ordinate and contain the energies of its subjects. The authoritarian character of colonialism meant that for the greater part of its duration the development of administrative structures was unaccompanied by the emergence of political modes of expression such as parties and interest groups.

Secondly, this already-preponderant state apparatus was given a further boost by perceived development needs and independence. The ideological thrust of the independence struggle – the strong emphasis on liberty and equality – seem to point irrevocably in the direction of some form of socialist planning. The need for heavy state involvement which the latter implied was given an additional spur by economic reality: the absence of an economically strong indigenous bourgeoisie and the consequent shortage of acceptable (as opposed to now unacceptable colonial capital) seemed to require that the state step into the breech. As a consequence the state in most third world countries, through a variety of public bodies and parastatals, became involved in a wide range of activities: from steel-making to pig-breeding; running banks, airlines, TV stations; importing and exporting as well as regulating prices. In addition to these broadly economic activities underdeveloped states found themselves constrained to provide a range of welfare and educational services in line with the populist rhetoric of the independence struggle as well as meet the expectations – for jobs as well as services – that had been raised as a result of the increased political mobilisation associated with this period.

Thirdly, concerning this last point and relating to Huntington's argument referred to earlier in this chapter, the inbalance between the demands made upon the state and the latter's capacity to meet them, often augmented by serious communal divisions, created instability and a crisis of legitimacy. A typical response to this crisis has been attempts at state-orchestrated mobilisation through the setting up of corporatist structures. Whether directly or under the umbrella of a single state-sponsored party, peasants, urban labour, professionals, women, students, religious and other communal groups are marshalled involuntarily in state-run organisations. The countries of Latin America clearly differ from those of Africa, Asia and Oceania, having thrown off the yoke of colonialism more than one hundred and fifty years ago. Nonetheless Latin America too exhibits a strong statist and corporatist character. For some writers this character has its roots in Iberian colonialism and arises out of the exigences of colonial administration as well as the influence of an organicist conception of the state (see for example Morse, 1964 and Sarfatti, 1966). This etatist tradition was given a powerful boost during the world slump of the

1930s when the collapse of commodity prices and the drying up of foreign investment forced Latin American governments to take the lead in economic development. There are, of course, variations between countries in the extent to which the state promoted 'import substitution industrialisation', with Brazil's 'Estado Novo' (1930–40) under Getulio Vargas providing the exemplar of this type of development. Mexico since Cardenas represents a variation on this pattern whilst in Chile and Argentina statism is less apparent (Cardoso and Faletto, 1979). In addition to state involvement in the economy political corporatism is also widespread in Latin America. Political corporatism, anyway, tends to be associated with extensive state involvement and was therefore particularly apparent, at least in its modern form, under Vargas. After 1964 the Brazilian military resurrected the corporatist trappings of Estado Novo in an attempt to contain the high levels of mass mobilisation that had been unleashed during the post-war populist phase. No doubt because of their effectiveness in containing mass pressure corporatist modes of political organisation have since been adopted in countries (such as Chile and Peru) where they had previously not been so evident (see Drake, 1978; Malloy, 1977; Skidmore, 1973).

Thus despite a highly specific pattern of historical evolution the state apparatus in Latin America shares with its counterparts in the third world a marked tendency to overdevelopment. This means that countries not at all well-endowed with material resources must bear the economic burden of an inflated public sector. In many if not most cases the burden is quite simply not bearable. A major consequence, and one that is at the very core of the problem of corruption, is serious institutional instability in the public sector. At the level of formal organisation this manifests itself in unclear lines of authority, overlapping jurisdictions and under-elaborated procedures.

In more mundane terms institutional instability means that public servants are irregularly as well as badly paid. Not only are they unsure about receiving their salaries at the end of the month, but because of frequent and sudden cutbacks they don't even know if they will be in the post. They are reasonably sure, by contrast, that they will never see the pension towards which they are compelled to make regular contributions. In other words the notion of a stable and secure career structure, one that is central both to the idea and the reality of public service as it developed in Europe is, to say the least, not well-entrenched in the third world. Insecurity and instability are hardly conducive to high levels of morale and efficiency, to the development of a strong professional ethic of service. In fact low morale (as it does anywhere) results in poor work performance: bad timekeeping, absenteeism, over- or under-observance of procedures which anyway are unclear. Not surprisingly administrative business is conducted at a snail's pace: files cannot be located, necessary forms are unavailable, decisions are not taken because no one is sure who has the competence; much sought after officials are 'not on seat' despite the fact that the crowd waiting to see them spills out on to the street. Under such circumstances it is inevitable that those who are able to resort to informal influence to get what they want. Strings are pulled where personal contacts exist, bribes placed where they do not. From the point of view of the public servant himself the temptation to accept or extort bribes is irresistable. He not only has a large extended family to maintain but a distinctive lifestyle in a situation where chronically high rates of inflation put basic necessities beyond the reach even of middle-class salaries. The opportunity to extract payment for the services he is supposed to give free is enhanced by the substantial gap in terms of status and education between the bureaucrat and a sizeable section of his clientele. The illiterate peasant or town labourer is unlikely to know his rights and may actually believe that he is supposed to pay to get his documents stamped, or hand over a regular tally from his wage packet to his superior. Even if he realises that he is being squeezed there is very little he can do about it. Since nepotism, bribery, extortion and misappropriation are widely held to pervade every level of society, from the very bottom to the very top, then there is no one to complain to.

This brings us to an additional source of pressure on third world bureaucracies, a further twist in the spiral of material scarcity → low morale → inefficiency → corruption → greater inefficiency: that is excessive politicisation. We saw that although patrimonialism is still widespread in DCs routine administration is on the whole insulated from direct political pressure. In UDCs, by contrast, patrimonialism is believed to pervade virtually the whole political system which suggests that all levels of administration down to the lowliest functionary are politicised. In order to understand how this operates and why such a degree of politicisation exists it will be necessary to look in some detail at the literature on patrimonialism in the third world.

PATRIMONIALISM IN UDCS

In 1966 Aristide Zolberg suggested that the 'party-states' (single party regimes) of West Africa approximated in a number of ways to Weber's ideal type of patrimonial domination. This is primarily because the most salient feature of these regimes is the private appropriation of public office by rulers and their followers. This tendency is, for Zolberg, reinforced by the pursuit of etatist economic policies, usually in the name of some brand of socialism, but whose end result is the redistribution of income in the interests of incumbents of positions in the state apparatus. Zolberg did not develop at length his ideas about the relevance of patrimonialism to the study of African politics, restricting his efforts largely to noting the similarily between the party-states and Weber's ideal type (Zolberg, 1966). Two years later Guenther Roth criticised the indiscriminate use of the concept 'charisma' by political scientists, particularly in the study of political change in the third world. The over-reliance on charisma, Roth suggested, had led to a neglect of Weber's notion of patrimonial domination. Pre-modern forms of organisation may survive into the modern era even though the traditionalist legitimation that once underpinned them is disintegrating. Patrimonialism is one such form and Roth identifies two basic variants: the first is to be found in those increasingly rare regimes where legitimacy is still primarily based upon traditional grounds. Pre-revolutionary Ethiopia, the kingdom of Morocco and the Gulf sheikhdoms are examples of what appears to be this disappearing form. The second and much more common type of patrimonialism, which Roth labels 'personal rulership', does not require any belief in the ruler's or leader's personal qualifications being based entirely upon material incentives and rewards. Personal rulership is usually subsumed under such terms as 'clique', 'clientele', 'machine', 'faction' and so forth, and is by no means absent from modern societies. In the USA the old political machines may have disappeared but personal rulership has not. Behind the alleged charisma of J. F. Kennedy, for example, lay an organisational apparatus which, for Roth, had a distinctly patrimonial flavour. Far from being a declining phenomenon modern forms of patrimonialism have been encouraged by the expansion of state activity in industrial societies, both capitalist and socialist.

In the underdeveloped world personal rulership is probably the most dominant form of government. The Thai bureaucracy, permeated by networks based upon the exchange of material and other rewards, which Edgar Shor (1960) regarded as a deviant case is, for Roth, by no means abnormal. In fact he believes that some of the new states are not properly speaking states in the modern sense at all but virtually the private instruments of those powerful enough to rule. A major reason for the survival of patrimonialism in UDCs, Roth believes, is the cultural and political heterogeneity of the new states. This heterogeneity confronts their governments with the problem of welding disparate social entities into a single nation. A bureaucracy run along patrimonial lines with a division of spoils is probably the only way in which these 'empires' – Roth believes that the scale of the diversity in some of these states makes them more akin to pre-modern empires – can be pulled together (Roth, 1968). One notes that Roth is here imputing to the patrimonial state the kind of intergrative role that other writers have attributed to the city machines.

The 1970s witnessed an outpouring of books and articles on third world politics in which patrimonialism featured as a central if not the principal tool of analysis (see for example Willame, 1972; Roett, 1972; Eisenstadt, 1973; Bill and Leiden, 1974; Heeger, 1974; Crouch, 1979 and Springborg, 1979). So far as the first half of the 1980s were concerned this tide showed little sign of abating (see for example Levine, 1980; Clapham, 1982; Callaghy, 1984 and Clapham, 1985). However my purpose here is not to engage in an extended review of the literature on patrimonialism but to explore the way in which it operates in the third world as well as to clarify the relationship between patrimonialism and corruption. With this aim in mind I propose to look briefly at a couple of examples, beginning with one of the first works to utilise the concept in a full-length study of politics in a particular society: Riordan Roett's *Brazil: Politics in a Patrimonial Society* (1972).

Roett's aim is to show how since independence a minority has maintained a firm grip on Brazilian society even during the era of so-called democratic politics from 1948 to 1964. The key to understanding the basis of this control lies in the ability of dominant groups to manipulate the distribution of public resources so as to create a series of clientele blocs radiating from the centre. Brazil is pre-eminently a patrimonial society which for Roett is a society based upon a highly flexible and paternalistic public order in which the spoils of office are used by ruling groups to reward friends, co-opt potential and actual opponents, satisfy local and regional allies, as well as to incorporate newly-emerging groups into the system. The possibilities of incorporation have been significantly enhanced by the rapid expansion of the federal bureaucracy since the 1920s. Whereas in 1920 one in 195 actively employed Brazilians was working in the federal bureaucracy, by 1940 this figure had become one in 142 and by 1960 one in 65. Roett brings out very well what is central to the understanding of the workings of a patrimonial state; the ways in which personal connections ramify from the public sector into other areas of society. In doing this he draws upon an extremely penetrating analysis of networks in Brazil by social anthropologist Anthony Leeds (Leeds, 1964). Of pivotal importance in the Brazilian socio-political system, maintains Leeds, is the *panelinha*, literally a little saucepan, but metaphorically a relatively closed informal group held together by common interests as expressed in the interpersonal contacts of its members *Panelinhas* exist in all walks of Brazilian life – recreational, cultural, literary, academic – but politico-economic *panelinhas* lie at the heart of the patrimonial regime.

A politico-economic *panelinha* typically consists of a customs official, a lawyer or two, a businessman or accountant, a municipal, state or federal deputy and a banker. No formal commitment is made by these people and no formal meetings are held. The cohesion of the group or 'quasi-group' (see Mayer, 1966) depends upon self-interest and the potential sanctions which arise out of this. Quite simply the member who leaves or does not measure up to expectations risks losing his connections and the resources they embody which are usually important if not essential to his work and position in society. Members may enjoy a good deal of immunity from the law because of pressure that can be brought to bear by associates with connections with the police or judiciary. If the banker leaves he loses the deposits of his peers which may be substantial. The banker will have difficulty in finding replacements as most persons of substance will already be connected with other *panelinhas*. The deputy to some extent depends upon his fellows for both electoral finance as well as the votes they can muster. These votes may come from friends, employees, tenants, debtors or other individuals and groups who in some way are obligated to *panelinha* members. These members in turn depend upon the deputy, whose connections with various government departments are invaluable for a host of reasons: obtaining import licences, contracts, building permits, inside information and so on. Brazilian society is conceived as a reticulated structure of cells whose members are bound together by the anticipation of the benefits that should accrue from their association. But, of course, not all Brazilians are members of *panelinhas* since one must be invited to join and the invitation will be issued only to those in possession of resources: wealth, power, connections, knowledge and the like. As the overwhelming majority of Brazilians have very few or none of these resources they will not be included in the patrimonial system. We can be confident that the Sao

Paulo autoworker or the sharecropper in the Northeast will never, throughout their lives, be asked to join a *panelinha*.

Thus the essence of patrimonialism is that the majority of the population are more or less permanently excluded from this scramble for spoils. In the past this exclusion was effected almost automatically by the social and geographical isolation of the masses, the fact that the bulk of the population were located within thousands of remote peasant villages. However rapid economic development since Vargas launched his industrialisation programme in the 1930s has resulted in substantial urbanisation and the formation, in more developed regions, of a sizeable proletariat. The concentration of this proletariat in and around major industrial cities like Sao Paulo led to the emergence of trade unions and eventually to mass mobilisation against the patrimonial regime through strikes, demonstrations and the support for radical politicians such as João Goulart. The military coup of 1964 and subsequent repression – the widespread arrest, imprisonment and torture of trade unionists, students and radical politicians – was aimed at insulating the patrimonial regime from a challenge from below. In the longer term overt repression has been transformed into a more subtle blend of corporatist containment and sustained ideological manipulation alongside nationalistic lines (see Schmitter, 1973, p. 217).

A similar concoction of co-operation through patrimonialism, repression and manipulation has been clearly evident in Indonesia, according to Harold Crouch, since General Suharto's rise to power in 1966. In consolidating his position Suharto was initially highly dependent upon the army because of its role in liquidating the Indonesian Communist Party (PKI) after an attempted coup in 1965, and subsequently in purging and containing other political parties. Accordingly army officers have been rewarded with lucrative government positions, loans with which to start businesses, substantial rake-offs on government contracts, as well as jobs, import licences and the like for relatives and friends. Since the early 1970s Indonesia's increased revenue and the influx of foreign capital has enabled Suharto to broaden his base of support through the judicious distribution of spoils. But as in Brazil the arteries along which flow these much-prized resources circulate only within the country's dominant groups, bypassing completely the Indonesian masses. Whilst poverty and frustration are rampant, political passivity is encouraged by the memory of the pogrom against the PKI in which probably half a million communists were massacred. Carefully orchestrated political participation is permitted, the ritual of elections celebrated. But since such occasions are dominated by fraud and intimidation a sweeping victory for the government corporatist body, Golkar, is a forgone conclusion. Despite these tactics of containment the Suharto regime is facing increasing popular disaffection from more mobilised sections of the population: students, professionals, a petty bourgeoisie being squeezed by foreign capital and the urban poor (Crouch, 1979).

One could go on to cite numerous other examples from the third world but the pattern, the articulation of social groups, would be fundamentally similar: a patrimonial regime which strives to contain the forces actually or potentially ranged against it through some combination of co-option, manipulation and repression. Rather than move on to consider further cases it is more important to address ourselves to the question of the apparently greater significance of patrimonialism in UDCs. We saw in the previous chapter that although patrimonialism survives in DCs the general consensus seems to be that it is something of a marginal phenomenon there. We do not expect to come across articles or books with titles like 'Patrimonialism in the Federal Republic of Germany' or 'Patrimonialism and Political Change in Norway'. We are not, on the other hand, surprised to encounter titles such as 'Patrimonialism in Indonesia' or *Patrimonialism and Political Change in the Congo* (Willame, 1972). Is this because of prejudice and the subtle influence of evolutionary social science models, or are there conditions inherent in less developed economies which make patrimonialism more likely? Having dealt with this question we can move on to explore the relationship between patrimonialism and corruption in UDCs.

WHY IS PATRIMONIALISM MORE APPARENT IN UDCS?

Since by patrimonialism we mean patronage and other forms of personalism operating within and radiating from the state apparatus then clearly the larger this apparatus the higher the potential for patrimonialism. As we have seen third world states exhibit a marked tendency towards overdevelopment in that they typically engage in a range of activities which in industrial capitalist societies would be left to private business and market forces. An expanded state apparatus, however, does not of itself account for a higher incidence of patrimonialism. The mere opportunity to use public resources for private purposes does not guarantee that they will be so used. If this were the case one would expect patrimonialism and corruption to be much higher in the US than in Britain whereas the consensus would seem to be that it is considerably lower (see Benson, 1978; and note the absence of a chapter on Britain in Clapham, 1982). In order that the opportunity be transformed into relevant action it is necessary that there be motivation or pressure. So far as third world states are concerned I would suggest that there are three crucial sources of pressure on this expanded state apparatus: the first derives from the nature of politics in UDCs; the second from the process of class formation and the emergence of a bourgeoisie; and the third from the inter-relationships between the state, the emerging bourgeoisie and the international capital.

We saw in the previous chapter that it is quite usual in industrial polities for prime ministers, presidents, ministers and senior politicians in general to gather around them a small group of personal associates: J. F. Kennedy had his 'clan', Harold Wilson his 'kitchen cabinet', Leonid Brezhnev his cronies from the Ukraine and Ronald Reagan his 'Colorado Crazies'. All of us like, even need, to associate with people of similar mind who share our views, our interests, our prejudices and who therefore provide us with reassurance. For those in politically exposed positions – who must take decisions which will have far-reaching consequences and whose words and deeds are under constant scrutiny by opponents, the press and the public – advice, support and reassurance are even more crucial. In return for support leaders bestow on their trusties favours, honours, titles, prestige, opportunities for self-aggrandisement and access to scarce resources generally.

Now if top politicians in DCs feel exposed their counterparts in the third world feel positively naked. This is because of the praetorian nature of politics in UDCs (see Huntington, 1968). Third world states are invariably riven by deep internal cleavages centred upon ethnic, religious, linguistic or regional divisions which are over-laid by extremes of wealth and poverty. Under such conditions it is extremely difficult if not impossible for an overall consensus, in the sense of basic agreement on the rules of the political game, to emerge. An atmosphere of acute distrust prevails; politics becomes a ruthless zero-sum contest in which contending parties strive not simply to stay on top but to eliminate their opponents altogether. The political style is, therefore, conspiratorial: characterised by constant maneouvring, the making and breaking of alliances, carpet crossing, character assassination and sometimes physical assassination. Those in power use every means to hold on to it for once out they believe, usually rightly, that they will never get back in. Accordingly elections are rigged, opposition leaders jailed on trumped-up charges, newspapers closed down and radio and TV used assiduously to promote the regime. Under such circumstances it is easy to appreciate the immense significance that will be attached to building up and maintaining the cohesion of clientele networks. And given our extensive state apparatus it is probably inevitable that it provide the resources (the 'glue' according to Riding, 1987) which binds these networks together.

The second major source of political pressure on the public sector in the third world stems from the material weakness of the bourgeois class. We recall from Chapter 2 that the state apparatus in pre-modern Europe was firmly in the grip of the landed aristocracy. This meant that the rising bourgeoisie had to make its way in trade and industry outside the state, indeed *in spite of* the state and its petty restrictions on economic activity. The evidence suggests that where members of the bourgeoisie were able to make incursions into the state say through the purchase of office or the acquisition of a tax farm, few were prevented by puritan-type work ethics from doing so. This is hardly surprising since no sane entrepreneur would choose to run a time-consuming and bothersome cottage-weaving business if he had the opportunity to make just as much creaming off a nice percentage from the excise. The point is that such opportunities were few and far between because they were monopolised by an aristocracy and gentry who used them to reward dependents and supporters. When the bourgeoisie finally entered or was permitted to enter the political arena it had generally already acquired a considerable degree of economic power. Its drive for political power was motivated by the desire to secure and consolidate its material position, in particular to protect itself and its property from the arbitrary depredations of the aristocracy. In short, the European bourgeoisie did not go into politics in order to accumulate capital.

The USA makes an interesting contrast to Europe because once the British had been ejected (the first stage of America's bourgeois revolution, the second being the Civil War), there was no aristocracy (except of course in the South) against which the rising bourgeoisie had to struggle. The development of capitalism was therefore unrestricted by the kind of paternalistic outlook which in Europe seems to be the outcome of the dialectical struggle between bourgeois utilitarianism and an aristocratic ethos of *noblesse oblige*. This together with the fluidity of a national culture-in-the-making imposed few restraints on the use of public office to make money. In terms of this fluidity, coupled with rapid economic expansion and accompanying social change, North America shares many similarities with UDCs. The crucial difference, of course, is that unlike Africa, Asia and Latin America, the USA expanded autonomously on the basis of abundant natural resources under the complete control of what had effectively become an indigenous bourgeoisie. The countries of the third world, by contrast, have been thoroughly penetrated by Euro-American capital, their economic structures and their labour forces marshalled according to the dictates and needs of the industrial heartland. For those which were until recently colonies formal indepence has not lessened the predominance of Euro-American capital, technology and expertise. This predominance and the overall underdevelopment which it expresses (and for some writers is the major cause, see A. G. Frank, 1969, 1971) considerably restricts local opportunities for economic advancement: access to lucrative and prestigious occupa-tions, to markets and to capital and wealth. In this situation it is not surprising that political power and the opening it gives to the wide range of resources, including opportunities under the control of the state, plays a major role in the emergence of a bourgeoisie. In fact the notion of a *bureaucratic* bourgeoisie, a bourgeoisie which uses political power to acquire wealth, is well-entrenched in the development literature (see Randall and Theobald, 1985, ch. 5). In this vein Huntington suggests that the following statement, although made in relation to the Philippines, has general applicability in the third world:

> Politics is a major industry for the Filipinos; it is a way of life. Politics is the main route to power, which, in turn, is the main route to wealth . . . More money can be made in a shorter time with the aid of political influence than by any other means. (Huntington, 1968, p. 67)

The main point is that in the absence of adequate alternatives the state apparatus becomes the main vehicle of economic advancement and capital accumulation.

Moving on to our third source of pressure on the third world state, not only is the scramble for public resources accelerated by the strong presence of international capital but the ensuing competition between the latter's various agents to expand this presence notches up the pressure even further. That is to say third world countries by the very nature of their underdevelopment offer attractive investment opportunities, are a lucrative source of contracts especially in the area of infrastructure, and provide promising markets for capital and consumer goods, increasingly agricultural commodities as well as arms. The attractions are enhanced by the fact that the kinds of restrictions which industrialists and businessmen find so irritating – regulations regarding safety, environmental pollution, product standards and the like – either do not exist or are not taken too seriously in UDCs. Consequently the competition to break into and expand in these countries is to say the least intense. Since outside agencies are likely to have fewer scruples about the social consequences of their actions, normal business ethics, in so far as they exist, can be dispensed with. The offer of substantial material inducements to government personnel who are in a position to award contracts, concessions and the like seems to be so normal that I could spend the rest of this chapter detailing examples. But in order to convey something of the scale of this form of patrimonialism I will confine myself to the following examples.

In 1975 the Nigerian Federal Military Government (FMG) under General Yakubu Gowon was rocked by the 'cement scandal' when around 20 million tonnes of cement were ordered by the Nigerian authorities, with 16 million tonnes earmarked for defence purposes. Since the estimated cement needs of Africa as a whole at this time were only 30 million tonnes it became clear that there had been massive over-ordering, which obviously pleased the overseas suppliers whose profits received an enormous boost. But not only the suppliers benefited from the cement bonanza: an unknown number of middlemen, civil servants and army officers were also taking huge rake-offs from contracts in which prices were carefully set at 15 dollars a tonne over the going rate. Shippers also were able to partake of the generosity of the FMG whose Ministry of Defence agreed to pay demurrage charges (compensation for cargoes unloaded by the contract date) which were 60 per cent higher than normal. With more than 360 ships lying off Lagos waiting to be unloaded, by November 1975 and the FMG paying out over $500 000 per day in demurrage charges, a nice return was to be had simply by chartering a rusting hulk, loading it with cement and pointing it in the direction of Nigeria. The whole exercise is thought to have cost at least two billion dollars or one quarter of Nigeria's oil revenue for 1975 (Williams, 1987, pp. 67–70).

In the mid-1970s a large Asian country called for tenders for the construction of a new sugar mill. The lowest bid of around $50 million came from a US firm, whereas a British company bid $55 million, the extra $5 million comprising a customary 10 per cent built into all tenders in anticipation of necessary 'side payments'. A French firm, by contrast, put in a very high bid of $75 million. The Asian country's officials not wishing to offend a major American company with an outright rejection visited its executives and gently suggested that a higher bid might be more in tune with current thinking in government circles back home. However because of current Congressional interest in bribery scandals involving US corporations overseas the executives were unwilling to raise their bid. The British also refused to raise their figure so that in the end the French got the contract. It is thought that their very high figure included between $15 to 20 million as bribes for the politicians. This figure is small beer, however, compared to the $80 million the appalling former president of the Phillipines, Ferdinand Marcos, allegedly received as a kickback for concluding a deal with Westinghouse for the supply of a nuclear power plant. It seems that Westinghouse's rival General Electric's much lower bid had already been approved by a panel set up by Marcos himself. Marcos nonetheless overruled this decision before Westinghouse had even submitted a detailed bid leading his outraged Secretary for Industry to protest, courageously but fruitlessly, to the singing dictator that he was buying 'one reactor for the price of two' (George, 1988, p. 19).

Given the intensity of the competition in the international arms trade it is not surprising that a number of corruption scandals have revolved around the purchase of military hardware. It was rumours of a £22 million kickback on the sale of jet fighters by a British aircraft manufacturer to Nigeria's Shagari regime (1979–83) that were thought to have triggered the military coup which brought it to an end. In July 1987 Rajiv Ghandi's government in India was severely shaken by allegations of huge kickbacks for the supply of military equipment from the Swedish firm, Bofors, as well as on a German submarine deal. But perhaps the most shocking affair of this kind was the deal concluded in 1976 between President Mobutu of Zaire and the German rocket corporation, OTRAG. The arrangement gave OTRAG exclusive rights including subsoil rights to an area of Southeast Zaire as large as the Bundesrepublik itself. As a result OTRAG's position in Southeast Zaire was not unlike that of the East India Company in Bengal: effectively it assumed the mantle of a government responsible only to itself. We have no record of the minutiae of the transactions that lay behind this agreement but in the light of Citizen President Mobutu's record we may be sure that they materially assisted the upkeep of his seven chateaux in France and Belgium, not to speak of additonal residences in Spain, Italy and Switzerland (see Kalamiya, 1979; George, 1988, ch. 7).

Before leaving the international level it is worthwhile noting that the stakes in that arena were raised significantly after the oil price hikes of 1974 and 1979. The resulting surge of petrodollars washing around the world economy inaugurated a scramble on the part of international banks to press huge loans on third world countries. These loans were often tied to specific projects, for instance road construction, the provision of piped water, electricity power supply and so on, to be undertaken by Euro-American consortia put together by the banks themselves. Since these consortia usually included the banks' own customers back in the USA, the UK, France or Germany the arrangement had an obvious appeal for the parties concerned. It also proved appealing for the third world politicians who negotiated the loans since they were able to impose their 'price' for accepting them. As a consequence many third world countries have not only been encumbered with inordinantly expensive and in a number of cases totally inappropriate technology, but in addition with ruinously high debt service payments (in 1987 an estimated $20 million per day for Mexico. See George, 1988).

It is very difficult to decide to what degree these huge gratuities are the result of extortion by strategically placed national leaders and their cronies, or a cost which western governments and multinational companies (MNCs) are prepared to take on board in order to do business in the third world. It is almost certainly a combination of both. The key point is that the opportunities for massive self-aggrandise-ment afforded by these international connections places a truly fantastic premium on incumbency of office. Clearly only a tiny minority are able to avail themselves of this gold-plated patri-monialism. But the mere existence of such opportunities and the returns they bring in the form of air-conditioned Mercedes, luxury villas and extensive próperties overseas intensifies the predatory view of public office. And if one cannot jump aboard the international gravy train then one must make do with what is available locally. As a result virtually every position in the bureaucracy, from permanent secretaries to market inspectors, from economic advisers to mes-sengers, is targeted by contending politicians eager to incorporate as much as possible into their patrimony. In concrete terms this means that political nominees – relatives, friends, clients – are regularly appointed to positions in the administration especially the more attractive ones, i.e. those with the greatest opportunities for graft. Since many of these nominees will not have the appropriate qualifications or experience – some will have neither – then the effect on the morale of other public servants is obvious.

Let us take the hypothetical but not unrealistic case of a clerk who has worked for eleven years in the department of customs and excise and who sees the semi-literate relative of a crony of the state governor appointed to a post in his area, a post which unlike his deals directly with the public thereby offering attractive opportunities for extortion. Our clerk will very likely be unable to do anything about the situation not least because he will be intimidated by the assumed consequences – suspension or transfer to another region – of offending the powerful. Nonetheless, the appointment finally confirming his growing disillusion, he decides that he must start a business on the side to supplement his meagre salary. With a brother he buys a taxi and although they employ a driver, running the business demands frequent absences from the office. Job performance suffers accordingly. Alternatively the clerk and some of his colleagues, possibly belonging to the same caste or religious group, feel strong enough, because one or two of them occupy fairly senior positions, to move against the nominee. They therefore set out to undermine his position by scandal-mongering, character assassination, accusations of incompetence, indiscipline, dishonesty and the like. Whatever the outcome the physical and emotional energy that must be devoted to 'departmental politics' must detract further from work performance, morale and efficiency. The fundamental point is that excessive politicisation of the bureaucracy, the inability of routine administrators to insulate themselves from the depredations of the politicians, further undermines their performance, giving an additional thrust to the cycle of material scarcity → low morale → inefficiency → informal pressure and so on.

PATRIMONIALISM AND CORRUPTION IN UDCS

If patrimonialism pervades all levels of the state apparatus in third world countries, is normal to the extent that, although not approved is widely accepted, under what circumstances is this widespread appropriation of public office likely to be labelled 'corruption'?

Firstly, it needs to be understood that where the administrative process itself is underdeveloped then even with the best will in the world illegal behaviour is not easy to detect. Detection demands that there be clear-cut rules and norms the illegal departure from which can be unequivocally identified. Such situations are not easy to achieve even in the developed bureaucracies of the industrialised world, as we saw in the previous chapter. Where rules and procedures are inadequately articulated and lines of authority are unclear and where, above all, accounting techniques are primitive, it will be extraordinarily difficult to determine where or when serious irregularities have occurred. In other words, the fact that large sums of money cannot be accounted for does not necessarily mean that they have ended up in someone's Swiss bank account.

Such difficulties can be illustrated by the affair of the 2.8 billion naira (about £2.2 billion) which allegedly went missing from the accounts of the Nigerian National Petroleum Corporation (NNPC). In the first months of 1980 the normally abrasive Nigerian press had a field day with rumours that a large sum had disappeared from the nation's oil company. Accusation followed accusation with opposition politicians seeking to use the issue to discredit the NPN (National Party of Nigeria) regime whose appointees were running the NNPC (the chief one, ironically, being the Major-General Buhari who was to lead the coup against the very same regime four years later). Such was the outcry that President Shagari was forced to set up a tribunal of enquiry to look into the affair. In its report the Irikefe Commission found no evidence of corruption and dismissed the allegations as the 'greatest hoax of all time' (Williams, 1987, p. 107). In the prevailing atmosphere this conclusion was met with a good deal of scepticism and the affair of the missing billions continued to be a matter of speculation long after Shagari was removed from office. Even as late as March 1988 a former secretary to the Nigerian government was offering the 'conclusive' explanation of the disappearing naira. Mr Allison Ayida claimed that the money had been transferred in late 1979 from NNPC's account in London to a private account because it was feared that the British Government might seize it after Nigeria had nationalised BP's interests in retaliation for British support for South Africa. Whether this is an accurate account of what happened (the current public affairs manager for NNPC refused to confirm that it was), we shall probably never know (see *West Africa*, 4 April 1988, p. 613). The main point is that the Irikefe Commission found that the NNPC laboured under a severe shortage of qualified staff and had no proper accounting system. The fact that the accounts department was in a state of disarray meant that the mis-appropriation of even massive sums was difficult to detect (Williams, 1987, p. 107).

But seldom is the will there to tackle seriously the abuse of public office. True, politicians throughout the world affirm their belief in the absolute necessity of efficient and honest government and are appropriately censorious about the misuse of public resources. When he came to office in 1976 President Lopez Portillo fumed angrily against the extent of corruption in Mexico. But as he was nearing the end of his six-year term Portillo was being asked by Congress to justify the use of vast sums of money for the construction of four large mansions and a library on the outskirts of Mexico City, apparently for the use of his family (Rettie, 1982). One writer goes so far as to claim that Portillo absconded with more than $1 billion when he left office and moved to Rome (see George, 1988, p. 20). But perhaps the most ironic piece of self-righteousness, in view of what subsequently happened, was made by the then General Mobutu by way of justifying his military coup of 1965:

> What could the army high command do? Only what it has done: sweep the politicians out . . . Nothing counted for them but power . . . and what the exercise of power would bring them. Filling their pockets, exploiting the Congo and its inhabitants seemed to be their only purpose (quoted in Heeger, 1974, p. 107)

Although the private appropriation of public resources seems normally to emanate from the very centre of government and not infrequently the head of state, charges of corruption are nonetheless made, tribunals of enquiry set up, bureaucrats dismissed and officials and politicians sent to prison. This raises the obvious question of why it is that, in an overall context of widespread and pervasive patrimonialism, official moves are made against certain individuals or groups? It seems that the most likely situation in which charges of corruption are pressed is when there has been a change of regime. Setting up commissions and tribunals of enquiry to expose the improprieties of politicians of the old order is a useful tactic for discrediting it and them. This is particularly important when the new government comes to power by means which are strictly speaking illegal, most notably the military coup.

In Sierra Leone the 1967 coup was followed by the Forster Report which targeted the previous regime of Sir Albert Margai (especially Sir Albert himself who was criticised for a number of specific abuses of office). Although Sir Albert was certainly corrupt the exercise was aimed primarily at smearing his administration thereby rendering his party, the Sierra Leone People's Party, leaderless so that Siaka Steven's All People's Congress could be assured of victory in the elections of 1968 (Riley, 1983). Similarly the overthrow of Nkrumah in Ghana in 1966 was followed by over 40 commissions of enquiry, which by exposing the extensive abuses that took place during his personal rule helped to provide legitimacy for the army officers who brought it to an end. Likewise Suharto after seizing power in Indonesia in 1965 set up a 'Corruption Eradication Team', and the officers who in 1983 terminated Nigeria's second experiment with 'democracy' arrested most of the leading politicians of the Shagari era and charged them with corruption. But in all three cases there was a fair amount of selection with regard to the personnel who were to be 'processed' by whatever means were chosen. It seems that many 'big fish' escaped the trawl of the Ghanaian commissions possibly because the net, as one Ghanaian novelist put it, was made 'in a special Ghanaian way that allowed the really big corrupt people to pass through it' (see Werlin, 1972, p. 248). In Indonesia some of the most corrupt elements of the 'Guided Democracy' era were shielded from investigation by the Corruption Eradication Team by powerful politicians who had survived into Suharto's 'New Order' (see Palmier, 1983). Again a number of commentators have noted that southern opposition governors predominated among the politicians arrested and charged by the Nigerian military, suggesting a greater degree of continuity between the officers and the Shaghari regime than their public stance was intended to convey (see for example Williams, 1987, p. 110).

Change of regime is not the only situation which tends to be associated with official attempts to 'do something' about the 'problem' of corruption. Where the volume of abuse reaches such a level as to become a major issue of public concern and where this concern can be articulated, say through the media, then some form of official reaction is required (see Riley, 1983). The Irikefe Tribunal is an obvious example of this type of situation. The 'Mr Kilowatt Affair', which broke in Sierra Leone in the mid-1970s, is another. The affair involved the large-scale misappropriation of funds from the country's Electricity Corporation, revelations of which provoked a public scandal. The scandal was carefully manipulated by the All People's Congress newspaper, *We Yone*, to point in the direction of a public enquiry which resulted in the detention of a number of the Corporation's leading officials. (Riley, 1983).

In 1981 Oscar Flores Tapia, governor of the Mexican state of Coahuila, resigned after charges that he had amassed a fortune somewhere between $30 million and $84 million when his official salary was $1 600 per month. The charges, first laid by the editor of a newspaper in Tapia's state capital, were subsequently taken up by the national press in Mexico City. The public outcry forced the ruling Institutional Revolutionary Party (PRI) to agree to the setting up of a congressional committee to investigate the charges. Finding that Mr Tapia had indeed accumulated a fortune of around $30 million, the committee recommended that he be impeached for 'inexplicable enrichment' during his term of office. That the committee found Mr Tapia's self-enrichment 'inexplicable' may seem to be somewhat disingenuous in a country where misappropriation, nepotism, bribery and extortion permeate every level of the political system; where Luis Echeverria Alvarez left the presidency in 1976 as one of the country's richest men, and where his successor, José Lopez Portillo, began his term by appointing his wife to head a large government agency, his sister to run government-owned television, radio and movie-making companies and his son to a position concerned with the evaluation of public spending (Seibel, 1981).

The targeting of Tapia points up the highly political character of accusations of corruption in the third world. By the 1980s public tolerance of corruption in Mexico was wearing thin, especially in the context of the growing austerity that was being forced on the country by its creditors. In the face of escalating and increasingly well-organised opposition the PRI had to go through the motions of taking corruption seriously. Tapia was, then, a lamb to the sacrifice, someone whom the PRI bosses agreed could be processed through the appropriate rituals in an attempt to appease public opinion. As with the Mr Kilowatt affair popular outrage was focused on a scapegoat – in that case Electricity Corporation employees with politicians being left alone. In the early months of 1988 South Korean President Roh Tae Woo made an even bigger sacrifice – his own brother! Since his party, the Democratic Justice Party, had failed to win an absolute majority in the National Assembly, Roh was on the lookout for new political allies. The approaching Olympic Games, furthermore, placed a premium on securing a stable social order. By distancing himself from military hardliners and having his brother taken into custody on charges of corruption, Roh attempted to signal to the Korean public that a clean break was being made with a repressive and corrupt past.

One more example will serve to illustrate the selectiveness of corruption charges in the third world. In 1964 King Hassan of Morocco made the grand gesture of establishing special corruption courts.

However a government minister predicted at the time that only unimportant and dispensible public figures would be brought before them. True, in 1972 the King did put several ministers and high officials on trial for misappropriating several million dollars. But this was after two attempted coups and was Hassan's way of dealing with those he believed to be opposed to him as well as a means of 'encouraging the others' (Waterbury, 1976).

CONCLUSION

The consensus of writings on patrimonialism seems to be that whereas in DCs it is a marginal phenomenon, confined largely to dominant political and economic groups, in UDCs it pervades the entire political system. The reasons why patrimonialism survives among dominant groups in DCs is not entirely clear from the literature that deals with it. In fact I attempted to suggest a number of reasons in the conclusion to the previous chapter. Without repeating these I will add that patrimonialism in the sense of some degree of personal appropriation of public resources exists at *all* levels of the state apparatus (in fact all formal organisations. See Rudolph and Rudolph, 1979, and the discussion in Chapter 1 of this work). The key point is that in developed economies patrimonialism at routine levels of administration is normally sufficiently constrained within bounds set by rational-legal principles as to be non-problematic. Only at the upper levels of the state where administrative and political roles cannot be so rigidly codified is the scope for appropriation much greater, so that it is here that appropriation more frequently verges on abuse.

In UDCs, by contrast, routine administration is badly under-institutionalised primarily because of a weak material base and associated bureaucratic instability and discontinuity. This means that the scope for serious deviations, on the part of poorly-trained and badly-paid public servants – from norms which, anyway, are in-adequately articulated and under- or over-enforced – such scope is extensive. The potential for such deviations is given additional impetus from two sources. Firstly, the salience of personalism in social relations in UDCs, a personalism which survives from earlier modes of social organisation based on kinship, clanship and the like, means that where possible personal ties will be invoked in transactions with the bureaucracy. The continued importance of ethnic and other primor-dial attachments in the new states of Tropical Africa, Asia and

Oceania gives a further thrust to the desire for personal intervention in dealings with public servants. Where no common ground exists the usual presumption is that some form of cash payment is needed to bridge the chasm of anonymity which separates petitioner and bureaucrat.

Secondly, the impact of personalism on public administration is augmented by the nature of the political game in UDCs. This game consists primarily of a struggle for control of the state apparatus and for the resources which this control will yield. The principal aim of the leading participants in the struggle is to arrogate to themselves or their faction as big a slice of the public sphere as possible. As a number of writers have observed this can result, in extreme cases, in the virtual privatisation of the state so that it can become simply the personal instrument of those who are powerful enough to gain control of it (see especially Roth, 1968; Gilsenan, 1977; Medard, 1982). The intervention of international capital at the underdeveloped periphery raises significantly the value of public office and with it the intensity of the competition to gain access to it.

The extent of abuse of public office will obviously vary from UDC to UDC and it is extremely difficult to formulate any generalisations which will adequately explain these variations. It is not possible to claim, for example, that the poorer the country the greater the abuse. If this were the case then corruption would be more of a problem in Tanzania than Nigeria, and in Nigeria than Mexico. The consensus seems to be, however, that Tanzania is the least corrupt of the three. Mexico, in fact, is an interesting example since it has existed as a nation-state for over 150 years, it is unaffected by serious communal divisions and is firmly in the World Bank's 'upper middle income' category alongside South Africa, Greece and Yugoslavia (*World Development Report*, 1987). Such a continuity and relative prosperity one would expect to be associated with a highly institutionalised public order. Yet, as we have seen, flagrant abuse of office permeates the entire Mexican political system. Chile, by contrast, with less than 70 per cent of Mexico's GNP per capita, is widely held to be the least corrupt country on the Latin American continent.

It is not possible here to embark upon an exhaustive comparison of the two countries. However it would seem that Mexico's higher propensity to abuse of office has to be explained in terms of a specific pattern of interrelationships between the processes of economic and political change. In Mexico a single party, the PRI, has maintained its dominance over 60 years through its control over the spoils yielded by high levels of corporatist involvement in the economy. This pool of spoils was enormously swollen by the inflow of oil wealth after 1974 and subsequently further enlarged by the eagerness of western bankers to lend the Mexican state vast amounts of money. Chile, on the other hand, has experienced much more gradual economic growth, lower levels of state intervention articulating with a tradition of independent political parties competing (until 1973) for the votes of a largely literate, urbanised and mobilised public. These two brief examples will serve to emphasise that whilst economic underdevelopment appears to be linked with administrative instability and under-institutionalisation in the public sector, mere economic growth does not automatically enhance the quality of public administration. On the contrary, it may well be that a sudden increase in wealth (or expectations of such an increase) is associated with an upsurge of administrative abuse.

In societies where abuse of office is pervasive the selection and processing of specific abuses as corrupt actions tends to be highly unsystematic. This is because the systematic investigation and prosecution of deviations requires well-established administrative procedures and, as we have seen the very pervasiveness of patrimonialism signifies that these are lacking. In such a context accusations of corruption tend to take two forms: firstly *ad hoc* purges or campaigns launched either after a change of regime or as a reaction to what are widely held to be unacceptable levels of abuse. The second form is where charges of corruption are used to target political enemies. Generally speaking where the political contest consists primarily of a factional struggle for control of the state apparatus, and where the masses are largely peripheral to this struggle, accusations of corruption will be a frequently-used political weapon. This contrasts with those developed polities where a consensus has emerged between contestants so that defeated parties are prepared to relinquish control of the state apparatus. Under these circumstances it is more productive for politicians to bend their efforts to persuading the electorate that they are fit persons to govern.

Finally, we need to ask is a high degree of patrimonialism not inevitable and necessary in UDCs? Bearing in mind the fragmented nature of many if not most of these societies is not some fairly extensive spoils system essential in order to integrate their disparate segments rather as the graft of the machines pulled American cities together?

5   Is Corruption a Problem?

'They [US Congressmen] believed in the glorious future of their
country, and said so at every opportunity. They had never pre-
tended to be disinterested; they were in politics to make a living and,
if possible, get rich: it was the American way, and only while such
benefits seemed likely would enough able recruits be found to fill the
innumerable posts which the federal system created.'

Hugh Brogan, *The Pelican History of the United States of America*

The very term 'corruption' with its connotations of disintegration and
decay, of perversion from a state of innocence, makes it difficult for us
to assume other than that its consequences are always bad. The title of
Lincoln Steffens' epochal exposure of municipal corruption in the
USA – *The Shame of the Cities* – leaves us with few doubts about the
nature of the author's opinion (Steffens, 1904). Wraith and Simpkins
liken corruption in Africa to the 'bush and weeds' which flourish
luxuriantly 'taking the goodness from the soil and suffocating the
growth of plants which have been carefully and expensively bred and
tended' (Wraith and Simpkins, 1963 p. 12, 13.) In a recent introduction
to African politics Richard Hodder-Williams sees corruption as a
'cancer . . . which is dysfunctional to the political and economic
system' (Hodder-Williams, 1984, p. 111). And of course statesmen
and politicians throughout the third world habitually and regularly
fulminate against corruption as the primary obstacle to development,
freedom, national regeneration and virtually everything else.

Notwithstanding this widespread condemnation there is a line of
thought, quite evident in certain social science writings, which views
corruption in nothing like so negative a light, which on the contrary
maintains that at certain stages of development corruption can play a
positive role. This line of thinking can be traced back at least to the
critical reaction of some American journalists and political scientists to
the exposés of writers like Steffens. As a result of his and other
journalistic crusades the very terms 'boss' and 'machine' acquired

strong perjorative overtones. The city machines subverted everything that America stood for in the way of constitutional legality. They were the antithesis of good government, a disease which wracked the body politic and must necessarily be cut away. Not so, countered certain critics: the machines represent a set of informal arrangements which are the necessary antidote to a legal framework of government which simply cannot and does not work in practice. These writers refer especially to two features of American government as formally constituted. The first is the large number of elected positions together with short terms of incumbency and rotation. Although introduced as a safeguard against abuse of authority the need to elect a gallimaufrey of officers – 'from president to pound keeper' – reduces the average voter to a state of bewilderment. In Chicago, for example, during the first decades of this century, there could be as many as 6000 nominees in a single primary election. A typical ballot for offices in that city might carry the names of over 250 candidates for around 50 municipal posts. In his confusion it is inevitable that the voter look for guidance to the only professional adviser he knows and trusts, the local precinct captain (see Sait, 1930–5).

The second feature associated with the rise of the machine is the division of authority within government. Again we find that a device aimed at avoiding the concentration of power by spreading it thinly, in the world of practical affairs, leads to administrative paralysis. That is to say the dispersion of power produced a situation where no one had adequate authority to act in cases which cut across different departments of government. In such a situation the Boss provides the vital links between the various branches; the organic connections which are needed to bring an ossified formal structure into life. 'The lawyer', observes E. M. Sait, 'having been permitted to subordinate democracy to the law, the Boss had to be called to extricate the victim, which he did after a fashion and for a consideration' (Sait, 1930, p. 658; see also Ford, 1978). In this view the Boss and the machine provide a way out of the impasse created by well-intentioned but impractical constitutional lawyers thereby rendering municipal (and state) government both workable and efficient.

The positive aspects of the machine were re-iterated and complemented by Robert Merton within the overall context of the rise of the functionalist perspective in the social sciences after the Second World War. For Merton the machine performs functions for basically four subgroups. The first of these comprises the urban masses for whom the machine in the form of the agents who keep it in operation provides a direct, 'quasi-feudal' relationship with the political process. The personal support and friendship proffered by the machine is contrasted with the cold bureaucratic approach of the professional agencies. Whereas the latter must typically evaluate claims for assistance according to universalistic criteria, which often entail prying into personal circumstances, the precinct captain simply helps out where he can and asks no questions. The machine thus fulfils the important function of '*humanizing and personalizing all manner of assistance* to those in need' (Merton, 1968, p. 128, authors italics).

The second sub-group for whom the machine performs functions is made up of businessmen, primarily big but also small. Merton accepts Adam Smith's dictum that businessmen everywhere are averse to unregulated competition and invariably strive to create privileged positions for themselves. Accordingly businessmen are not unhappy when some agency regulates and organises competition thereby stabilising the situation and enabling them (or rather some of them) to maximise their profits. The political boss performs the role of a kind of 'economic czar' controlling and rationalising access to desirable resources in a way that avoids the chaos of unrestricted competition. In return for appropriate considerations the Boss doles out to business interests privileges that the formal system of government cannot legitimately grant. The most fundamental of these privileges is a safe passage through the alien and hostile labyrinth of public bureaucracy. The exchanges may not be exactly legal but in rationalising the relationships between business and government they are functional for both and presumably for society.

Thirdly, the machine provides opportunities for social mobility to sub-groups who are excluded from more conventional channels of personal advancement. As is well-known, American culture lays enormous emphasis on money and power as a success goal. Certain groups, however, have extremely limited access to legitimate means of mobility. Merton is thinking here primarily of certain ethnic groups, usually recent arrivals on the urban scene, who lack the educational resources and personal contacts which are needed to enter established elites. For such groups the machine fulfils the social function of providing alternative routes to success. The Irish and later immigrant groups, for example, had great difficulty in securing a niche in the urban social structure. By gaining control of the machines, however, usually through a combination of guile and strongarm tactics, such groups were able to obtain a base for social mobility. Politics and the rackets then are important means for self-aggrandisement for groups whose ethnic background and low-class position prevents them from advancing through 'respectable' channels.

Lastly, just as the machine performs certain functions for legitimate business so also is this the case with its illegitimate counterpart. Merton here makes the point that in strictly economic terms there is no difference between the provision of licit and illicit goods and services. Pizzas or prostitutes, bicycles or bootlegged liquor – it makes no difference from the point of view of supply and demand. Accordingly the racketeer basically finds himself in the same situation as the company boss: both aim to meet market demand for a particular good or service; both strive to maximise their gains; both hope to keep government (including police) interference to a minimum; and both would like an efficient, powerful and centralised agency to fix things when necessary with appropriate government officials. The Boss and the machine meet all four of these needs. (Merton, 1968, pp. 127–137). In summary the graft and personal exchanges which embody the political machines perform the following principal functions: in countering the excessive fragmentation of governmental authority they prevent bureaucratic paralysis and so enhance administrative efficiency; in enabling business interests to develop productive links with government the machine helps to promote a stable environment for profit maximisation and economic expansion; the machine also provides potentially disaffected groups with opportunities for self-aggrandisement and upward mobility; and, lastly, it offers a means by which the masses, especially the poor and the uneducated, can articulate their needs and influence the political process. In short, we can say that certain forms of corruption may be held to improve the administrative capacity of governments, encourage entrepreneurship thereby promoting economic growth and, by incorporating the dis-affected and the poor, foster social integration.

In effect precisely such functions (as well as others) have been imputed to corruption in the context of the third world although here the focus has usually been upon national government rather than city administration. By way of a critical reaction against what some have termed the 'moralistic' approach, the mid- to late –1960s produced a flurry of books and articles which questioned whether corruption was indeed the problem writers like Wraith and Simpkins claimed. One of the first contributions along these lines came from Nathaniel H. Leff, who in 1964 suggested that not only was (bureaucratic) corruption not a problem but that it could actually promote economic development. Critiques of bureaucratic corruption, for Leff, are invariably based upon a model of a government which is seen to be working purposefully and intelligently to promote economic development but whose efforts are constantly undermined by corruption.

If we subject this conception to critical scrutiny then we may be able to examine the consequences of corruption in a different light. During the first development decade of the 1960s economists and other observers became increasingly aware of the serious impediments to spontaneous growth in UDCs. Shortage of Capital, entrepreneurial talent, technical skills; structural features which could prevent such an economy from breaking out of a low-income equilibrium trap – these and other factors produced an orthodoxy which emphasised the indispensability of extensive government intervention for development. Economists, maintains Leff, 'collected their problems, placed them in a box labelled "public policy" and turned them over to the governments of the underdeveloped countries' (Leff, 1964, p. 9). In a situation where the state is heavily involved in the economy, links with the bureaucracy are essential for most economic activities. And it is here that graft – the illegal purchase of favours from the bureaucracy – can have beneficial effects.

Firstly, corruption can assist economic development by making possible a higher rate of investment than would otherwise have been the case. Investment decisions always involve risks but the risks are much greater in UDCs primarily because lack of data and (often arbitrary) government intervention make it extremely difficult to estimate future supply and demand. In such circumstances the existence of opportunities for graft provide some kind of guarantee that entrepreneurs will be able to continue influencing the administration despite shifts in policy. In another sense corruption acts as a form of insurance, this time against the pursuit by governments of bad policies. Where a government is proceeding energetically in the wrong direction, corruption can mitigate the losses in the sense that whilst the 'wrong' policy is busily implemented entrepreneurs are through graft subverting it and promoting another. For example, an important element in Latin American inflation in the 1960s, according to Leff, was stagnation in agricultural production leading to increases in the price of food. The governments of both Chile and Brazil attempted to deal with this problem by using the administration to hold down food prices. In Chile the bureaucracy behaved correctly, enforced price controls only to exacerbate the stagnation in food production. In Brazil, by contrast, a corrupt bureaucracy allowed the controls to be undermined with the result that food producers received higher prices which, in turn, stimulated agricultural production. We thus conclude that entrepreneurs together with corrupt officials produced a more effective economic policy than government.

Corruption can also promote competition and efficiency: entrepreneurs compete for scarce resources such as import licences, foreign exchange, government contracts and the like. Since payment of the highest bribe is one of the principal criteria of allocation then a premium is placed on ability to pay. Ability to pay depends upon the respective efficiency of the competing firms: therefore allocation of resources by bribery encourages efficiency and competition. Leff believes that the insinuation of this 'back-door' competition is particularly important as market imperfections tend to weaken competitive pressures in many areas of underdeveloped economies.

Regarding the alleged negative effects of corruption Leff believes that most of the arguments are based upon the assumption that development is best produced by an uncorrupted administration. This position assumes that governing elites are actually concerned about development, whereas in reality they may be more preoccupied with advancing their own interests. Again the view that corruption emasculates a government's ability to appropriate taxes, which can then be used for development, needs to be treated with caution. This argument probably attributes to elites a higher propensity to spend for development purposes than is actually the case. The goal of economic development often has much lower priority for indigenous elites that it does for western observers. This means that revenues that might have been collected (were there no corruption) are as likely to have been spent on jet fighters or luxury hotels as on hospitals, schools or irrigation projects. Furthermore if the propensity of entrepreneurs to invest is higher than that of governments, then the funds that elude the revenue collector will be a gain rather than a loss for development.

One of the most frequently voiced criticisms of corruption is that it engenders a climate of greed, selfishness and cynicism which drastically undermine if not destroy the willingness to make the sacrifices that are necessary for development. Leff is extremely dubious about this line of argument basically for two reasons: firstly, in so far as disillusion is engendered among the lower classes the consequences will be minimal as this sector is already being squeezed to a degree that makes further sacrifice virtually impossible. Secondly, he is sceptical about the view that development depends heavily upon a collective pulling-together. As far as he is concerned economic growth is much more likely to be the outcome of individual ambition and drive. Therefore an ethos of self-aggrandisement is not necessarily harmful to the social economic order. Not only may such an ethos produce growth but it can also assist the dissolution of the traditional ties and obligations that are often seen as an impediment to development.

The consequences of corruption, Leff concludes, are thus not as serious as is often assumed. And anyway corruption is deeply-rooted in the psychological and social structures of the countries where it is allegedly prevalent. Consequently its elimination cannot be realistically anticipated until certain fundamental changes have taken place. The most important of these are the rise to predominance of universalistic norms, the emergence of new centres of power outside the bureaucracy and the development of competitive party politics. Such changes, however, can come about only after a long period of social and economic development.

I do not, at this stage, propose to subject Leff's argument to critical scrutiny. Nonetheless, before we move on, it is worth noting two aspects of it: firstly, that it contains no clear distinction between 'economic growth' and 'development' and, secondly, that its conclusion is not untinged by an evolutionary perspective in that DCs, having evolved the appropriate features (universalistic norms and so on), are implicitly assumed to have a low or negligible levels of corruption.

One year after Leff's observations appeared Colin Leys was asking 'What is the problems about corruption?' Leys was thinking primarily about newly-independent Africa and especially about the moralistic condemnation of what were perceived to be high levels of corruption there by writers such as Wraith and Simpkins (Leys, 1965). The moralists, Leys suggests, whilst recognising that many corrupt activities may serve a purpose, insist that this always entails a high cost. Like Leff, Leys questions the basic assumption that lies behind this argument: that funds saved from misappropriation will necessarily be spent on desirable projects. Spending public money properly does not guarantee that it will benefit those most in need. The economic costs of corruption, furthermore, are not necessarily higher than those that would have been incurred had transactions been entirely proper. Leys quotes that example of a Ugandan minister who was much criticised for giving a lucrative monopoly for the sale of TV sets to an American contractor in return for the supply of a transmission station at cut rates. Even if corruption had been involved Uganda did get a TV station and got it more quickly and more cheaply than was the case in neighbouring Kenya, where an administratively more correct policy had been pursued. Again, would Russian consumers be better off, asks Leys, if the fixers, who derive an illegal income from getting round bottlenecks in the supply of materials for production, were somehow eliminated?

Huntington too, in a section on corruption in his influential *Political Order in Changing Societies* (1968, pp. 59–71), agrees that it can often promote economic development. During America's 'gilded Age' (the 1870s and 1880s) the notorious corruption of state legislatures and city authorities by business interests and those seeking franchises for public utilities is widely held to have accelerated the growth of the American economy. It may be doubted, for example, whether the necessary levels of investment needed to build America's railways would have been forthcoming without what many considered to be the excessively generous land grants that went with the contracts (see for example Brogan, 1987 ch. 17). Similarly during the Kubitschek era in Brazil (1954–60), according to Huntington, a high rate of economic development corresponded with an upsurge in corruption as entrepreneurs bought protection and assistance from conservative rural legislators. Huntington quotes Myron Weiner who, in relation to India, asserts that the country would be paralysed by administrative rigidity were it not for the flexibility introduced by *baksheesh*. Indeed attempts to reduce the latter in countries such as Egypt served only to produce additional obstacles to economic developments.

From the point of view of economic growth there is only one thing worse than a 'rigid, overcentralised dishonest bureaucracy' and that is 'a rigid overcentralized honest bureaucracy' (Huntington, 1968, p. 69). Huntington recognises that although contributing to economic development by oiling the wheels of bureaucracy, in that it undoubtedly weakens administrative capacity corruption, is incompatible with *political* development. This appears to be offset, however, by the contribution that a corrupt bureaucracy can make to the development of political parties. Historically strong party organisations have emerged either out of a revolution from below or patronage from above. England in the eighteenth and the USA in the nineteenth centuries provide clear cut examples of the use of public resources – offices, pensions, sinecures – to build party organisation. Huntington believes that the repetition of this pattern in third world states has significantly assisted the development of effective and stable political parties. The role of patrimonialism here is particularly important in societies where the volume of private wealth is too small to make an effective contribution to party development. Accordingly, in the 1920s and 1930s Ataturk used the resources of the Turkish state to promote the development of the Republican People's Party. In Mexico government patronage played a vital role in the emergence and institutionalisation of the PNR (National Revolutionary Party, subsequently PRI – Institutional Revolutionary Party). In Korea the Democratic Republican Party, in India Congress and in Israel Mapai – were all launched down a ramp of official patronage. And a good deal of the misappropriation of public monies in West Africa, Huntington believes, derived from the financial needs of fledgling political parties. Lastly, and for Huntington most blatant of all, are communist parties which, having once gained power, proceed directly to subordinate the state apparatus to their own needs. Huntington here is presumably thinking of the use of public office for the purposes of faction building.

In the process of promoting the emergence of political parties, indeed of some form of 'modern' political system, corruption also facilitates the expansion of mass participation. Recently urbanised and enfranchised elements can use their votes to secure jobs and other favours from the party machines. That is to say, corruption in the sense of the possibility of concrete returns provides an incentive for hitherto marginal groups to get involved in politics. However, and paradoxically, corruption in fostering the development of parties and mass participation assists in its own demise. The historical experience of the West reflects the operation of the principle that corruption varies inversely with political organisation. Although parties in their early stages may have played a parasitical role – 'leaches on the bureaucracy' – they are eventually transformed into 'the bark which protects it from destructive locusts of clique and family'. Partisanship and corruption, as Henry Jones Ford recognised, are basically antagonistic principles. Partisanship entails commitment to a set of principles and goals which transcend individual interests, whereas corruption embodies the clandestine pursuit of private ends in a way that seeks to escape accountability of any kind: 'The weakness of party organisation is the opportunity of corruption' (Ford, quoted in Huntington, 1968, p. 71).

Having outlined some of the principal so-called functions of corruption it would seem appropriate at this stage in the argument to attempt to summarise them before moving on to its negative consequences or dysfunctions. In doing this I will be drawing particularly on two articles by J. S. Nye and David Bayley respectively, both of which set out to weigh the benefits of corruption against its costs. Since the two articles appeared more than twenty years ago I will be complementing them with ideas and arguments which have been developed over the last two decades (Bayley, 1966; Nye, 1978).

BENEFITS

Put most simply corruption is held to promote economic growth and political development. The two are of course closely interrelated: economic growth is crucial if a government is to maintain legitimacy in the face of increased mass mobilisation that rapid social change produces. Corruption is believed to promote economic growth in the following ways: it assists capital formation; it fosters entrepreneurial abilities; allows business interests to penetrate the bureaucracy and, lastly, permits the logic of the market to insinuate itself into transactions from which public controls attempt to exclude it.

A   Economic Growth

1   Capital formation   Indigenous capital is scarce in UDCs for basically two reasons: the very condition of underdevelopment itself – the predominance of peasant agriculture, low cash income, limited opportunities for commercial transactions, poor communications and so on – both signifies a shortage of capital as well as serious obstacles to its accumulation. Secondly, the predominance of international capital backed by sophisticated technology and marketing techniques makes it difficult for local entrepreneurs to break into and reap adequate profits from such markets as exist. Under these circumstances the public sector offers a convenient alternative source of capital. That is to say the politician or bureaucrat may use resources he has appropriated illegally to launch himself on a business career or significantly expand one he has already started. Whether we are talking about actual funds or such things as import licences, loans, timber, mining or land concessions, their appropriation can play a key role in the emergence of an entrepreneurial class. In fact a number of writers have imputed to corruption a significant part in the formation of a bourgeois class in underdeveloped economies. Applied usually to the newer states of Asia and Tropical Africa, the idea is that access to public resources may be necessary to fuel the take-off of indigenous enterprise. A study of private companies in Zambia, for example, revealed that public office had provided the main launching pad for a subsequent career in the world of business (see Szeftel, 1982; see also Crouch, 1979). There are certain parallels here in the relationship between the state and the rise of a commercial bourgeoisie in Europe from the sixteenth century onwards. Then the sale of monopolies, tax farms and other forms of privileged access to economic opportunities provided the kinds of guarantee needed by a nascent commercial class. Returning to the contemporary context this argument is obviously valid only if the accumulated capital is used inside the country in 'productive' economic activities.

2 Entrepreneurialism Sustained economic growth clearly requires capital, but capital alone is not enough. The ability to indentify markets, to develop products, to mobilise and coordinate factors of production, to adjust quickly to changing circumstances – all are equally indispensible. It is assumed that such a complex of abilities was a necessary ingredient of industrial development in Europe and that without the 'entrepreneur' the industrial revolution could not have taken off. The failure of many UDCs to exhibit appropriate levels of growth, expecially in their manufacturing sectors, is often attributed to the relative scarcity of entrepreneurial talent plus the traditional restraints on entrepreneurship posed by kinship obligations, norms of hospitality, ceremonial and the like. In so far as entrepreneurialism is important for economic development, then corruption may encourage the associated talents. Where corruption is normal and widespread it is likely to generate a climate of opportunism, risk-taking and profit-seeking. Indeed, recalling Merton's argument earlier on in this chapter, from an economic point of view there is no difference between legal and illegal enterprises. Illegal enterprises require planning, forethought, ingenuity, a careful (no doubt even more careful) assessment of risks and costs, adaptability and so forth. Clearly more mundane acts of corruption – the policeman who extracts a bribe at a checkpoint, the immigration officer who refuses to stamp your passport without 'dash' – amount to little more than the unashamed abuse of public authority and require little in the way of 'enterprise'. (Although it would be wrong to assume that such acts were completely devoid of an ability to estimate the market value of one's 'product' and the risks entailed. See for example Riding on Mexican traffic policemen, 1985, ch. 6.) More grandiose examples of corruption, however, often suggest a striking degree of ingenuity. Take for example the case of Joseph Gomwalk, sometime governor of Benue-Plateau state, Nigeria, subsequently executed for alleged complicity in an attempted coup in 1976. When Gomwalk took office he was reputed to have the sum of ₦200 (about $200) in his savings account and ₦430 in his current account. By the mid-1970s his material position had improved appreciably the Governor now having acquired:

(a) a house in Naraguta Avenue, Jos, valued at ₦70,000; (b) a block
of four flats in Pankshin, valued at ₦60,000 for which he collected
rent of ₦40,000 from the Federal Military Government.; (c) a house
in Langtang Street, Jos, which was rented by Voteniski (a firm of
contractors in which the Governor had an interest) for the sum of
₦24,000 per year; (d) another house . . . in Jos rented by Voteniski
for ₦20,000; (e) a house . . . in Pankshin, said to have been bought
from another contracting firm, Bepco, for ₦26,000 but which was
valued at ₦140,000 . . . (g) two blocks (each of six flats) of flats at
Victoria Island, Lagos, built for the governor by Julius Berger (a
West German contracting firm) for having been awarded the
contract for the Liberty Dam (Jos) and the Jos Waterworks . . .
(Dudley, 1982, p. 318)

As Dudley points out the spectacular increase in Governor
Gomwalk's fortunes was not at all untypical for members of the
political class during this phase of military rule in Nigeria and was
almost certainly exceeded during the Second Republic which followed. Nor is this degree of self-enrichment peculiar to Nigeria (as
previous chapters in this book will have made clear); neither is it
confined to political elites (see for example Szeftel on the deceptions
practised by government clerks in Zambia, 1982, p. 12). The point
about such behaviour is that, however, reprehensible, it does require a
fair amount of skill and ingenuity. Indeed it seems that for the corrupt
politician or bureaucrat to be successful he must have many of the
attributes of the entrepreneur. He must make optimal use of the
resources at his disposal: contacts, information, the ability to deploy
inducements and pressure. He must be able to negotiate an appropriate price for the goods he is offering as well as deal with competition
especially from new entrants into the industry. The corrupt politician
or bureaucrat must, above all, be able to handle those who would force
him 'out of business' through exposure, character assassination, threat
of prosecution, perhaps outright violence. This may entail in him co-
opting certain opposition elements in order to limit the impact of
coalitions formed against him. Although we might dub the talents
required for such operations with such negative terms as 'guile',
'cunning', 'duplicity', 'machiavellianism' and the like, there can be
little doubt that exercising them effectively demands a marked ability
to 'organise' to 'manage' and, above all, to react quickly to rapidly
changing circumstances. The fact that such abilities express themselves
in undesirable pursuits, it may be argued, is a reflection of a specific

opportunity structure. Change that structure and the talents nurtured in illegal activities can be channeled into productive enterprise.

3 Red tape It is well established that bureaucracies in UDCs move at a snail's pace. Anyone who has had to deal with formal organisations, both public and private, in the third world will usually have experienced the interminable waiting: the inexplicable absence of necessary forms, the inability to locate the one official who has the authority to countersign your application and so on. In the previous chapter. I suggested a number of reasons as to why such conditions exist. These reasons apart, the delays produced by a situation where it can take three hours to cash a cheque constitute an obvious burden, in terms of time and money, for entrepreneurs.

Accordingly the ability through bribery or nepotism to short-circuit the decision-making process, to 'oil the wheels' of the administration, can result in considerable savings. There is furthermore an underlying economic logic in that those able to pay the biggest bribes are likely to be the most businesslike since the bribes represent a cost of their enterprise. Hence the allocation of public resources such as import licences, market stall places or taxi licences on the basis of size of bribe may be held to lead to more efficient outcomes than had their distribution been on the basis of official non-market criteria.

Those who have emphasised the necessity of informal perhaps even illegal influence in making large and cumbersome bureaucracies work have often cited the example of the Soviet Union, because the degree of central planning there bears some similarities with that in many UDCs. It seems to be widely accepted that without pervasive deviations from rational-legal norms the Soviet economic system would grind to a halt. When Soviet managers are unable to fulfil plan targets through adherence to normal regulations they are expected to innovate. This will usually entail resorting to formally illegitimate practices such as report padding (inflating output), the diversion and hoarding of materials, the production of shoddy goods to meet plan targets, as well as 'blat' – the use of various inducements to extract favours from other officials in the state apparatus. Not infrequently bending the rules crosses over into breaking them: report padding is extended into outright embezzlement; lavish entertainment becomes bribery. As a result some managers end up in court but, on the whole, are treated leniently signifying, it seems to be agreed, the underlying official tolerance of fairly pervasive shady practices in the economic system. Without such practices there would be no possibility of plan targets being approached let alone met (Schwartz, 1979; Lane, 1985).

However we should bear in mind that substantial deviations from rational-legal norms are by no means confined to bureaucracies in the USSR. As we saw in Chapter 1 a degree of flexibility in the interpretation of bureaucratic roles is essential in all formal organisations to counteract the rigidities which are a consequence of strict conformity with formal rationality. It may be expected that the incidence and degree of flexibility in public bureaucracies will increase to the extent that there is a disjunction between planning targets and the means of achieving them. That is to say conditions of scarcity and institutional weakness – conditions typical of UDCs – may well require a substantial degree of nonconformity with bureaucratic norms if the administrative apparatus is not to seize up.

4   Market forces   On the theme of state involvement in various areas of social and economic life, governments everywhere intervene to influence and sometimes control the production and distribution of certain goods and services: healthcare, education, law and order, municipal services, roads and railways, as well as regulatory 'goods' such as passports, driving licences, building permits and so forth. Such resources are usually allocated on the basis of non-market criteria, according to what Robert Tilman has termed a 'mandatory pricing system' (Tilman, 1968). In addition governments may intervene to determine the monetary price of certain goods and services.

In developed countries this is most apparent in the case of state monopolies under which the price of, say, a unit of gas or electricity, a railway or bus journey, is the outcome of an administrative decision which does not necessarily correspond with the market value of that particular good. In the third world this type of intervention is more common and is particularly apparent in two areas: the use of government subsidies to keep down the price of certain basic food items such as bread and rice; and the payment of fixed prices for designated agricultural commodities.

In the second case the government is acting as a (monopsonistic) consumer whose aim is to cream off the difference between farmgate prices and those which prevail on international markets. Such a policy is justified on the grounds that it allows the state to accumulate hard currency from these sales. Now if subsidised rice is diverted by corrupt officials and sold at three times the fixed price on the open market, or if farmers bribe border guards so that they can trade their cocoa for a substantially higher price in a neighbouring country, it is not easy to see that there is any overall gain for society at large. Yet there is an argument that such transactions, in highlighting the existence of a parallel market, force governments to recognise the disparity between their mandatory price and that which operates on the open market. Whilst the usual reaction is then for the state to attempt to suppress unofficial or 'black' markets, there is always the possibility that pricing policy will be amended in line with the forces of supply and demand.

For those who advocate this line of argument such a shift would represent a distinct improvement since the market is seen as the most efficient mechanism for the allocation of factors of production and goods and services. Attempts to circumvent its logic accordingly, entail substantial costs. Food subsidies, for example, could be better spent paying higher prices to agricultural producers with a view to stimulating food production and allowing market forces eventually to drive down food prices in the cities. The abandonment of price controls leads in addition to administrative savings since the costs of policing them is no longer incurred. Corruption, then, is an important medium through which the logic of the market can express itself.

B Political development

A vast amount has been written on the meaning of the term 'political development' (see for example Huntington, 1971; Eckstein, 1982). However there would probably be general agreement that political development has two basic aspects: firstly, an increase in governmental capacity in the sense of the ability to formulate and implement policy decisions as well as to enforce laws and regulations through out the territory under jurisdiction. But administrative gains alone do not imply that political development has taken place. Most writers would insist that improved capacity must be accompanied by the maintenance of legitimacy *vis-á-vis* the mass of the citizenry. This is usually taken to imply accountability and consent which in turn requires the institutionalisation of mass participation in the political process. Participation seems to demand independent political parties, and institutionalisation implies overall agreement or consensus on the rules of the political game. In short we can say that political development has four basic ingredients: enhanced administrative capacity; the development of political parties; mass participation and national integration.

1   Administrative capacity   We have already encountered, in the context of American cities, the argument that corruption can overcome the administrative fragmentation which results from the division of authority. Whereas the problem for American municipal government was mainly that of decentralisation, third world states are usually afflicted by over-centralisation, with decision-making authority concentrated at the top. This usually results in a pronounced unwillingness at lower levels to act in the most routine of cases so that minor decisions are passed up the hierarchy. Over-centralisation is aggravated by administrative confusion, unclear lines of authority, inadequate role definition, poor training and low morale. In short all the characteristics outlined in the previous chapter and which together conspire to produce administrative paralysis.

Under such conditions nepotism and bribery can elicit adminstrative action where adherence to formal procedures would yield none at all. The possibility of misappropriation can form the basis for informal coalitions which can provide a focus for policy formulation and implementation. In the absence of a strongly institutionalised ethic of public service, self-interest may be the only means of securing co-operation both within and across departments of state. The possibilities of gains through corruption may, in addition, have the positive consequence of attracting to the public service talented individuals who might otherwise be discouraged by poor career prospects. As stated earlier corrupt public officials are not necessarily incompetent nor inefficient. On the contrary, those at the top will be keen to advance the careers of the more ambitious and resourceful. Political appointees are therefore likely to be more innovative and flexible than career officers who have entered the service on the basis of minimal educational qualifications and are likely to be obsessed with formal rules and procedures. In short, nepotism, bribery and spoils may be the only means of making a remote and rigid administration responsive to the needs of various groups in society, of teasing out some minimal level of service. Their absence, by contrast, is likely to enable public servants simply to further their own interests effectively shielded from outside criticism and scrutiny (see Abueva 1978; Greenstone, 1978; Riggs, 1971).

2   Development of parties   We saw in Chapter 2 how in Europe the prospect of spoils played a key role in binding together the factions out of which were to emerge political parties. In the USA, too, graft played a pivotal role in galvanising nascent parties into action. Not all parties, however, developed in this way. European social democratic and communist parties emerged from the trade union movement and matured on the basis of support, both financial as well as political, from a mass membership. This last pattern is unlikely to be replicated in UDCs primarily because, with certain exceptions in the more economically advanced countries of Latin America, the trade union movement is extremely weak. That is to say because of economic backwardness the proportion of wage labour in organisable work situations is low.

Also in poor countries the vast mass of the population living at or near subsistence level is unable or unwilling to meet the costs of participating in voluntary associations. This unwillingness is furthermore intensified by the persistence of primordial loyalties and the atmosphere of mistrust that surrounds universalistic organisations. It thus seems that the spoils option presents possibly the only means of building followings and transforming them into political parties, of providing the incentives for those disposed to devote their energies to a political career. Politics, as Colin Leys has pointed out, must be made to pay, must offer sufficiently desirable inducements to attract the ambitious and the able from other career trajectories (Leys, 1965). The likelihood of tangible returns also promotes the formation of opposition parties. In fact, according to Riggs, without the prospect of spoils opposition parties are unlikely to flourish. Where there is no hope of getting into power and reaping the rewards of power, opposition politicians will simply carpet-cross to the main party, abandon the game altogether or resort to extremist tactics. Riggs goes even further to maintain that without the expectation of electoral victory and spoils there can be no consensus for one cannot invest in a political system which offers nothing in return (Riggs, 1971).

3 Mass participation In so far as corruption promotes the development of political parties with politicians seeking election, it may be claimed to encourage mass participation in the political process and so enhance government accountability. But the character of the 'mass' in rapidly changing societies makes it unlikely to respond to the issue-based political style we associate with developed polities. For a start the majority of voters will be living in rural communities where social exchanges are dominated by cross-cutting ties of kinship, clanship and other village-based associations as well as, for some; clientelism. Most of their urban counterparts will have moved to the city only recently and will be quite unaccustomed to the impersonal character of urban life. Both sets of voters, then, will be looking for a politician who can broker the remote and anonymous government departments to them; who can intervene personally to 'fix' things for them: get their children registered for school; put them in touch with the right official who will stamp their tax form with a minimum of fuss. Corruption in the form of nepotism and favouritism thus humanises an impersonal state apparatus and so helps to assimilate newly enfranchised masses to national politics, to national life generally. Even bribery provides a means of interest articulation for those who lack the organisational base for expressing their needs through more formal channels. In this respect the peasant who bribes a government official is using such means as are available to him to influence the political process just as the wage earner may press his needs through his trade union (see Scott, 1972, p. 24–26).

4 National integration Lastly corruption is held to be of major significance in promoting national integration. Underdeveloped countries tend to be riven by serious communal differences such as those based upon tribe, race, caste, language and religion. In the absence of an overall consensus the distribution of public resources along communal lines may be the only way of drawing disparate segments together, of providing the necessary connections between the individual and his/her group, the state and other groups. This is the 'empire-building' function which Roth and numerous others have explored and which was discussed extensively in the previous chapter.

The role of patrimonialism, or what Waterbury has termed 'planned corruption' (Waterbury, 1976), in nation-building is essentially that of enabling an emerging state to move beyond a stage of protracted internecine struggle by using public office to weld contending factions together. Wraith and Simpkins note that in England by the end of the seventeenth century bribery and corruption had replaced resort to armed force in the struggle for power (Wraith and Simpkins 1963, p. 60). It is highly likely that the spectacular graft which characterised the 'gilded age' which followed the American Civil War played a major role in national re-integration. Again the deeply-entrenched corruption without which the Mexican political system could not function (see Riding, ch. 6) was crucial in enabling Mexican political development to transcend the decade of bloodletting which followed the Revolution. On this Walter Lippmann cites the president of a Latin American republic explaining that he was in the process of consolidating his regime by giving his most dangerous political enemies ambassadorships with extra large grants. In the past, he explained, they would simply have been shot (Lippmann, 1978).

We saw in the previous chapter, however, that those who have employed the notion of patrimonialism to explain political integration have usually been thinking of the circulation of spoils within hegemonic groups. That is they have in mind primarily *elite* integration. If it is to be held that graft contributes significantly to *national* integration then clearly some, if not a sizable proportion of these spoils, must filter down to the masses. In other words one would need to show that jobs, schools, development projects and sundry favours are channeled along personal networks to the periphery. To the extent that they are it could be argued that in the absence of effective institutional arrangements for allocating such resources according to universalistic criteria, then nepotism, cronyism and graft constitute the most rational alternative.

COSTS

Those who would emphasise the negative side of corruption maintain that it impedes rather than promotes economic growth, stifles entrepreneurialism as well as squandering scarce national resources. And far from promoting political development, corruption leads to serious political decay in that it weakens administrative capacity and undermines democracy, stability and national integration.

A Impedes economic growth

1 Dissipation of capital The argument that corruption assists the accumulation of capital assumes that its proceeds are invested in economically desirable activities within the country concerned. 'Economically desirable' activities are usually understood to refer to commercial agriculture, extractive industries, heavy and light engineering, manufacturing and the provision of certain services such as transport, catering, maintenance and repairs.

Now, opponents of the argument that corruption promotes economic growth insist that there is no adequate evidence to support the idea that corrupt gains are systematically invested in desirable areas. On the contrary, the evidence that exists suggests that the proceeds are not infrequently channeled into unproductive and wasteful pursuits. Corrupt politicians and bureaucrats, the argument goes, seem to be more interested in importing BMWs, imitation Louis Quinze furniture or, in the case of Nigeria, private jets, than investing in manufacturing or road haulage. The building of luxury dwellings such as Lopez Portillo's five-mansion complex on the edge of Mexico City seem to elicit a good deal more enthusiasm than the construction of warehouses or bottle factories. Again it is by no means unusual for politicians to spirit their loot overseas, investing in property such as Mobutu's chateaux in France or the Marcos' extensive holdings in Manhattan; or simply to stow it away in numbered accounts: 'I have billions abroad . . . ' admitted Côte d' Ivoire President Houphouët Boigny in 1983. Ivoirians could, however, take comfort from the fact that Houphouët insisted that he also had billions in the Côte, proving that 'I have confidence in my country' (quoted in *West Africa*, 9 May 1983, p. 1142).

2   *Stifles entrepreneurialism*   Rather than encouraging it, corruption stifles entrepreneurial activity in basically two ways: firstly, those with innovative capacities and a risk-taking disposition are deflected from a business career into what appears to be the vastly more lucrative opportunities in the public sector. Why invest an inordinate amount of time and energy in developing a small manufacturing business when you can make four times as much in bribes as a customs officer or a hundred times as much in kickbacks on government contracts. In short, the predominance of 'crony capitalism' (using one's position in the state to dispense favours to cronies in the business world) and the stupendous fortunes made out of it is a major disincentive to embarking on a career in legitimate business.

Secondly, those actually engaged in commerce and industry must spend a vast amount of time and money simply dealing with a corrupt administration. The road haulage contractor must set aside a substantial amount to take care of bribes to policemen at checkpoints; the small-scale manufacturer of plastic items must employ extra staff simply to develop the necessary contacts with and bribe appropriate officials with regard to the importation of the chemicals he needs. In extreme circumstances the depredations of bureaucrats and policemen may drive businesses to the wall. Accordingly the idea that corruption assists businessmen by oiling the wheels of the administration is firmly rejected. A corrupt administration, on the contrary, represents a serious cost for business interests, and draining away of scarce resources which could have been put to more productive use.

3   *Squandering national resources*   We have seen that, for a number

of reasons, the state in the third world plays a major role in economic development, not only in laying the foundations of infrastructure, but also in owning and controlling a wide range of industries and services. Given the scale of this involvement it follows that any significant diversion of public resources into the private sphere is likely to have far-reaching consequences for overall economic and social development. Accordingly corruption, in that it entails precisely such a diversion must, it is argued, result in a significant squandering of scarce national resources. Investment decisions are distorted by corrupt interest: development projects are sited not where they are most needed but according to the machinations of politicians who need to pay off the businessmen who have bank-rolled their election campaigns. Tenders for government contracts are accepted not according to economic criteria but on the basis of who will offer the largest bribe. The argument that the contractor who can offer the largest bribe is, anyway, likely to be the most efficient is challenged. The cost of kickbacks is invariably recouped by charging higher prices (i.e. building the cost of the kickback into the initial tender) or by delivering an inferior product. For example, Nigerian building contractors during the Shagari era put up numerous public buildings and blocks of flats many of which deteriorated very rapidly and in some cases collapsed altogether, bringing death or injury to their hapless occupants.

In Mexico, a few years ago, a pharmaceutical company sold millions of below-strength pills to the Social Security Institute causing serious problems for those to whom they were prescribed (Riding, p. 128). Sometimes no product is delivered at all: again in Nigeria it was not unusual for contractors who had been granted a mobilisation fee (often running to several hundred thousand naira) to begin a project, immediately to abscond resulting in the disappearance of millions of naira. Whether in the form of kickbacks or the delivery of inferior goods of services, pervasive venality must result in a serious dissipation of a nation's capital. Whereas a strong economy like that of the USA can no doubt withstand a not insignificant level of mis-direction and misappropriation of public resources, (possibly around 10 per cent of the Federal Budget according to Toinet and Glenn, 1982), the consequences for a poor country will obviously be profound. In a country like Zaire where 60 per cent of the national budget is allegedly lost, they are likely to be catastrophic (see Jackson and Rosberg, 1982, p. 10).

4   *Weakens administrative capacity* Corruption debilitates administrative capacity in that widespread venality, far from drawing together the different departments and areas of the public service, provokes fragmentation, dissension, inter-and intra-departmental rivalry. The struggle for access to illegal perquisites which are usually available only to some, possibly only a minority of public servants, stimulates envy, backbiting, constant manoeuvring and factionalism. Where public office is a highly-prized commodity those powerful enough to do so will be able to extract a regular toll from subordinates to stay in their jobs. The subsequent costs in terms of the time and energy which must be devoted to (invariably clandestine) stratagems aimed simply at surviving, the low levels of morale and paranoia which are typically associated with an acutely unstable work situation, will have very marked negative consequences for job performance. A corrupt bureaucracy, furthermore, implies nepotism, political patronage and bribery all of which conflict with the fundamental principle of appointment and promotion according to universalistic criteria. Where such practices are common there is little incentive for functionaries to work efficiently or honestly. Nepotism, patronage and bribery also deprive the public service of appropriately qualified and talented personnel who lack the necessary contacts or funds. Where all these conditions prevail it is extremely difficult, if not impossible, for an ethic of public service to take root. Lastly corruption further depletes scarce administrative resources in terms of the time and organisational talent that must be deployed in trying to contain it.

5   *Undermines democracy*   Far from promoting political parties, corruption results in their atrophy. This is because the very existence of extensive opportunities for self-enrichment through control of the state apparatus places a fantastic pemium on actually being in power. The over-riding goal of politics then becomes to capture and retain the fortress of public power. This situation generates not political parties in the sense of organisations whose basic aim is promote a programme or ideology, but political machines: loose coalitions of vested interests who join together to get themselves into power. Once in power the victors do everything they can to stay there – from ballot-rigging to censorship; from the imprisonment of political opponents to death squads and terror. Since the opposition is unlikely to dislodge the incumbents through constitutional means it seems to have two alternative courses of action: firstly, its members, at least those who are quick enough off the mark, can 'carpet-cross' to the government side; alternatively, it can resort to unconstitutional means: economic sabotage, conspiracy, fomenting mass discontent, communal tension,

riot, urban insurrection, perhaps even armed rebellion. Party politics as conventionally understood is very remote from a power struggle which takes on a distinct zero-sum character and which in extreme circumstances becomes (as General Buhari observed of the political struggle during Nigeria's Second Republic) 'a matter of life or death'.

In addition to encouraging the growth of parties, corruption is supposed to foster mass participation; to promote a kind of 'proto-democracy' in which the newly mobilised, the recently urbanised and the illiterate are assimilated to an unfamiliar political system through personalism and graft. The problem with this type of argument is that it derives from a somewhat simplistic and cosy view of American political machines and the way in which they worked. Much of the writing on machines (as well as on rural clientage systems) is informed by the notion that they function rather on the lines of a primitive welfare system distributing largesse according to need, the assumption being that everyone's turn will come. An alternative view, however, maintains that far from being oriented to the mass allocation of welfare, machines are based rather on the manipulation of scarcity. The essence of this process is acutely caught by Judith Chubb in her study of the Christian Democrat machine in Palermo:

> In the last analysis, the system works less through the mass distribution of benefits to all comers than through the astute management of *scarcity*, above all, the critical element of hope. The key to the successful politician is not mass patronage but the maintenance of the maximum clientele with the minimum payoff . . . (Chubb, 1981, p. 242, authors italics; see also Theobald, 1983)

Similarly, at the level of national politics the distribution of spoils in return for political support is primarily to members of the various elites. In so far as public resources penetrate the periphery they are restricted to strategically placed individuals such as village heads, landowning castes, co-opted trade union leaders (*pelegos* in Brazil), moneylenders, urban employers and landlords – all of whom are likely to have a 'bank' of dependents whose votes, physical presence at meetings or chants of support can be delivered when required. A few crumbs are undoubtedly scattered to the masses. The landless labourer or petty trader may indeed have the vote, may sometimes be provided with a meal or a temporary job by the local 'big man', but *effective* political participation, in the sense of ability to influence the political process and the distribution of resources, is non-existent. Not only this, regimes based heavily on the distribution of spoils among hegemonic groups are invariably characterised by a marked degree of mass manipulation and repression. Whether we are looking at the Shah's Iran, the Bokassa empire in Central Africa, the cocaine generals' Bolivia or the Duvalier 'family business' in Haiti (see Latin American Bureau, 1980 and 1985), there seems to be a strong inverse relationship between level of corruption and respect for human rights. Accordingly corruption is anti-democratic in two senses: if corruption is the primary form of political influence then by definition only the wealthy and the well-connected have it. Secondly, corrupt regimes are invariably ones in which basic democratic rights are minimal.

Undermines national integration and promotes instability

The idea that graft fosters social integration by pulling together the various segments of which society is composed has already been questioned in the previous section. Far from uniting the contending factions, it has been argued that the state apparatus becomes an eagerly-sought prize to be seized and carried off by one of them. Widespread corruption seems to be associated with a pathological political style, an ethos of mistrust, subterfuge and conspiracy.

This ethos cannot be confined to the political arena but seeps into all other areas of social life, having a corrosive effect on confidence and trust generally. Where everything in the public realm seems to be up for grabs, where, as in Zaire, no one bothers to post letters anymore because the postal workers steal the stamps (see Gould, 1980), it is extremely difficult to sustain any conception of civic virtue and the belief that it is possible to act disinterestedly or altruistically. Whatever a person says or does s/he is maximising his/her short-term gains, finding jobs and other situations for relatives and friends, surreptitiously contriving to prevent others (including oneself) from getting to the trough. Such 'radical selfishness' is held to be incompatible with a just, stable and equitable political order (Dobel, 1978). The political ascendance of naked self-interest intensifies social inequalities, encourages social fragmentation and internecine conflict, and propels a corrupt society into an unremitting cycle of institutional anarchy and violence.

CONCLUSION

Having outlined the main costs and benefits of corruption it has to be admitted that it is extraordinarily difficult to balance one against the other in any concrete situation. This is primarily because corruption is frequently claimed to bring about diametrically opposed effects: promoting economic development and obstructing it; encouraging entrepreneurship and stifling it; furthering national unity and under-mining it, and so on. Whilst it is certainly conceivable that corruption may do all of these things, unless we can specify the point which benefits become costs such claims are relatively meaningless. To date no writer has been able to do this mainly because there are so many unknown and unquantifiable elements which interrelate in a variety of highly complex ways with basic variables such as economic growth and political development.

In the face of uncertainty the general consensus seems to be that whilst having some positive consequences corruption is generally speaking undesirable and should be controlled as far as possible. Not the least of the objections to it is that it is virtually impossible to confine corruption to those areas where its effects are deemed to be beneficial. The position of the World Bank here would seem to represent current development orthodoxy. Corruption, the Bank maintains, weakens the effectiveness of governments since attempts to contain or conceal it entail a diversion of scarce resources. If persistent, corruption may undermine popular confidence in the public service to the degree that it may provoke and provide the justification for violent changes of government. In states where corruption is pervasive 'rent seeking' becomes an obsession among public officials who will do nothing without bribes. In such situations members of the public are employed unproductively in buying their favours. In extreme cases, in countries which are major exporters of illegal drugs for example, whole areas of the administration come under the sway of private interests. Lastly, corruption favours the wealthy and those who have political power as well as benefiting unscrupulous people at the expense of law-abiding citizens (*World Development Report*, 1983, p. 17; see also Rose-Ackerman, 1978, ch. 1).

To relate the issue of the supposed costs and benefits of corruption to the underlying perspective of this book, it is worth re-iterating that no institutional apparatus can cohere on the basis of rational-legal principles alone. This means that the state apparatus is necessarily pervaded by personal exchanges expressed through networks which embody some combination of ideal and material interests and along which flow resources such as friendship, various forms of support, information, material inducements and suchlike. In no organisational context is it possible to maintain a permanent and impenetrable division between public resources and private interests. In other words patrimonialism is both normal and necessary at all levels of public (and private) bureaucracies. The basic problem for UDCs seems to be that the appropriation of office that is part of normal patrimonialism too often becomes outright abuse, apparently because of the weakness of institutional restraints. The key question would therefore seem to be: are there ways in which these restraints can be strengthened?

6 Can Corruption be Controlled?

'What is government more than the management of the affairs of a nation? It is not, and from its nature cannot be, the property of any particular man or family, but of the whole community, at whose expense it is supported; and though by force or contrivance it has been usurped into an inheritance, the usurpation cannot alter the right of things.'

Thomas Paine, *The Rights of Man*

Whatever the strength of their underlying commitment statesmen throughout the world, especially the third world, constantly extol the virtues and absolute indispensibility of efficient and honest government. If politicians and administrators cannot be relied upon, are not dependable nor above suspicion, the whole process of planning and policy implementation, any prospect of social and economic progress is undermined; the very notion of development itself becomes a chimera. Accordingly the fight against the abuse of public office is more or less a permanent feature of the political scene in many if not most UDCs. It is a struggle which takes a wide variety of forms individually too numerous to catalogue but which, for convenience, I propose to review under six broad headings:

Firstly, is the attempt to drive out corruption by means of usually one-off purges or campaigns. The idea here is that an immediate and powerful offensive is needed not only to punish wrong-doers but to serve as a lesson to others. A second strategy is one that bases itself on the setting-up of anti-corruption boards, commisions and the like, which subject the administrative apparatus to more or less permanent scrutiny investigating specific cases of abuse as they are revealed. Thirdly, we encounter not so much a strategy but more an ethos associated particularly with military regimes and which locates the root of corruption in politics and the antics of politicians. The antidote is,

133

therefore, conceived in terms of severely constricting if not the curtailing of the political contest, effectively of inaugurating a process of depoliticisation. Fourthly, and again more of an ethos, situates the abuse of office within the larger problem of a general social malaise, a kind of moral vacuum or anomie the remedy for which is some form of moral regeneration or moral re-armament. Fifthly, is the long-established tradition which sees corruption to be fundamentally about the abuse of power and accordingly looks to the strengthening of the checks on the abuse of power, the enhancement of the accountability of the powerful, as the principal means of combating the phenomenon. Lastly comes the view that the only effective way of dealing with this abuse is drastically to reduce the opportunities for corrupt trans-actions. This is to be achieved primarily by cutting back on the state's activities, a strategy which is supposed to be particularly appropriate for UDCs with their over-expanded public sectors. It also resonates with the current faith of international agencies such as the IMF in the efficacy of free market forces.

Before moving on to look at the main characteristics of each approach it is worthwhile pointing out that in the most general of senses all UDCs are continually preoccupied with the problem of abuse of office as part of the overall concern with administrative efficiency. Administrative reform is an ongoing process in all societies, but where the public sector plays a pivotal role in bringing about desired change then the character of the administrative apparatus becomes absolutely central to the process of development. Accordingly, there has emerged over the past two decades a sub-stantial policy-oriented literature which usually comes under the rubric of 'development administration' and whose main focus is the study of the administrative arrangements which are most appropriate for the implementation of development policies in economically backward societies.

This is not the place at which to embark on even a cursory survey of development administration literature. But in order to orient the subsequent discussion it will serve to point out that the overall enhancement of administrative capacity of the third world is usually thought to have two basic aspects: the first concerns the structural arrangements which are deemed most appropriate to the development needs of respective countries. The number, size and functions of ministries and departments of state, their relationship to each other and to other government bodies, and to the supreme executive authority; the number and size of departments within ministries, the division of functions between departments, the layers of authority within them, the most appropriate elaboration of rules and procedures as well as definitions of bureaucratic roles, the design and implementation of effective accounting and budgetary controls – all are central foci of development administration. And since the overwhelming majority of citizens in UDCs encounter government only at its lowest levels, then a major concern of this area of study is or should be the pursuit of those arrangements which permit the simplest and speediest resolution of the myriad routine decisions which, although individually undoubtedly trivial, collectively constitute the heart of public administration and its problems.

The second principal focus of development administration is on the quality of the personnel who occupy bureaucratic positions. Precisely because development administration is concerned with societies which are in the throes of rapid social and economic change, an accelerated transition from traditional to modern forms, the administrative arrangements in these societies are allegedly susceptible to certain 'pathologies'. The more dominant of these are held to be: resistance to change, commitment to traditional relationships and customs, bureaucratic formalism in the sense of a rigid adherence to rules and procedures with a concommitant indifference to or ignorance of the rationale behind these rules and procedures, a reluctance to delegate, an obsession with status and its symbols and lastly nepotism, favouritism and corruption (see Montgomery, 1972). Strategies aimed at curing such pathologies tend to emphasise effective programmes of recruitment, training and staff development coupled with the institutionalisation of a stable career structure. The primary goal of such policies is to inculcate the kind of public service ethos, the administrative professionalism which, along with occupational security, is seen to be an indispensible component of modern government everywhere. Accordingly most UDCs have the equivalent of a civil service commission (often part of the colonial heritage) one of whose basic tasks is to urge the supremacy of the principle of merit in recruitment and promotion as well as adherence to rational precepts generally in the conduct of all administrative affairs.

Whilst adminstrative reform is a permanent and continuous process the amount of time it takes for supposed improvements to percolate through bureaucratic structures is invariably considerable. The time-lag between the conception of an idea for reform, its transformation into a concrete programme and the appearance of discernible and attributable results is seldom less than five years and may take as long as ten (see for example Reilly, W., 1979, ch. 2). Since corruption is a live political issue and since those who have political power are pre-occupied with short-term results, the malady sems to require more immediate and visible surgery. Taking visibility in its most literal sense the cure might take the form of the public execution of discredited politicians in front of the world's TV cameras as happened in Liberia in 1980. Less dramatic but still highly visible, within the countries concerned, are the campaigns and purges periodically unleashed against the politicians and bureaucrats whose rapacity and indiscipline are held to have undermined the social order.

PURGES AND CAMPAIGNS

As we saw at the end of Chapter 4 major drives against corruption are usually associated with political upheaval, typically a change of regime. These purges may take the form of the careful targeting of certain prominent representatives of the *ancien regime*, the primary goal being to discredit it and establish the legitimacy of its successor. Thus when Lopez Portillo assumed the Mexican presidency in 1976 an atmosphere of widespread public disenchantment with government corruption prompted him to jail several senior officials of the preceeding Echeverria regime on charges of extortion, the solicitation of bribes and embezzlement. By means of this ostensibly radical action Portillo was signalling to the Mexican public that he, unlike Echeverria, took the problem of corruption seriously and was deter-mined to do something about it. Jailing some of Echeverria's leading cronies also served as a warning to the former president to stay out of politics now that he was no longer in office (Riding, 1987, ch.6).

An offensive against corruption has also been a prominent feature of First Secretary Gorbachev's audacious attempt to shake up the hitherto largely inert political edifice of the USSR. Senior party members, administrators, policemen, even high-ranking KGB officers have been dismissed or put on trial for corruption or for illegally harassing citizens, journalists and the like who had laid charges of abuse against them. Undoubtedly the most sensational move to date in Gorbachev's often breathtaking assault against the past was the arrest and bringing to trial in 1988 of Yuri Churbanov. Churbanov was not only First Deputy Minister of the Interior (which meant that he was virtually in charge of the national police) but also had the good fortune to be a son-in-law of former General Secretary of the Soviet

Communist Party Leonid Brezhnev. Churbanov's privileged position brought him many benefits, not least around £600 000 being his cut from the massive fraud involving state payments for a non-existent cotton crop in Soviet Central Asia. However, as the *Independent* Moscow correspondent pointed out at the time, it was not just Churbanov and eight accomplices who were put on trial in the autumn of 1988 but the whole Brezhnev era, now villified as the 'period of stagnation' in *glasnost* demonology (Cornwell, 1988). In fact the Gorbachev offensive was not confined to hitting a limited number of powerful figures from the past. Taking up an initiative begun by Andropov a thorough-going purge of the party and administration has resulted in the dismissal or prosecution of around 4000 officials.

Such far-reaching campaigns have also been a prominent feature of the political scene in China since the Revolution. Soon after the Chinese Communist Party came to power in 1949 a series of campaigns was launched against corrupt dealings between cadres and officials and certain surviving factions of the pre-revolutionary bourgeoisie. The 'Three Antis Campaign' of the early 1950s exhorted ordinary people to criticise favouritism and graft among party members. Ad hoc committees and mobile investigation teams were encouraged from above and pressure put on officials to confess publicly their misdemeanours. A crucial feature of the campaign was that protection was extended to members of the public who were prepared to expose cases of abuse. As a result of this and a follow-up campaign large-scale corruption based on links between officials and businessmen was virtually eradicated from the urban context (see Østergaard, 1983). After another major social upheaval, the Great Leap Forward (1958–61), corruption was perceived to be a major problem in China. This was because the large-scale disruption provoked by the Leap led to demoralisation and withdrawal among lower level party cadres (who generally took the blame for its often spectacular failures) with the result that many members and minor officials concentrated on feathering their own nests. Accordingly in the early 1960s the 'Four Clean-ups' or 'Socialist Education Movement' was launched. Focused on the countryside, now the epicentre of China's revolutionary road to modernisation, the movement was ostensibly directed at helping the peasantry acquire the confidence and organisation to criticise effectively anti-socialist behaviour by local cadres and elites. In fact the campaign developed into a contest between, on the one hand, higher party echelons seeking to contain it and, on the other, local activists keen to promote Mao's emphasis on popular mobilisation embodied in his notion of the 'mass line' (see especially Gray, 1972). The outcome was that the Socialist Education Movement was largely diverted into an operation whose character differed markedly from the proclaimed intention. It became an exercise in which the Party dispatched special teams to the countryside to conduct low-key investigations keeping the peasantry in the background as much as possible. Cases of corruption were exposed but the aim was now to ensure that the investigations were kept firmly under the control of the Party (see Østergaard, 1983).

'Operation Purge the Nation' was in no sense intended to be a mass movement, being a major assault launched by the Nigerian military against the public sector in the wake of the coup that removed General Gowon from power in July 1975. With their reputation at its nadir following the cement scandal and the depredations of the hated military governors (now dismissed), the soldiers, under Murtala Muhammad, needed a dramatic gesture both to restore public confidence in themselves as rulers as well as in the Nigerian state at large. The purge affected all public sector organisations, including parastatals and the universities, but was concentrated on the federal civil service and the administrative organs of the country's twelve states. Between 10 000 and 12 000 public servants were dismissed for such offences as 'abuse of office', 'decline in productivity', 'divided loyalty' and 'corruption' (see Adamolekun, 1986, pp. 120, 122; Williams, 1987, p. 109). A similar but much more drastic exercise was carried out almost a decade later after General Buhari had removed the recently re-elected civilian government of Shehu Shagari. In addition to arresting most of the leading politicians of the Shagari era the military dismissed, demoted or retired probably more than 100 000 public officers between January and October 1984. The federal civil service lost no fewer than 17 of its 33 permanent secretaries and the purge spread to the universities, the military and the police (see Oluwu, 1985; *West Africa*, 26 March 1984).

The dismissal of personnel on this scale will clearly have far-reaching consequences for the subsequent quality of the public service, especially in terms of loss of trained manpower and effects on morale. With regard to the latter 'Operation Purge the Nation' is held to have had profoundly negative effects on civil service morale primarily because it banished completely the notion of security of tenure. One may well imagine the inertia and defensiveness that this type of exercise is likely to produce amongst those who survive it. Despite this such an operation might be justified if it could be shown that it helped to cut away some of the dead wood – the relatives, friends and political appointees, often untrained and incompetent, who constitute a considerable burden on the public purse in most UDCs. Unfortunately there is no evidence that this is the case. On the contrary the very character of such purges, the need for immediate and highly visible effects, means that they are invariably carried out in haste without sufficient time for proper consideration of the cases they deal with. This was certainly what happened in Nigeria in 1975, when the newly-appointed military governors were given hardly any time to appraise the situation in their respective states and were under strong pressure to provide lists of malefactors as soon as they had assumed office. They therefore had to embark upon an arbitrary and indiscriminate removal of top civil servants relying on very dubious advice from vested interests: 'favour-seekers, cringers and stooges' according to one well-known ex-civil servant and expert on public administration (Adebayo, 1981, pp. 149, 50). The fact that the situation provided a wonderful opening for opportunism and the settling of scores was subsequently conceded by head of state General Obasanjo (Adamolekun, 1986, pp. 121, 22).

In sum, one-off purges and campaigns seem to have extremely limited impact on the level of corruption in a given polity. On the contrary in so far as such measures promote an atmosphere of mistrust and paranoia they may be held to encourage bureaucratic pathologies such as cronyism, factionalism and excessive politicisation, if not actual corruption. The main function of these exercises seems to be to discredit and possibly eleminate opponents whilst at the same time whipping up popular support by means of a political 'show' of 'doing something' (on the importance of the show in politics see Nettl, 1967, pp. 264–5).

LEGAL ADMINISTRATIVE MEASURES

Legal-administrative measures aimed at controlling corruption are specialised and semi-permanent bodies whose sole responsibility is to investigate alleged infringements of the law relating to behaviour in public office with a view to bringing them before the courts. Such organisations would seem to have a number of advantages over campaigns and purges: since they exist over the long term they should be able to acquire a corpus of trained staff who are able to develop a specific expertise in investigating cases of abuse. In an age of large-scale and complex financial transactions such expertise, not least a sound knowledge of public finance and accounting, would seem to be essential for effective operation. Furthermore, in so far as the enquiries of anti-corruption bodies are based upon careful and painstaking investigations, striving to avoid arbitrary or tendentious accusations, they are more likely to win the confidence of the civil service and the general public.

In India the fight against corruption goes back at least to Lord Cornwallis (appointed Governor-General in 1786) and his insistence that Company servants abandon involvement in commercial transactions confining their activities to public business. Whilst petty corruption – 'speed money' – is tolerated in modern India by the recognition that probably nothing can be done about it, various attempts have been made to keep in check abuses by senior or 'gazetted' public servants. Official concern about corruption intensified after independence had brought a massive increase of state involvement in the economy thereby greatly expanding the opportunities for graft. Since 1964 a Central Vigilance Commission with branches in each ministry has been the principal watchdog over the civil service. Branches report suspected abuses to the Central Commission who pass on cases to a special department of the police, the Central Bureau of Investigation (CBI). The Bureau investigates and brings suitable cases before the courts. The fact that the Bureau acquires resources on the basis of the number of convictions it secures is supposed to be some kind of guarantee against the lethargy that is often attributed to such institutions elsewhere. According to Palmier these arrangements have proved reasonably effective in containing corruption without actually reducing it. Despite strenuous efforts the CBI has not been able to increase the number of convictions of corrupt public servants even though opportunities for abuse continue to increase. Weighing this record against the alleged extent of corruption in contemporary India one may liken the position of the Central Vigilance Commission to a thumb in a dyke that crumbles irreparably under the swell of a 'sea of corruption' (Palmier, 1975, 1981; see also *Guardian Weekly*, 10 January 1988).

Interestingly Palmier also discusses the activities of the Independent Commission against Corruption (ICAC), set up in Hong Kong in 1974 in the aftermath of a scandal over the escape from the island of a senior police officer who was under investigation for corruption. The ICAC is independent of the police and of any government department reporting directly to a judge. Although technically a civilian organisation it has many police powers including the ability to detain suspects without trial. In addition to investigation and prosecution the ICAC has sought to make it easier for members of the public to report instances of corruption and has used the media to emphasise its anti-social consequences. As a result public confidence in the ICAC has grown as have the number of cases reported to it. Three years after it was established the Commission had broken the major syndicated corruption rackets in the police force. Unfortunately, though, its very success provoked a police mutiny against its activities. The concessions to the force that Hong Kong's governor consequently had to make have probably weakened the ICAC's clout (Palmier, 1983).

Since the turbulence and chaos of the Cultural Revolution China's leaders have jettisoned mass campaigns against corruption in favour of relying on mass education coupled with administrative measures. The Party's main organisational device for combating corruption since 1979 has been the Discipline Inspection Commissions which operate at all levels under the direction of a central body. The commissions are supposed to ensure that standards of behaviour regarding the use of public funds, especially in the area of entertainment (often a form of covert bribery), are strictly adhered to. Despite a strong emphasis on the role of the commissions in the fight against corruption since 1981 there is no evidence that they have made a serious impact. On the contrary, with the enthronement of the profit motive under the post-Mao modernisation programme, there is speculation that corruption may be increasing (see for example Gittings, 1981). The thrust, anyway, of the commissions seems to have been attenuated by a difference of interests between the Party on the one hand, and law enforcement and judicial agencies on the other. The need for Party supremacy means that it, rather than the impartial application of legal criteria, ultimately determines which cases of abuse are to be processed (Østergaard, 1986).

Despite the acknowledged failure of 'Operation Purge the Nation' the crusade against corruption in Nigeria was continued under Obasanjo with the setting up of a Public Complaints Bureau (PCB) and a Corrupt Practices Investigation Bureau (CPIB). The Public Complaints Bureau, theoretically with a branch in each state, was supposed to deal with administrative abuse generally. The commissioner of the CPIB was to investigate all allegations of corruption reported to it and was empowered to command the production of whatever evidence was required. The commissioner was not able to initiate proceedings against suspects having to recommend cases for action to the Criminal Investigation Department of the police. The CPIB achieved little being hampered by a lack of resources and the vagueness of its relationship with the police. It and the PCB, supposedly more successful but also poorly staffed, were abolished at the transition to civilian rule in 1979 to be replaced by a Code of Conduct, a Code of Conduct Bureau and a Code of Conduct Tribunal.

Under the prescriptions of the Code senior politicians and civil servants were forbidden from accepting a loan from other than certain specified financial institutions and were precluded from deriving any benefit of whatever nature from a company, contractor or business-man. Politicians and civil servants were also not allowed to hold bank accounts outside Nigeria. In addition *all* public officers were required to submit to the Code of Conduct Bureau 'a written declaration of all his properties, assets and liabilities and those of spouse and unmarried children under 21 years old' (Dudley, 1982, pp. 136, 7). In addition to receiving declarations of assets the Bureau was to investigate all complaints about non-compliance with the Code and where contravention was proven recommend one of a number of specified penalties. As Dudley has pointed out the provisions on the declaration of assets is bizarre for it could mean that within the space of four years the Bureau would have to process some four million declarations. This would need any army of public servants who would themselves need to declare their assets. The logical outcome could be that every Nigerian citizen is employed processing each others' assets! (Dudley, p. 137). Whilst such absurd prescriptions cannot be translated into political reality, Dudley's observation does point to one of the principal weaknesses of anti-corruption agencies: that such bodies depend upon administrative resources which in UDCs, as emphasised throughout this book, are in extremely short supply. In concrete terms this means that the availability of adequate buildings, typewriters, filing cabinets, telephones, motor vehicles, secretaries and competent investigators will be grossly inadequate. Staffing seems to present particular problems as investigating officers must have exceptionally high levels of skill and motivation if they are to be effective and, most of all, constitute a deterrent. They must, first of all, be able to develop the investigative talents that will enable them to penetrate the often formidable defensive screens which departments under scrutiny typically throw up in self-protection. These screens will comprise such tactics as non-cooperation, withholding information, laying false trails, accusing investigators of victimisation, ethnic bias and so on. Agents must also be highly motivated because the task on which they are engaged is fairly unrewarding. Firstly, the perquisites with which a large number of public servants regularly supplement their incomes are not available to anti-corruption officers; and, secondly, since their job is to cut off or reduce the supply of these perquisites they will be the focus of considerable hostility and resentment. Anti-corruption work is therefore not popular and does not generally attract the brightest and most ambitious of individuals, especially when there are more promising alternatives. In Shagari's Nigeria the clamour among graduates to join the customs service was not matched by a rush to the Code of Conduct Bureau. But this, after all, was not so astonishing for nobody really took the Code of Conduct seriously. For more than three years the national assembly refused to pass the law which would give the Tribunal the powers required to compel political office holders to abide by the provisions of the Code. Not until 1983, the final year of his first term, did Shagari ask his ministers and other office holders to declare their assets. In the event only Shagari and his vice-president did so declare.

The Nigerian experience highlights the main weakness of legal administrative attempts to combat corruption: that they ultimately depend upon the commitment and good intentions of those who hold political power. Where the political will is absent no amount of laws, bureaux, commissions or draconian punishments will even begin to make an impact on let alone deal with corruption. Where the politically powerful use their position to shield relatives and friends, where public offices are normally doled out to kinsmen, cronies and financial backers, administrative measures against corruption will have minimal effects. In fact they too are often employed to target relatively unimportant bureaucrats or politicians who have fallen from grace, whilst the real culprits in the political class are left to their own devices. This seems to suggest strongly that the political class itself must be subjected to greater regulation and many would argue that the most effective way of achieving this, especially where the means of administration are weak, is by strengthening political accountability. The accountability option I will come to presently. Before turning to it I want to consider first a more drastic alternative, one that had not only been attempted in a large number of UDCs but for which it is possible to find some support in a certain type of development literature. I refer to the depoliticisation option under which an authoritarian (usually military) government by effectively banning politics and politicians, in theory, greatly reduces the pressure on the public sphere. If you don't have parties and elections then you don't need to pay off your backers with contracts and jobs!

DEPOLITICISATION

In his penetrating study of long-established attempts to reform the Brazilian civil service, L. S. Graham focuses on the central role played by the State Department of Public Service (DASP) set up in July 1938 during the authoritarian rule of Getulio Vargas. DASP acted as Brazil's civil service commission the primary goal of which was to curtail the system of patronage which had dominated government both before and since independence. In its efforts to substitute a merit system DASP was given the authority to monitor all placements, transfers, as well as disciplinary procedures to ensure that they conformed with rational-legal criteria. DASP also had responsibility for pre-service and in-service training together with the promotion of organisational efficiency and effective co-ordination within the civil service.

Now, the most important point that comes out of Graham's careful analysis is that DASP was able to operate most effectively under Vargas achieving considerable success in institutionalising the supremacy of rational and universalistic principles within the civil service. With the onset of the era of democratic politics (1945–64), however, DASP went into a marked decline in the face of a significant resurgence of patrimonialism. The decline is explained by Graham in terms of the integrative needs of the Brazilian state during a period of rapid industrialisation accompanied by high levels of mass mobilisation. That is to say in their attempts to come to terms with the demands of a mass electorate Brazilian politicians increasingly turned their sights on the state bureaucracy, thereby making an upsurge of patrimonialism inevitable. With the need to incorporate the masses the Brazilian political elite were quite uninterested in DASP's basic goals. As a consequence the civil service was transformed from a 'guardian' bureaucracy into a patronage bureaucracy in which principles of merit and efficiency played a fairly minimal role (Graham, 1968, ch. xi). Crucial for the issue of depoliticisation, Graham suggests that the return to power of the military in 1964 saw a resurgence of commitment to the principles of economy, efficiency and merit. On this point Graham receives support from Thomas Skidmore who notes after 1964, and especially after 1967, a concerted effort by the military to suppress brokerage networks in the civil service and establish a thoroughly technocratic system (Skidmore, 1973).

A situation with a number of parallels with Brazil was to be found in Indonesia after the coup which brought General Suharto to power in

1965. Under the 'New Order' a commission was set up to examine the problem of corruption. The commission identified two fundamental causes: the first was the general lack of efficient administrative and budgetary controls which allowed civil servants to use their positions more or less as they pleased. To counter this defect it was recommended that opportunities for corruption be reduced by cutting back on the activities of state agencies as well as retrenching staff. The bureaucracy was also to be subjected to greater surveillance and more frequent deployment of legal sanctions against offenders. However the commission also identified the over-politicisation of the civil service as a second major cause of corruption. To remedy this situation three steps were taken: firstly, political nominees in the civil service were replaced by army officers loyal to Suharto. Secondly, an Inspector General was appointed to make sure that policies agreed by ministers and senior officials were actually implemented and appropriations used for the intended purpose. Finally, the number of political parties was reduced to two, both of them effectively controlled by the state. Civil servants were involuntarily organised into a corporatist body (KORPRI) which was grouped within the state-sponsored party, GOLKAR. As a consequence the civil service was allegedly de-politicised and corruption, or at least of the kind that was seen to threaten national integrity, declined appreciably (Palmier, 1983).

From these two brief examples arises the notion that a military or at least highly authoritarian regime, by restricting if not outlawing entirely competitive politics, significantly reduces political pressure on the administration and with it the abuse of public office. Co-incidentally, such a view chimes with a conception of the military which was popular with some social scientists in the 1960s and has by no means disappeared (not least among army officers themselves). According to this conception the military in UDCs plays the progressive role in development allegedly played by the bourgeoisie in Europe. Since in most UDCs a well-established bourgeoisie has not emerged, the military steps into the breech. Thus, according to Huntington, the officers corps, at certain stages of modernisation, like the protestant entrepreneurs of Europe, embrace a form of puritanism attacking waste, inefficiency and corruption and promoting economic and social reform. Brazil and Mexico in the early decades of this century and Bolivia, Peru, Ecuador, Egypt, Syria and Iraq in the post-Second World War period are cited by Huntington as examples where the military has played this progressive role (Huntington, 1968, ch. 4).

Similarly, Manfred Halpern has argued that army officers form a sort of vanguard of what he calls the New Middle Class (NMC). In the absence of entrepreneurial elites in UDCs the historic task of modernisation falls upon other sectors of the middle class, mainly bureaucrats and professionals. The officer corps, as the most cohesive sector of the NMC, provides it with leadership. Not only is the officer corps cohesive but it also seems to be free of the pettiness, venality and obsession with self-aggrandisement which bedevil civilian politics: 'In civilian politics corruption, nepotism and bribery loomed much larger. Within the army a sense of national mission transcending parochial, regional or economic interests or kinship ties seemed to be much more clearly defined than elsewhere in society' (Halpern, 1962, p. 74).

But to what extent does the military measure up to these high expectations? Firstly, it has to be admitted that the term 'military' is a catch-all covering a vast range of organisations which probably have in common only that their members wear some kind of uniform and that they have a legitimate monopoly of armed force. The difference between long-established and highly institutionalised militaries of say Argentina and Brazil on the one hand, and their much more recently-created counterparts in Uganda or Togo on the other, are so marked as to question the utility of using a single term to describe them. In effect the armies of some of the new states of Tropical Africa are in reality so highly factionalised, internally divided by clan and other personal loyalties, that the expression 'organisation' seems barely appropriate (see for example Mazrui, 1976; Decalo, 1986).

However despite such variations there is no evidence that soldiers in power are less likely to use their position for self-aggrandisement than civilians. On the contrary, there is a good deal of evidence of extensive if not pathological corruption under military or 'civilianised' military regimes. In Tropical Africa some of the most corrupt governments of the independence era have been headed by army officers – one thinks of Acheampong in Ghana. Gowon in Nigeria, former sergeant later 'Emperor' Jean Bedel Bokassa of the Central African Empire, Macias Nguema of Equatorial Guinea who stored all the state's banknotes in his village – 'I am the chief of my people, everything belongs to me' (Medard, 1982, p. 186) – and last but by no means least Colonel now 'Citoyen' Mobutu Sese Seko of Zaire. In Bolivia senior army officers including a former head of state were deeply implicated in the cocaine trade. The coup which brought the army to power in July 1980 has been referred to as the 'cocaine coup' following allegations by a US senator that its leaders were heavily involved in large-scale smuggling operations (Latin America Bureau, 1980, pp. 78, 79). Likewise high-ranking army officers in Turkey, Lebanon and Syria are held to play a pivotal role in the transhipment of heroin from Pakistan and Iran to western Europe (see Arlacchi, 1988, ch. 8). In Thailand, where opportunities for enrichment play a key role in maintaining cohesion within the military, senior officers preside over a vast range of government enterprises most of which have little connection with the armed forces. In Burma the army until 1988 had a virtual monopoly of the nation's economic activities, of productive, financial and foreign exchange resources all affording endless scope for graft. In Indonesia although the military may have been successful in depoliticising and hence reducing corruption within the administration, rampant abuse among favoured army officers persists (Ball, 1981; Palmier, 1983). Concluding an international comparison of the consequences of military rule Nicole Ball observes that whilst it would be simplistic to argue that ideology and other political factors are absent from the motivations that lie behind military coups, it is certain that the enhancement of personal wealth and power has a high priority (Ball, 1981).

Notwithstanding evidence of widespread corruption among army officers, in that the military does invariably curtail political activities, bans elections and proscribes political parties, pressure on the public sector probably does decline and with it certain forms of abuse. Whether this signifies a real reduction in the overall volume of corrupt transactions or that they are now hidden from view, more tightly controlled and concentrated in the hands of a repressive military elite, is extremely difficult to determine. Even if the former is true, any gains would need to be offset against the costs in terms of the well-attested abuse of human rights that are a salient feature of such regimes.

The view that looks to the military as a repository of virtue and efficiency is befogged by a tendency to assume that the armed forces are somehow outside and above the rest of society: like the Ottoman janissaries untouched and untainted by the collision of forces of which the social order is composed. The military reacts with and refracts societal tensions and tendencies. It also reflects prevailing norms and values. Consequently if politics in a given society has become 'a sea of corruption' then it is highly unlikely that the soldiers will be able to resist taking a dip. It is no use, some would argue, expecting the army to act as lifeguards when the sea itself is so grossly polluted as to taint all who enter. It is the water itself that must be purified or, translating the metaphor, society as a whole is in need of some kind of moral regeneration.

MORAL RE-ARMAMENT

A dominant theme in the development literature is one that stresses the centrality of a moral revolution, a thorough-going ethical re-orientation in the process of modernisation. 'Becoming modern', that is, entails the acquisition of a distinct set of values and attitudes. This would include, according to two leading proponents of this line of thought, being 'an informed participant citizen', independent and autonomous', 'ready for new experiences and ideas', 'open-minded' and 'cognitively stable' as well as having 'a marked sense of personal efficiency'. Left behind are the fatalism, conservatism, superstition and unthinking attachments to established folkways and relationships which are alleged to characterise traditional societies (see Inkeles and Smith, 1974, p. 290). This line of thought goes back to Max Weber's writings on the role of protestantism in the modernisation and industrialisation of Europe. In various branches of protestantism Weber claims to have located the orientation or *weltanschauung* which, in sanctifying the acquisition and accumulation of wealth, gave a vital impulse to the development of industrial capitalism. The protestant ethic not only venerated the rational pursuit of profit but also urged the virtues of sobriety, frugality, hard work and honesty; condemning strongly all manifestations of idleness, indulgence, time-wasting and sloth. Above all protestantism stressed the paramountcy of work as a religious duty.

This is not the place even to begin to assess the importance of the protestant ethic for the emergence of capitalism. What is, nonetheless, indisputable is that industrialisation in Europe coincided with the rise of a distinctive bourgeois ideology which emphasised the value of work, the link between work and achievement, the necessity of planning, of making sacrifices for future rewards and, above all, identified the good of society and national well-being with the dissemination of these characteristics (see for example Perkin, 1969, ch. VIII. Whether this bourgeois ideology caused or was produced by capitalism, or whether each reacted on the other dialectically, is not an issue with which we can be concerned here. The relevant point is that the need for some form of moral transformation for the attainment of modernity is widely accepted throughout the world not least by leading statesmen and ideologues.

Paradoxically given the supposed role of ascetism in the development of *capitalism*, a pre-occupation with the need for discipline, hard work and frugality has been particularly evident in socialist countries and in the writings of socialist leaders. Lenin recognised that the industrialisation of the USSR could not be achieved without the internalisation of a work ethic. In *The Immediate Tasks of Soviet Power* (1918) Lenin observed that the Russian 'is a bad worker compared with the workers of advanced countries'. Accordingly a major task for the Revolution is to teach people how to work. Love of one's work is one of the most important principles of Leninist morality, with slovenliness, carelessness, untidiness, unpunctuality, nervous haste and the inclination to substitute discussion for action all roundly condemned. Lenin as a secular revolutionary did not turn to the writings of the puritan divines for inspiration but to exponents of 'scientific management' such as F. W. Taylor, at that time the leading high priest of America's capitalist class. The Soviet Republic must at all costs adopt as much as is relevant of Taylor's scientific method for studying the work process (Bendix, 1964, p. 154). In the writings of other Soviet industrialists Bendix has noted a similarity with the ideas of protestant ascetics. Exhortations to make time count, to cultivate work habits of steady intensity and the need for systematic planning figure prominently. The techniques advocated to develop these attributes also bear echoes of the seventeenth century: the revolutionary worker is enjoined to keep a record of his activities, to examine his conscience and scrutinise his conduct each day (Bendix, pp. 154–7). As David Lane has pointed out, the Bolshevik new morality was by no means confined to the workplace: the revolutionary *life* rejects disorderly and anarchic behaviour; immediate gratification is abandoned in favour of self-discipline and deferred reward (Lane, 1976).

If we turn to revolutionary China a heavy emphasis on the need for profound cultural change is not simply more apparent than in the USSR, but at times becomes pre-eminent. Maoism as it evolved in the 1950s expressed growing disillusion with centralised planning and increasing support for the idea that the local community could become the base from which development projects were launched. The notion of self-development threw the emphasis on to local institutional arrangements, political leadership as well as social and psychological attitudes. Mao well understood that the ultimate success of community-based development projects in a peasant society would require certain radical cultural and institutional changes. On the cultural dimension the inculcation of certain modern attitudes is demanded. Jack Gray has listed these as follows:

the ability to apply rational calculation to the use of scarce resources; some simple appreciation of the idea of controlled experiment; readiness to accept change; the ability to recognize new opportunities; willingness to cooperate in communal improvement; the foresight necessary for long-range planning; the discipline to accept and carry out majority decisions; and the capacity for honest, diligent and economical administration. (Gray, 1973, p. 117)

The dissemination of such values would necessitate a fundamental shake-up in China's educational system. Highly specialised education for a small minority of experts would be down-graded and priority given to the promotion of mass literacy and the teaching of skills relevant to rural needs. China's moral revolution would also need a new type of local leader, someone who could mediate between national leadership and the local community, who could re-formulate national policy goals into realistic and practical local schemes. Above all community leaders must be able to secure consent and cooperation in the adoption and implementation of local schemes. This accords with Mao's 'massline' theory which insists upon the primacy of consensual leadership and mass participation.

In Cuba policies employed to mobilise the labour force during the first half of the 1960s were considerably less successful than had been expected. Labour indiscipline, bad timekeeping, absenteeism, lack of respect for superiors as well as damage to the means of production were publicy acknowledged problems after 1961. Accordingly the second half of the 1960s saw the emergence of a fresh mobilisation strategy centred around a new-model Cuban – *el Hombre Nuevo*. The New Man (New Women were apparently not needed) would dedicate his life to the needs of the revolution, to fellow Cubans and to humanity as a whole. He was to be self-disciplined, hard working, ascetic and incorruptible. He was therefore to be free of egotism, selfishness and materialism and would especially not indulge in the three principal malpractices that were undermining the revolution: privilege-taking, *amiquismo* and black marketeering.

Privilege-taking refers to the practice of party members and high officials arrogating to themselves special privileges such as access to automobiles, special restaurants, better housing and overseas travel along similar lines as the *nomenklatura* in the USSR. *Amiquismo* might be translated as friendship, favouritism or cronyism and denotes the practice of giving preference to friends and friends of friends in the allocation of goods and services in the expectation of some return whether in cash or in kind. Black and gray markets are ubiquitous in

Cuba and, as is the case with other centrally-planned economies, play a crucial role in the informal distribution of all goods and services. In order to transform Cubans into *hombres nuevos* the educational system, the media and corporate bodies such as unions, farmers, womens' and youth organisations and the army were to bend their energies to the transmission of appropriate values. As Arnold Ritter has pointed out the mobilisation strategy during this period envisaged the virtual militarisation of Cuba and its transformation into an immense column with Fidel Castro at its head (Ritter, 1975, ch. 7).

These moral crusades are much more visible in centrally-planned economies because of their formal rejection of the profit motive and material incentives. But they are by no means confined to such societies and in fact appear in various guises in most UDCs whether organised around some central concept of negritude, self-reliance, authenticity, Arab resurrection, shia millennialism, rectification, a war against indiscipline or, as in contemporary Togo, a religious cult celebrating the 'miraculous' escape of 'president-founder' Eyadema (the cult's high priest) from an aircraft accident in 1974. Whatever their rhetoric the primary function of such campaigns is to attempt to incorporate a diverse and often divided populus behind the drive for economic growth. Whether there is any connection between certain types of mass mobilisation strategy and actual growth is extremely difficult to determine and cannot detain us here. What seems certain is that their ability to bring about far-reaching attitudinal and moral change is minimal. Commenting on the Cuban search for a new morality Ritter somewhat drily observes, 'Given the relative lack of success of almost two thousand years of Christianity in creating an altruistic New Christian Man, it is probably too much to expect the Cuban Revolution to create a similar man in five years . . .' (Ritter, p. 295).

One may add that repeated calls for sacrifice for the good of the country and panegyrics on the virtues of hard work in societies where basic necessities are extremely scarce and when access to them is spectacularly unequal, will almost certainly fall upon deaf ears. Is it realistic to expect a policeman, directing traffic in the broiling sun, to pass up an opportunity for petty extortion for the sake of some remote and nebulous ideal, when the air-conditioned Mercedes that glide past him are an open mockery of that ideal? Clearly far-reaching behavioural changes were associated with the industrial revolution in Europe. But it is crucial to bear in mind that these changes coincided with dramatic economic expansion. It thus seems likely that the 'civilising' or 'gentling' of the European masses had more to do with the fact that they were eventually permitted to share in the fruits of this expansion than with some mass internalisation of the 'gospel of work'. The twentieth century saw the progressive political incorporation of the common people with the growth of mass democracy and welfarism. As a result the 'state' ceased to be a distant and alien entity, a mere tool in the hands of the powerful, to become an institution which embodied the people's interests, underwrote their basic needs and was accountable to them for its actions. It is the development of public accountability and awareness of its necessity, rather than some alleged diffusion of greater honesty that, many would argue, lies at the heart of the question of political corruption.

ACCOUNTABILITY

As we all know Lord Acton believed in the inherent corruptability of power. Accordingly the most effective way of containing corruption seems to be that of strengthening the restraints on the exercise of power. Certainly the increase in the accountability of European governments, initially to elected representatives, then to the middle classes and ultimately to a mass electorate, acted as a major constraint on the behaviour of those who held public office. The existence of rights of free association, the emergence of independent interest groups and mass media were indispensible components of this accountability. However it is important to remember that the consolidation of bourgeois democracy in the west was inextricably linked with certain socio-economic conditions. Not the least important of these was the emergence of an industrial working class which eventually acquired the organisational means to articulate its needs and interests: initially through trades unions, subsequently mass political parties. Obviously the granting of full rights of citizenship to the European masses was not simply a response to pressure from below. The need for efficient work and fighting forces coupled with a sharp sense of enlightened self-interest on the part of the ruling classes were also of pivotal importance. Nonetheless it is hard to envisage the development of European parliamentary democracy without this mass pressure.

Now in most third world countries the socio-economic situation is quite different from that which obtained in late nineteenth and early twentieth-century Europe. Firstly, in the majority of UDCs the bulk of the population is located in the rural sector living in peasant villages which are separated from each other and from the towns and cities. The geographical and cultural isolation of these communities, low levels of education together with their inward-looking traditional cultures, provides a poor base for effective political mobilisation. Secondly, so far as the minority that works in the urban sector is concerned, the deprivation and squalor its members endure might seem to conduce to high levels of political consciousness. Whilst not denying that consciousness exists the chances of its expressing itself through co-ordinated and directed political action are not great. The predominance of small units of production and petty trade in the urban economy means that the number of unionisable workers is low. Furthermore any collective identity that is generated by the division of labour is often attenuated by the continuing importance of communal attachments and the associated tendency to resolve difficulties and problems through kin, clan or village associations, or through patron-client relationships. Thirdly, the serious civic tensions that are usually associated with widespread poverty and deprivation, often exacerbated by communal differences, frequently panics dominant classes into structuring the political game in such a way as to stifle independent pressure. Hence regimes which either repress outright all forms of political expression or attempt to absorb and neutralise them by means of corporatist organisations are virtually the norm in UDCs.

It is worth noting here that even in the more developed countries of Latin and Central America a relatively large and often well-organised working class has been unable to prevent the establishment of authoritarian corporatist regimes. Whilst such regimes in general often set up elaborate arrangements in the form of congresses, councils, rallies and the like which permit a degree of formal mass involvement in decision-making and policy formulation, it is doubtful that this type of participation constitutes an effective check on executive authority. Certainly there is no evidence that such arrangements have played any role in limiting the abuse of office by the politically powerful in Brazil, Mexico, Egypt, Libya, Syria, Iraq, Côte d'Ivoire, Mali, Indonesia, South Korea or elsewhere.

In the absence of the structural conditions which are generally considered to be a necessary (but not sufficient) condition for western-style democracy, an alternative tradition has developed which focuses on the local community – the village or neighbourhood – as a potentially viable base for effective mass participation. The model for this type of democracy is Mao's China, where the people's communes supposedly achieved a considerable degree of autonomy as largely self-governing entities in which administrators and party cadres were subjected to the democratic control of the mass line. Following China's example other socialist societies such as Cuba, Tanzania, Angola, Mozambique and Ethiopia have emphasised the centrality of community organisations for the realisation of popular democracy. However it is not only socialist societies that have advanced the cause of grass-root organisations. The 1980s have seen a surge of support for a view which stresses the need for popular involvement in the formulation and implementation of development policies. This has been particularly evident in relation to rural development programmes where the participation ideal seems to have acquired almost universal acceptance on the part of major multilateral aid bodies such as the principal UN agencies (see Hall, A., 1986). Even the not noticeably radical World Bank is showing signs of moving away from an obsession with sophisticated and expensive mega-projects towards programmes which give priority to the notion of 'putting people first' (the title of a collection of essays put out by the Bank in 1985 – see Cernea, 1985).

But what is the likelihood of community-based popular organisations acting as an active constraint on the exercise of power by central and local government agencies? Unfortunately there is not enough evidence available on the performance of local political organisations to permit us to draw firm conclusions. For a start the data on China is to say the least equivocal. It varies from writings which on the one hand regard the commune movement as the embodiment of government by the people to those, on the other, which views virtually the whole Maoist period as an aberration, synonymous with extreme fanaticism and mindless persecution (compare for example Aziz, 1976, with the first hand account of Heng and Shapiro, 1984). A more cautious estimate admits the existence of both tendencies, the predominance of either varying significantly with time and place (Stiefel and Wertheim, 1983). But even had the commune movement succeeded in establishing a genuine peoples' democracy in which power-holders were truly accountable, the course of economic and political change since the death of Mao have moved firmly away from the commune model. China's new road to modernisation entails not only a shift in the direction of capitalist farming ('kulakisation'), but a renewed emphasis on hierarchical decision-making and the assertion of managerial prerogatives.

China's experience points up one of the essential weaknesses of attempts to base structures of accountability on local communities (rural or urban): this is that the needs of communities as expressed through their organisations must be reconciled with national needs and that in the event of conflict the latter will invariably prevail. For example, there is some evidence that the peoples' defence committees set up in Ghana after the Rawlings coup of 1981 have had some success in checking abuses of power at the local level. British judge Lord Gifford, after monitoring the operation of public tribunals in 1983, claimed that Ghana was in the process of being transformed from a society 'where the laws were flouted by the powerful, into a society where the laws are obeyed' (*West Africa*, 10 October 1983, p. 2342). It is noteworthy that earlier in the same month the Canadian High Commissioner in Ghana went so far as to assert that the Rawlings regime had 'succeeded to a large extent in eradicating corruption' as well as 'bringing sanity into the economy' (*West Africa*, 3 October 1983, p. 2320). The fact that Rawlings himself has subsequently fulminated on a number of occasions against the high level of corruption and irresponsibility on the part of people in positions of trust, including the police force, seems to suggest that the High Commissioner was being over-optimistic (see for example *West Africa*, 8 October 1984, p. 2026); and 3 December 1986, p. 2334).

The main point is, however, that no matter how committed or successful the Provisional National Defence Committee has been in establishing effective local defence committees, Ghana's acute economic problems and the decisions these impose on the country's rulers (e.g. drastic cuts in public expenditure, devaluation of the cedi), will conflict with and almost certainly over-ride the expressed needs of the people (for jobs, affordable food, cheap items of consumption etc). We can say generally that the dependent character of third world economies and the drastic surgery which this frequently demands means that ruling elites, however well-intentioned, must adopt policies which are highly unpalatable to the bulk of their citizens. Under such circumstances democratic arrangements of whatever hue would seem to be at best of marginal importance. That good intentions are seldom there is readily apparent from the alacrity with which many third world rulers have deployed arbitrary arrest, imprisonment, torture and death against independent sources of criticism. In the light of these facts we must therefore conclude that the prospects for checking corruption by making power-holders in UDCs more accountable are not encouraging.

PRIVATISATION

Privatisation involves reducing the size of the public sector by selling off nationalised industries. Since the enthusiasm for privatisation derives from a firm belief in the virtues of unrestricted competition, it is invariably associated with deregulation; that is to say, the removal of 'artificial' impediments to the free play of market forces. The impetus behind the privatisation drive initially had nothing to do with the problem of corruption but reflected an upsurge in the 1970s in the popularity of *laissez-faire* economics and a growing conviction among certain economists and politicians that it offered the only means of regenerating the stagnant capitalist economies of the developed world.

Privatisation and deregulation, coupled with a tight monetary policy to combat inflation, became the economic orthodoxy of the 1980s, especially in Britain and the USA as well as in the latter's client states such as Chile and South Korea. The economic predominance of the USA ensured that *laissez-faire* ideas were given a new lease of life in key international agencies such as the IMF and the World Bank, for whom the notions of privatisation and deregulation seemed particularly relevant to the economic problems of many UDCs. By the 1980s the most urgent of these problems was chronic indebtedness and the serious balance of payments it had produced in countries of the third world. In return for re-scheduling agreements on increasingly unpayable loans more and more UDCs were constrained to implement structural adjustment programmes involving drastic cuts in domestic consumption and investment. Given the heavy burden of an inflated and invariably inefficient public sector absorbing a huge proportion of government revenue, it was probably inevitable, given the new orthodoxy, that it became a prime target for retrenchment. Accordingly the late 1980s have witnessed the widespread adoption of privatisation programmes by formerly statist and in some cases unequivocally socialist governments throughout the third world (see Shackleton, 1986). Where organs of state, for various reasons, cannot be sold off, restructuring has or will entail stringent cutbacks (not least in staffing) and in some cases winding up altogether. Accompanying privatisation, deregulation has involved dispensing with such controls as import licences, tariffs, food or petroleum subsidies as well as the flotation of currencies.

Notwithstanding the economic impetus to privatisation the World Bank has explicitly recognised a link between *laissez-faire* economics and the control of corruption. Whilst agreeing that corruption is undesirable and that steps should be taken to reduce it, the Bank has little confidence in anti-corruption drives. These tend to be short-lived and are largely ineffective because they concentrate on punitive measures and rely on the imposition of greater controls. Fewer controls in the form of deregulation is the best way of dealing with corruption since this reduces the opportunities for abuse. Corruption can be limited by striving to avoid administratively created scarcities of the kind which in centrally-planned economies have led to the emergence of a second economy. Abandoning attempts to regulate markets enables the state by cutting back on its activities to perform those it retains that much more effectively. The reduced demand for public servants should permit improved salaries and conditions for those who remain: 'Corruption is usually better fought by a combination of fewer, better-paid officials controlling only what needs to be (and can effectively be) controlled in the full light of public scrutiny, than by occasional anticorruption "campaigns"' (*World Development Report*, 1983, p. 117).

In the light of this position the Bank is appropriately enthusiastic a few years later about what it sees as the 'impressive' results achieved by the Brazilian Debureaucratisation Programme. Set up in 1979 the Programme aimed to simplify administrative procedures as well as reverse what seemed to be a relentless trend in the growth in government, excessive centralisation and the proliferation of regulations. Modern Brazil inherited from centuries of Portuguese colonialism a highly centralised and formalised administrative system. Bureaucratic formalism manifests itself in an excessive preoccupation with amassing documents, to such an extent that what should be straightforward and simple transactions become enormously complex and time-consuming. A case reported recently claimed that obtaining an export licence required 1470 separate legal actions, involved 13 government ministries and 50 agencies. Such a situation cries out either for 'speed money' or for an intermediary who can find his way through the maze of regulations and departments cutting the time it takes to obtain a necessary document from weeks to hours.

In Brazil these intermediaries, known as *despachantes*, not only exist but are widely recognised as a legitimate and indispensible feature of the administrative scene. The *despachante* for a fee will purchase and complete the multiplicity of forms, deliver them to the appropriate officials and obtain the licence, permit or whatever is required. The *despachantes* are a thriving profession with their own trades unions and competitive examinations. Their role, however, seems to be threatened by the Debureaucratisation Programme since it, on the basis of extensive citizen-based surveys, has been able to identify and eliminate a large number of inessential administrative procedures. As a result, over the five year period 1979–84, some 600 million documents a year have been removed from circulation at the instigation of the Programme. This has led to savings of $3 billion or 1.5 per cent of Brazil's GDP. In concrete terms rural credit programmes have been vastly simplified and it now takes only three days to form a company instead of 3 to 6 months (*World Development Report*, 1987, p. 73).

CONCLUSION

I have separated out the various approaches to the problem of corruption only for the purposes of analysis. In reality these approaches invariably co-exist: most UDCs have established anticorruption agencies which usually function alongside intermittent purges and one-off campaigns. National programmes of regeneration are virtually ubiquitous and are usually accompanied by attempts to establish structures of mass participation. The fact that all of these approaches face major impediments should not permit us to conclude that they should be abandoned. For example, whilst the outlook for democracy in the third world is bleak, recent experience of *glasnost* in the USSR, particularly its role in exposing rampant and sustained abuse of office, would seem to suggest that the possibility of genuine reform should not be dismissed.

On this point it is worth mentioning Susan George's appealing suggestion that debt re-scheduling agreements with third world states could be made contingent upon the acceptance by the debtor countries of development policies derived from genuine consultation with the masses (George, 1988, ch. 14). Whatever the merits and practicalities of George's proposal it is certainly the case that industrialised countries could bring greater pressure to bear on repressive third world regimes. The fact that they do not, or do so only very selectively, could be regarded as a manifestation of the developed world's complicity in the abuse of power in UDCs.

Given the ambivalence of the 'Free World's' commitment to reform it may be that privatisation offers the only viable prospect of curtailing corruption in the third world. On economic grounds alone the burden of an inflated state sector is one that few poor countries can bear. Any lessening of this burden alone would seem to yield certain gains. The additional benefits in terms of reducing the opportunities for abuse plus the possibility of improving the salaries and working conditions of those public servants that remain, might seem to make the case for privatisation almost unassailable. Whilst it would be refreshing if a social scientist could for once commit him/herself unequivocally to a particular policy line, the need for critical analysis requires that I raise a note of caution.

I mention but cannot explore here the technical difficulties of privatisation: whether the institutional means for selling off state enterprises actually exist in the form of developed capital markets and so on; whether there will be enough buyers for what are usually inefficient and run-down undertakings; whether the sums realised represent an acceptable return in the light of the vast amounts of public money that have been invested in the state sector over the years? In addition the amount of time it will take to complete a privatisation programme (seldom less than five years) needs to be offset against the urgency of the problem of corruption (see Shackleton, 1986; and *West Africa*, 9 May 1988, pp. 824, 5).

More seriously, if the argument outlined in Chapter 4 is accepted to the effect that politics in UDCs – the politics of scarcity tends to take the form of a frenetic scramble to appropriate public resources, then a reduction in the supply of these resources is likely to screw up the intensity of the competition to a point where it has serious de-stabilising consequences. An example of this is to be found in Nigeria where a drastic curtailment of public employment and contracts since the military coup of December 1983 has cut off a significant fraction of the bourgeoisie from its principal source of wealth and power. It seems certain that elements within this disaffected bourgeoisie – former regional 'big men' – have recently played a key role in fomenting communal tensions, especially in the serious religious rioting in the North in March 1987. The fact that on the latter occasion large numbers of ordinary Nigerians were prepared to join in the looting and burning highlights another dimension of privatisation. Where the state is a major employer cutbacks in the public sector must inevitably exacerbate already high levels of unemployment.

In evaluating the seriousness of the consequences of such cutbacks we should be aware that a public servant's salary in the third world will be supporting at least twice the number of people than is the case in developed countries (see for example Morice, 1987, p. 134. Furthermore, since privatisation is usually linked with de-regulating policies such as currency devaluation and the removal of subsidies on basic necessities, it also leads to a decline in levels of consumption. It is not therefore surprising that attempts to implement such structural adjustment programmes have in various countries provoked serious civil disorder (for example Sudan, 1985, Zambia 1986, Guinea, 1987 and Nigeria, 1988). Even when austerity has not unleashed a specific outburst the long-term consequences of the resulting increases in poverty, disease, crime and general demoralisation are impossible to estimate (see for example 'The poor become poorer, admits IMF', *West Africa*, 27 June 1988, p. 1172).

Here we get to the heart of the problem of corruption: that it is inseparable from the problem of underdevelopment and it is inconceivable that the former can be seriously tackled apart from the latter. When in the world's seventh industrial state, Brazil, inflation is running at over 1000 per cent, where two thirds of the population can't get enough to eat and one tenth don't legally exist because their parents could not afford the £3 for a birth certificate, and where a leading politician believes his country is on the brink of 'total political and economic disintegration', the prospects for administrative reform are, to put it mildly, dismal (Rocha, 1988; Vanhecke, 1988).

7 Conclusion: Corruption, Development and De-development

'We're being killed. Nothing has any meaning. That is why everyone is so frantic. Everyone wants to make his money and run away. But where? That is what is driving people mad. They feel they are losing the place they can run back to . . . It's a nightmare. All these airfields the man has built, the foreign companies have built – nowhere is safe now.'

V. S. Naipaul, *A Bend in the River*

The basic argument of this book has been that the phenomenon of political corruption – the illegal use of public office for private gain – can be understood only against a background of social and economic change. We have seen that in pre-modern societies some notion of the abuse of office certainly existed but since access to and behaviour within office were deeply embedded in the network of personal exchanges which underpinned the social order, a distinctive public sphere could not be clearly differentiated from private interests. Accusations of corruption, therefore, had about them a good deal of arbitrariness in the sense that they seldom conformed to legal criteria objectively applied. Generally speaking such accusations were closely bound up with and tended to reflect the interminable struggle between dominant factions for control over the state apparatus.

Capitalist industrialisation both required and made possible the re-structuring of social existence on the basis of rational-legal principles. The latter were now mediated directly through the mechanism of the market or more obliquely through the role structure of formal organisations predicated upon the goal of efficiency. However this restructuring did not eliminate personalism nor even confine it to a private sphere (e.g. family and friends) supposedly outside the bounds

161

of formal organisations. A considerable body of research on organisations since the Hawthorne experiments of the 1920s has clearly demonstrated that behaviour within them cannot be adequately understood in terms of a theory of rational means-ends activity directed to the attainment of organisational goals. Organisational goals, the literature clearly reveals, are constantly obscured, distorted, subverted and organisational resources appropriated under the emergent kaleidoscope of needs and interests which constitute the normal interactions of role incumbents. On the basis of an extensive survey of organisational studies M. Dalton has contended that conventional organisational theory 'slights the fact that in large organisations both local and personal demands take precedence in most cases', and that 'typical firm is thus a shifting set of contained disruption, powered and guided by differentially skilled and committed persons. Its unofficial aspects bulk large but are shrouded in bureaucratic cloak' (Dalton 1959, quoted in Anthony, 1986, pp. 178, 179). Dalton is here referring to business organisations but there can be no doubt that his observations also apply to public bureaucracies (see Downs, 1967, and Peters, 1978, and the discussion in Chapter 1 of this work).

Rather than a 'cloak' I would prefer to think of the formal structure of modern bureaucracies as a steel net, the flexibility and durability of which varies over time and from organisation to organisation: in some contexts strong yet subtle, able to respond to and bend with the informal pressures it seeks to contain; in others rigid and taut, just about holding its constituency together, but with its weaker areas rupturing under the strain. Whatever the age and quality of the net it seems clear that the lower down the bureaucratic hierarchy we travel, the finer its mesh and, therefore, the less scope there is for personal innovation, for the private appropriation of formal procedures and resources. As we ascend the hierarchy the constricting power of the net necessarily reduces as organisational roles demand and allow greater flexibility. At the apex the web is loose enough not only to permit much greater autonomy to role incumbents, but considerably to erode the division between a public and private sphere. Hence patrimonialism within and between dominant groups in industrial societies is both more evident and politically more significant.

This elite patrimonialism is, however, not normally perceived to be a problem in DCs basically for two reasons: firstly, it is partly concealed from public view by the social distance which obtains between elite and masses in predominantly urban societies: that is to say, the absence of direct personal contact which arises from the high degree of compartmentalisation inherent in a developed division of labour and class structure. Structural concealment or partial concealment is reinforced by the cultural imposition of a universalist ideology which expresses itself in an ethic of achievement. This states not only that the most qualified get to the top but that society has the necessary built-in mechanisms to ensure this. The second reason why patrimonialism is not normally considered to be a problem in DCs is that in the most visible areas of the state – lower levels of routine administration – the bureaucratic net is sufficiently strong and well-anchored to contain personalism to a degree that is compatible with accepted canons of honesty and efficiency. Only when personalism reaches a level at which it cannot be contained, or is no longer insulated by the process of socio-political compartmentalisation, does it spill into the popular domain and require some form of public reaction.

As a result of the growth of a world economy and its dissemination through colonialism to what we now call the third world, the capitalist system, its administrative instrument together with its accompanying universalist ideology, were implanted in societies at a quite different stage of social and economic development. That is to say, a modern state apparatus was erected on economic and social foundations which were ill-suited to bear the edifice. Here economic underdevelopment has meant that a materially weak but large public sector is subjected, in the first instance, to the immense pressure that derives from a chronic imbalance between the demand for and supply of public resources. This pressure is considerably augmented by the persistence of pre-capitalist forms of social exchange such as kinship, clanship, clientelism and the like which are regularly invoked in transactions with public bureaucracies. These conditions together with an ethos which expresses itself in what has been appropriately termed an 'extractive' approach to politics (Hodder-Williams, 1984, ch. 4.), gravely impedes the development of administrative stability and renders the public sphere *as a whole* (not simply its upper reaches) highly susceptible to appropriation for private purposes.

This seems to be tantamount to saying merely that corruption is a function of underdevelopment and that in the long term pervasive abuse of office will decline only to the extent that economic development takes place. Such a view is certainly evident, either implicitly or explicitly, in much of the literature and indeed is inherent in the basic and widespread assumption that corruption is primarily a problem for the third world. It is a view that, furthermore, carries a good deal of force, for the European experience strongly suggests that without having achieved a certain level of economic development no state can lay the foundations for a professional public service; without sustained economic growth no state can begin to meet the mass expectations which the dawn of 'modernity' has unleashed; and without a healthy private sector no state apparatus can insulate itself from the aspirations of the more able and aquisitive of its citizens. Conversely it seems inconceivable that public administration can even aspire to, let alone sustain, acceptable levels of honesty and efficiency against a background of punishing indebtedness, galloping inflation, chronic unemployment, dismal standards of living and the serious civic strains that such conditions inevitably produce.

However to assert that corruption is simply a consequence of underdevelopment runs the risk of embracing a crude evolutionism which envisages a proportionate decline in the volume of abuse with each percentage improvement in GDP. We have already seen that corruption in the more developed areas of the third world is not necessarily less of a problem than in poorer states. Even more important, when considering the relationship between corruption and development, it would be absurd to overlook the fact that the wealthiest country in the world, the USA, is widely held to have an unacceptably high level of abuse. Indeed as Ronald Reagan rode off into the sunset he left behind him an administration whose reputation for 'sleaze' has probably not been exceeded since the 'gilded Age' at the end of the last century.

During Reagan's two terms of office over 100 top officials and aides have been investigated for improper conduct. These include a former chief political adviser who hurriedly cleared his desk after rumours of his involvement in insider dealing, a senior White House aide who was prosecuted for perjury in relation to illegal lobbying activities, an Attorney-General who was forced to resign after being implicated in a bribery scandal, and a former National Security Adviser who has been charged with conspiring to defraud the American government. In addition to individual breaches of public trust there is the vast and tangled lobbying undergrowth (more than 23 000 lobbyists according to a recent count by H. Smith, 1988) where a range of inducements are exchanged for political influence in ways that are often difficult to separate from outright bribery (see for example Barry Goldwater on Political Action Committees in H. Smith, 1988, ch. 9).

One of the most notorious areas for profitable back-scratching is defence, where massive overcharging on government contracts seems to be the norm with the result that Pentagon officials hand over billions of taxpayers' money to their cronies in the defence industry for weapons systems that frequently do not work (see former fighter pilot and trenchant critic of defence procurement D. Smith, 1988: 'The problem is not that there is fraud in defence procurement. The problem is that defence procurement has itself become a fraud.') The fact that the bulk of these lucrative defence contracts are destined for an area of the country, the southwest, which plays a pivotal role in keeping the Republican Party in power betokens a degree of Federal patronage which renders the expression 'defence porkbarrel' not inappropriate (see Whitaker, 1987). In the prevailing atmosphere of *accumule qui peut* 13 000 Pentagon personnel leave government employment every year to market their knowledge and contacts to the private sector; senior officials and former friends of the president scramble to publish their memoirs for six-figure sums immediately they leave office (see Brummer, 1988); and CIA officers find it difficult to distinguish between their country's security needs and their own penchant for expensive first-class holidays in Europe (see Emerson, 1988). Confronted with such a record we have to conclude that an extractive approach to politics is by no means confined to Mexico and Zaire. The key question is whether the Reagan dispensation is an exception, an aberration, or whether the drift and instability it reflects is symptomatic of more fundamental changes in the nature of the advanced capitalist state.

It is crucial to appreciate, first of all, that our conception of the modern state with its 'clean' administration is the product of a particular period in the development of western capitalism. This was a period of enormous economic expansion generated by the massive reconstruction and investment which followed the Second World War, greatly assisted by technological advance – a 'phenomenal increase' in the quality as well as the quantity of the means of production (Armstrong, P., *et al.*, 1984, p. 168). The existence, furthermore, of a managed international economy based upon the system of stable exchange rates established at Bretton Woods in 1944 permitted within respective industrial states a form of managed capitalism founded upon Keynesian economics. The eventual outcome in European society was the attainment of high levels of mass consumption backed by a public commitment to full employment and welfare. In short the consolidation of a form of social democracy in which the state, in fulfilling a range of civic obligations, became as public a piece of property as it has ever been. In the USA, with its different pattern of economic and political development, very high levels of affluence for the majority made possible by America's global economic supremacy, a marked degree of depoliticisation achieved through the manipulation of Cold War rhetoric, together with the decline of elimination of more public forms of abuse (the machines), facilitated the widespread acceptance of the belief in America as a repository of civic virtue.

Since the 1960s a number of fundamental changes have conspired to shift the core industrial economies on to a quite different development trajectory. Firstly, the re-emergence of Germany and Japan as major industrial powers, followed more recently by the newly industrialising countries (NICs such as South Korea, Singapore, Brazil and Mexico), have severely eroded the economic supremacy of the USA as well as significantly stepping up the level of competition within the industrial orbit. One crucial aspect of this competition is the need to provide a favourable domestic economic environment for investment, especially on the part of increasingly powerful multi-national corporations. Secondly, the collapse of the Bretton Woods agreement in 1972 opened the door to an international speculative free-for-all in which the stakes were raised immeasurably by the oil price hikes of 1974 and 1979. The development of computer technology, furthermore, made it possible to move billions of dollars in and out of currencies, commodities and countries at the push of a button (Wachtel, 1987). The growing inability of the capitalist states to insulate themselves from the speculative waves of the international money economy called into question the efficacy of national economic planning and of Keynesian policies in particular. In addition, increased international competition meant that the older industrial economies, especially the weaker ones like Britain, could no longer continue unconditionally to underwrite ever-rising living standards for the masses. In such a situation the free market orthodoxy of the 1980s was a heaven-sent revelation to middle classes chafing under a redistributive state: in sanctifying drastic cutbacks in the public sector, the implementation of neo-Conservative policies pushed up unemployment to a level which significantly weakened the ability of the masses to defend their wage levels.

THE RE-PRIVATISATION OF THE STATE?

Guenther Roth has suggested that in extreme circumstances the state can become the private instrument of those who are powerful enough to gain control of it (Roth, 1968). Michael Gilsenan has claimed that such a situation indeed existed in pre-Civil War Lebanon (Gilsenan, 1977). Zaire is a country in which the private appropriation of public resources has reached such a scale that political scientists have begun to ask whether a state can be said to exist at all (see Newbury, 1984). In relation to such cases it is important to note that the retreat of the state from the public domain into private hands is paralleled by the withdrawal or 'disengagement' of the masses (Azarya and Chazan, 1987). In other words in an overall context of economic scarcity and political instability a growing proportion of people withdraw or are forced to withdraw into subsistence farming or, failing that, into a range of peripheral or 'informal' activities such as black marketeering, smuggling, drug-dealing, banditry and the economy of violence which such conditions tend to nurture. Such popular acts of disengagement, even protest, are usually haphazard and uncoordinated, without any over-arching organisation (Chazan *et al.*, 1988, pp. 198–201). However they may be drawn into or absorbed by what amounts to a highly structured counter economy, even counter state, the most obvious examples of which are the cocaine enclaves of Bolivia and Colombia (on the drug industry in Bolivia see especially Sage, 1988).

Since this type of situation is most readily associated with extreme cases of underdevelopment it may seem absurd to suggest that such tendencies are discernible in the affluent North. None the less I would argue that the ascendance of neo-Conservatism has produced certain parallels: firstly, the retreat from social democracy which the embracement of the enterprise culture has necessarily entailed requires that the state insulate itself from popular pressure to a much greater degree than was the case say twenty-five years ago. To some extent this has been achieved by normal processes of social and economic change which have led to the fragmentation, perhaps disintegration, of the working class in developed societies. This has been augmented by the depoliticisation that has been achieved through the manipulation of a materialist culture. But in addition it is possible to detect a number of areas where the power of the state has been used to weaken mass pressure or stifle sources of criticism: for example curbs on the power of trades unions and certain forms of political protest; the enhancement of police power, greater politicisation of the civil service and increased use of legal and disciplinary measures against refractory public servants and greater politicisation of the judiciary. Clearly such developments are still a long way from the situation where, as in some of the countries we have looked at, wholesale looting of the public treasury is accompanied by a deliberate reign of terror. Despite this, to the extent that the state is able to reduce its accountability, effectively to retreat from the public domain, the opportunity for abuse of office increases. Confirmation that this is indeed the case may be had from such American evidence as is available which suggests that some of the most serious abuses, most troubling breaches of public trust, take place in precisely those areas of the state which are the least accountable, the most secret: the security services (see especially Emerson, 1988; Cockburn, 1988).

Now, in the developed world too it seems that the converse of the retreating state is the retreating public. It is certainly true that unlike their counterparts in much of the third world the overwhelming majority of the citizens of DCs enjoy the privilege of a materially and politically secure existence. Not only are we much less likely to be unemployed, undernourished or see our children die of mundane and preventable diseases, the chances of our being arbitrarily imprisoned, tortured or our lives summarily terminated by armed robbers, death squads or freedom fighters are similarly remote. And yet there is in developed states a sizable minority of people whose allocation of the fruits of affluence is a good deal smaller than the rest of us. In fact the position of an apparently growing proportion is marginal in every sense of the word: marginal economically in that they not only endure very low living standards (see for example 'Starvation Stalks the US' and 'A Fifth of America Living on the Margin', *Guardian Weekly* 13 December 1987 and 20 December 1987), but subsist largely outside the formal economy; marginal politically in that they have little or no influence over the formal political process, (7 million out of the 17 million blacks in USA were not registered to vote in 1982: see McLennan, 1984, p. 249); and the marginal culturally since a significant proportion of this sub-proletariat belong to ethnic minorities and are cut off from the dominant culture by language and/ or deeply entrenched racism.

In other words, there exists in the USA and Europe a substratum of what probably amounts to several million 'citizens' who are increasingly peripheral to civil society and the state; who inhabit a social space largely outside the 'respectable' world and who, in order to survive, must engage in informal, semi-criminal and criminal pursuits. The fact that these apparently expanding underdeveloped enclaves in the cities of the industrial North are sometimes linked directly to their counterparts in the third world (e.g. through the cocaine connection) points up what seems to be the growing interdependence of the *informal* in addition to the formal world economy. The main point about such enclaves is that they could increasingly fall under the sway of private interests (e.g. peripheral entrepreneurs and racketeers) to such a degree that the state's writ could barely be said to run within them.

Clearly the phenomenon of the retreating state and its counterpart the retreating public is only beginning to make its appearance in the industrialised world. It is also more evident in the weaker economies of former imperial and declining imperial powers such as Britain and the USA. One would expect it to be less apparent in those countries (e.g. Denmark and The Netherlands) where such austerity as has been introduced reflects a necessary adaptation to a tighter world market rather than the active embracement of monetarism. Whether the phenomenon is symptomatic of a long-term trend or a shorter cycle in the development of capitalism is extraordinarily difficult to predict, not least because the outcome depends in no small measure on future developments in the world economy. Rather than venturing into a field where I tread with a good deal of unease, I will confine myself, at this final stage of the argument, to my principal purpose which is to stress again the historical specificity of the 'modern' state. That is that the conception of the modern state, which has informed so much of our thinking about corruption, is very much a product of specific period. This was an era when, for reasons already outlined, a public domain – an area of social space where civil society contends publicly with the state – was more firmly institutionalised than at any other time in European history. To the extent that this public domain is shrinking – and I have proposed that it is – the opportunities for corruption and the more general though not necessarily illegal abuse of public office are likely to increase.

If this seems a somewhat gloomy prediction we might reflect upon the following: firstly, to the extent that something becomes a problem for 'us' rather than for some remote 'them' we are more likely to take it seriously and try and do something about it. Secondly, since most of us in the developed world are still untroubled by the fundamental problem of staying alive and since we have behind us a strongly entrenched tradition of political participation, we are much better placed to attempt to re-assert society against the state. Lastly, in the light of the close interdependence on all levels, formal and informal, overt and covert, of the world system, we might reasonably anticipate that a concerted effort to re-develop the public domain in the North will have positive ramifications in the South.

Bibliography

AARONOVITCH, S. (1961) *The Ruling Class* (London: Lawrence and Wishart).

ABUEVA, J. V. (1978) 'The Contribution of Nepotism, Spoils and Graft to Political Development', in Heidenheimer (ed.) pp. 534–539

ADAMOLEKUN, L. (1986) *Politics and Administration in Nigeria* (London: Hutchinson).

ADEBAYO, A. (1981) *Public Administration in Nigeria* (Chichester: John Wiley and Sons).

ALAVI, H. (1972) 'The State in post-Colonial Societies: Pakistan and Bangladesh', *New Left Review*, no. 74, pp. 59–82.

ANDERSON, P. (1979) *Lineages of the Absolutist State* (London: New Left Books).

ANDRESKI, S. (1966) *Parasitism and Subversion: The Case of Latin America* (London: Weidenfeld and Nicolson).

ANDRESKI, S. (1968) *The African Predicament* (New York: Atherton Press).

ANTHONY, P. D. (1986) *The Foundations of Management* (London: Tavistock).

ARLACCHI, P. (1988) *Mafia Business*, (Oxford: Oxford University Press).

ARMSTRONG, J. A. (1972) 'Old-regime Governors: Bureaucratic and Patrimonial Attributes', *Comparative Studies in Society and History* 14/1, pp. 2–29.

ARMSTRONG, P., GLYN, A., HARRISON, J. (1984) *Capitalism Since World War II* (London: Fontana).

AZARYA, V. and CHAZAN, N. (1987) 'Disengagement from the State in Africa: Reflections on the Experience of Ghana and Guinea', *Comparative Studies in Society and History* 29/1, pp. 106–131.

AZIZ, S. (1976) *Rural Development: Learning from China* (London: Macmillan).

BAILEY, F. G. (1971) 'The Peasant View of the Bad Life' in Shanin, T. (ed.) pp. 299–321.

BALL, N. 'The Military in Politics: Who Benefits and How', *World Development* 9/6, pp. 569–582.

BANFIELD, E. C. (1958) *The Moral Basis of a Backward Society* (New York: Free Press).

BANFIELD, E. C. (1969) *Urban Government: A Reader in Politics and Administration* (New York, Free Press).

BANTON, M. (1966) *The Social Anthropology of Complex Societies* (London: Tavistock).

BARKER, E. (1944) *The Development of Public Services in Europe 1660–1930* (London: Oxford University Press).

BAYLEY, D. H. (1966) 'The Effects of Corruption in a Developing Nation', *Western Political Quarterly* 19, pp. 719–732.

BAYNHAM, S. (ed.) (1986) *Military Power and Politics in Black Africa* (London: Croom Helm).

BEARDSHAW, J. and PALFREMAN, D. (1985) *The Organisation in its Environment* (London: Pitman).

BENDIX, R. (1964) *Nation-building and Citizenship* (London: John Wiley and Sons).

BENDIX, R. (1966) *Max Weber: An Intellectual Portrait* (London: Methuen).

BENSON, G. C. S. (1978) *Political Corruption in America* (Lexington: D. C. Heath and Co).

BHALERAO, C. N. (ed) (1972) *Administration, Politics and Development in India* (Bombay: Lalvani).

BIENEN, H. (1970) 'The Economic Environment' in Hyden *et al.*, (eds) pp. 43–62.

BILL, J. A. and LEIDEN, C. (1974) *The Middle East: Politics and Power* (Boston: Allyn and Bacon Inc).

BOISSEVAIN, J. (1977) 'When the Saints Go Marching Out: Reflections on the Decline of Patronage in Malta' in Gellner, E. and Waterbury, J. (eds) pp. 81–96.

BRAUDEL, F. (1983) *The Wheels of Commerce* (London: Book Club Associates).

BRIGGS, A. (1967) *Victorian People* (Harmondsworth: Penguin).

BROGAN, H. (1987) *The Pelican History of the United States of America* (Harmondsworth: Penguin).

BRUMMER, A. (1988) 'The Quick-fix of the Washington Insider – memoir', *Guardian Weekly*, 15 May, p. 30.

BURCKHARDT, J. (1965) *The Civilisation of the Renaissance in Italy* (London: Phaidon Press).

BUTT, R. (1978) 'The Unacceptable Face of Patronage', *The Times*, 13 July, p. 16.

CALLAGHY, T. M. (1984) *The State-Society Struggle: Zaire in Comparative Perspective* (New York: Columbia University Press).

CARDOSO, F. H. and FALETTO, E. (1979) *Dependency and Development in Latin America* (Berkeley: University of California Press).

CERNEA, R. (ed.) (1985) *Putting People First: Sociological Variables in Rural Development* (Oxford: Oxford University Press).

CHAZAN, N., MORTIMER, R., RAVENHILL, J., ROTHCHILD, D. (1988) *Politics and Society in Contemporary Africa* (London: Macmillan).

CHIBNALL, S. and SAUNDERS, P. (1977) 'Worlds Apart: Notes on the Social Reality of Corruption', *British Journal of Sociology* 28/2, pp. 138–155.

CHUBB, J. (1981) 'The Social Bases of an Urban Political Machine: the Christian Democratic Party in Palermo' in Eisenstadt, S. N. and Lemarchand, R. (eds) pp. 91–124.

CLAPHAM, C. (ed.) (1982) *Private Patronage and Public Power* (London: Francis Pinter).

CLAPHAM, C. (1985) *Third World Politics: An Introduction* (London: Croom Helm).

CLARKE, M. (ed.) (1983) *Corruption: Causes, Consequences and Control* (London: Francis Pinter).

COCKBURN, L. (1988) *Out of Control* (London: Bloomsbury Press).

CORNWELL, R. (1988) 'Brezhnev Era in the Witness Box', *Independent*, 3 September.

CROUCH, H. (1979) 'Patrimonialism and Military Rule in Indonesia', *World Politics* 31/4, pp. 571–87.

DALTON, M. (1959) *Men Who Manage* (New York: John Wiley).

DAVIES, N. (1982) 'No Help With Their Inquiries', *Guardian Weekly*, 15 August, p. 4.

DECALO, S. (1986) 'Military Rule in Africa: Etiology and Morphology' in Baynham, S. (ed.) pp. 38–66.

De KADT, E. and WILLIAMS, G. (eds) (1974) *Sociology and Development* (London: Tavistock Publications).

DOBEL, J. P. (1978) 'The Corruption of a State', *American Political Science Review* 72, pp. 958–973.

DOIG, A. (1984) *Corruption and Misconduct in Contemporary British Politics* (Harmondsworth: Penguin).

DOWNS, A. (1967) *Inside Bureaucracy* (Boston: Little, Brown and Company).

DRAKE, P. (1978) 'Corporatism and Functionalism in Modern Chilean Politics', *Journal of Latin American Studies* 10/1, pp. 83–116.

DUDLEY, B. (1982) *An Introduction to Nigerian Government and Politics* (London: Macmillan).

ECKSTEIN, H. (1982) 'The Idea of Political Development: From Dignity to Efficiency', *World Politics* 34/4, pp. 451–486.

EDELMAN, M. (1975) 'The Patronage State' *New Statesman*, 11 April, p. 70.

EISENSTADT, S. N. (1973) *Traditional Patrimonialism and Modern Neopatrimonialism* (London: Sage Publication).

EISENSTADT, S. N. and LEMARCHAND, R. (eds) (1981) *Political Clientelism, Patronage and Development* (London: Sage Publications).

EISENSTADT, S. N. and RONIGER, L. (1984) *Patrons, Clients and Friends* (Cambridge: Cambridge University Press).

ELTON, G. R. (1977a) *Reform and Reformation: England 1509–1558* (London: Edward Arnold).

ELTON, G. R. (1977b) *England Under the Tudors* (London: Methuen).

EMERSON, S. (1988) *Secret Warriors: Inside the Covert Military Operations of the Reagan Era* (New York: Putnams).

ERLICHMAN, J. (1988) 'Saved from Washington's Own Gulag', *Guardian Weekly*, 7 August, p. 24.

ERMANN, M. D. and LUNDMAN, R. J. (eds) (1978) *Corporate and Governmental Deviance* (New York: Oxford University Press).

FEIT, E. (1973) *The Armed Bureaucrats* (Boston: Houghton-Mifflin).

FINER, S. E. (1978) 'Patronage and the Public Service: Jeffersonian

Bureaucracy and the British Tradition', in Heidenheimer, A. J. (ed.) pp.106–127.

FISCHER, W. and LUNDGREEN, P. (1975) 'The Recruitment and Training of Administrative and Technical Personnel' in Tilly, C. (ed.) pp. 456–561.

FOSTER, G. M. (1967) 'Peasant Society and the Image of the Limited Good', in Potter, J. M., Diaz, M. D., and Foster, G. M. (eds) pp. 300–323.

FRANK, A. G. (1969) *Capitalism and Underdevelopment in Latin America: Historical Studies of Chile and Brazil* (New York: Monthly Review Press).

FRANK, A. G. (1971) *Sociology of Development and Underdevelopment of Sociology* (London: Pluto Press).

FRANK, P. (1969) 'How to Get on in the Soviet Union', *New Society*, 5 June, pp. 867, 868.

FRIEDRICH, C. J. (1966) 'Political Pathology' *Political Quarterly* 37, pp. 70–85.

FORD, H. J. (1978) 'Municipal Corruption: a Comment on Lincoln Steffens', in Heidenheimer, A. J. (ed.) pp. 284–293.

GAUHAR, A. (ed.) (1988) *Third World Affairs* (London: Third World Foundation).

GELLNER, E. and WATERBURY, J. (eds) (1977) *Patrons and Clients in Mediterranean Societies* (London: Duckworth).

GEORGE, S. (1988) *A Fate Worse than Debt* (Harmondsworth: Penguin).

GILSENAN, M. (1977) 'Against Patron-Client Relations' in Gellner, E. and Waterbury J. (eds) pp. 167–184.

GITTINGS, J. (1981) 'China Cracks Down on Corrupt Party Officials, *Guardian*, 27 August, p. 7.

GOTTFRIED, A. (1968) 'Political Machines' in Sills, D. (ed.) vol. 12, pp. 248–252.

GOULD, D. J. (1980) *Bureaucratic Corruption and Underdevelopment in the Third World: The Case of Zaire* (New York: Pergamon Press).

GRAHAM, L. S. (1968) *Civil Service Reform in Brazil: Principles versus Practice* (London: University of Texas Press).

GRAY, J. (1973) 'The Two Roads: Alternative Strategies of Social Change and Economic Growth in China' In Schram, S. R. (ed.) pp. 109–158.

GREENSTONE, J. D. (1978) 'Corruption and Self-Interest in Kampala and Nairobi' in Heidenheimer, A. J. (ed.) pp. 459–468.

GROSS, J. (1964) 'The Lynskey Tribunal' in Sissons, M. and French, P. (eds) pp. 266–286.

GUASTI, L. (1981) 'Clientelism in Decline: a Peruvian Regional Study' in Eisenstadt, S. N. and Roniger, L. (eds) pp. 217–248.

HALL, A. (1986) 'Community Participation and Rural Development' in Midgley, J. (ed.) pp. 87–104.

HALL, S. (1984) 'The Rise of the Representative/Interventionist State' in McLennan, G., Held D and Hall, S. (eds) pp. 7–49.

HALPERN, M. (1962) 'Middle Eastern Armies and the New Middle Class' in Johnson, J. (ed.)

HANDY, R. T. (1971) *A Christian America: Protestant Hopes and Historical Realities* (New York: Oxford University Press).

HART, J. (1972) 'The Genesis of the Northcote-Trevelyan Report' in Sutherland, G. (ed). pp. 63–81.

HARTZ, L. (ed.) (1964) *The Founding of New Societies* (New York: Harcourt Brace).
HEEGER, G. A. (1974) *The Politics of Underdevelopment* (London: Macmillan).
HEIDENHEIMER, A. J. (ed.) (1978) *Political Corruption: Readings in Comparative Analysis* (New Brunswick: Transaction Books).
HEIDENHEIMER, A. J. (1978) 'Introduction' in Heidenheimer, A. J. (ed.) pp. 3–30.
HELLER, M. and NEKRICH, A. (1986) *Utopia in Power: The History of The Soviet Union from 1917 to the Present* (New York: Summit Books).
HENG, L. and SHAPIRO, J. (1984) *Son of the Revolution* (London: Fontana).
HICKSON, D. J. and McCULLOUGH, A. (1980) 'Power in Organisations' in Salaman, G. and Thompson, K. (eds) pp. 27–55.
HILL, C. (1972) *The Century of Revolution 1603–1714* (London: Sphere Books).
HILL, C. (1976) *Reformation to Industrial Revolution* (Harmondsworth: Penguin).
HODDER-WILLIAMS, R. (1985) *An Introduction to the Politics of Tropical Africa* (London: Allen and Unwin).
HUNTINGTON, S. P. (1968) *Political Order in Changing Societies* (New Haven: Yale University Press).
HUNTINGTON, S. P. (1971) 'The Change to Change: Modernisation, Development and Politics' *Comparative Politics* 3/3, pp. 283–322.
HURSTFIELD, J. (1967) 'Political Corruption in Modern England: the Historian's Problem', *History* 52, pp. 16–34.
HYDEN, G., JACKSON, R. H., OKUMU, J. J. (eds) (1970) *Development Administration: The Kenyan Experience* (Nairobi: Oxford University Press).
IGNATIUS, D. (1987) 'Ollie North and His Slapstick Militiamen', *Guardian Weekly*, 21 June, p. 18.
INKELES, A. and SMITH, D. H. (1974) *Becoming Modern: Individual Change in Six Developing Countries* (London: William Heinemann).
IONESCU, G. (1977) 'Patronage Under Communism' in Gellner, E. and Waterbury, J. (eds) pp. 97–102.
JACKSON, H. (1983) 'EPA Chickens Home to Roost', *Guardian Weekly* 20 March.
JACKSON, R. H. and ROSBERG, C. G. (1982) 'Why Africa's Weak States Persist', *World Politics* 35/1, pp. 1–24.
JOHNSON, J. J. (ed.) 1962) *The Role of the Military in Underdeveloped Countries* (Princeton: Princeton University Press).
KALAMIYA, C. K. (1979) 'OTRAG in Zaire', *Review of African Political Economy* 14, pp. 16–35.
KALDOR, N. (1963) 'Taxation for Economic Development', *Journal of Modern African Studies* 1/1, pp. 7–23.
KAMENKA, E. and KRYGIER, M, (eds) (1979) *Bureaucracy: The Career of a Concept* (London: Edward Arnold).
KEY, V. O. (1978) 'Techniques of Political Graft' in Heidenheimer, A. J. (ed.) pp. 46–53.

KING, J. P. (1978) 'Socioeconomic Development and the Incidence of English Corrupt Campaign Practices' in Heidenheimer, A. J. (ed.) pp. 379–390.

KITSON-CLARK, G. (1977) *The Making of Victorian England* (London: Methuen).

KNIGHT, S. (1985) *The Brotherhood* (London: Grafton Books).

KRYGIER, M. (1979) 'State and Bureaucracy in Europe: The Growth of a Concept' in Kamenka E. and Krygier, M. (eds) pp. 1–33.

LAMPERT, N. (1983) 'The Whistleblowers: Corruption and Citizens' Complaints in the USSR', in Clarke, M. (ed.) pp. 268–287.

LANDÉ, C. H. (1973) 'Networks and Groups in Southeast Asia: Some Observations on the Group Theory of Politics', *American Political Science Review* 67, pp. 103–127.

LANE, D. (1976) 'Leninism as an Ideology of Soviet Development' in DeKadt, E. and Williams, G. (eds) pp. 23–38.

LANE, D. (1985) *Soviet Economy and Society* (Oxford: Blackwell).

LaPALOMBARA, J. (ed.) (1971) *Bureaucracy and Political Development* (Princeton: Princeton University Press).

LATIN AMERICA BUREAU (1980) *Bolivia: Coup d'Etat* (London: Latin America Bureau).

LATIN AMERICA BUREAU (1985) *Haiti: Family Business* (London: Latin America Bureau).

LEEDS, A. (1964) 'Brazilian Careers and Social Structure: an Evolutionary Model and Case History', *American Anthropologist* 66, pp. 1321–47.

LEFF, N. H. (1964) 'Economic Development through Bureaucratic Corruption', *American Behavioural Scientist*, November, pp. 8–14.

LEMARCHAND, R. and LEGG, K. (1972) 'Political Clientelism and Development', *Comparative Politics* 4/2, pp. 149–178.

LeVINE, V. (1980) 'African Patrimonial Regimes in Comparative Perspective', *Journal of Modern African Studies* 18/4, pp. 657–673.

LEYS, C. (1965) 'What is the Problem About Corruption?', *Journal of Modern African Studies* 3/2, pp. 215–224.

LIPPMANN, W. (1978) 'A Theory About Corruption' in Heidenheimer, A. J. (ed.) pp. 294–297.

LOFCHIE, M. F. (1971) *The State of the Nations: Constraints on Development in Independent Africa* (Berkeley: University of California Press).

MALLOY, J. (ed.) (1977) *Authoritarianism and Corporatism in Latin America* (University of Pittsburgh).

MARSHALL, T. H. (1964) *Class, Citizenship and Social Development* (Garden City, N. Y.: Doubleday).

MARTIN, R. (1977) *A Sociology of Power* (London: Routledge and Kegan Paul).

MAYER, A. C. (1966) 'The Significance of Quasi-Groups in the Study of Complex Societies' in Banton, M. (ed.) pp. 97–122.

MAZRUI, A. (1976) 'Soldiers as Traditionalisers: Military Rule and the Re-Africanisation of Africa', *World Politics* 28, pp. 246–272.

McLENNAN, G. (1984). 'The Contours of British Politics: Representative Democracy and Social Class' in McLennan, G., Held, D., and Hall, S. (eds) pp. 241–273.

McMULLAN, M. (1961) 'A Theory of Corruption' *Sociological Review* 9, pp. 181–201.

MEDARD, J.-F. (1982) 'The Underdeveloped State in Tropical Africa: Political Clientelism or neo-Patrimonialism?' in Clapham, C. (ed.) pp. 162–192.

MERTON, R. (1968) *Social Theory and Social Structure* (New York: The Free Press).

MEYERSON M. and BANFIELD, E.C. (eds) (1969) 'A Machine at Work' in Banfield, E. C. (ed.) pp. 169–179.

MIDGLEY, J. (1986) *Community Participation, Social Development and the State* (London: Methuen).

MILIBAND, R. (1969) *The State in Capitalist Society* (London: Weidenfeld and Nicolson).

MILIBAND, R. PANITCH, L. and SAVILLE, J. (eds) (1987) *The Socialist Register* (London: Merlin Press).

MONTGOMERY, J. D. (1972) 'The Bureaucracy as a Modernising Elite: the Possibility of Reform' in Bhalerao, C. N. (ed.) pp. 431–441.

MOORE, B. (1973) *Social Origins of Dictatorship and Democracy* (Harmondsworth: Penguin).

MORICE, A. (1987) 'Guinée 1985: Etat, Corruption et Trafics', *Les Temps Modernes*, pp. 108–136.

MORSE, R. M. (1964) 'The Heritage of Latin America' in Hartz, L. (ed.) pp. 123–177.

MYRDAL, G. (1968) *Asian Drama: An Inquiry into the Poverty of Nations* (Harmondsworth: Penguin).

NETTL, J. P. (1967) *Political Mobilisation* (London: Faber and Faber).

NEWBURY, M. C. (1984) 'Dead and Buried or Just Underground? The Privatisation of the State in Zaire', *Canadian Journal of African Studies* 18/1, pp. 112–114.

NYE, J. S. (1978) 'Corruption and Political Development: A Cost-Benefit Analysis' in Heidenheimer, A. J. (ed.) pp. 564–578.

OLOWU, D. (1985) 'Bureaucratic Corruption and Political Accountability in Nigeria: an Assessment of Recent Developments', *International Review of Administrative Sciences* 51/1, pp. 7–12.

ONOGE, O. F. (1982) 'Corruption in Development' – Keynote Address to Nigerian Anthropological and Sociological Association Annual Conference, Ahmadu Bello University, Zaria, Nigeria.

ØSTERGAARD, C. S. (1983) 'Political Corruption and Local Administrative Elites in the Peoples' Republic of China – Paper given at the workshop on Comparative Political Corruption, ECPR, Freiburg, 20–25 March.

ØSTERGAARD, C. S. (1986) 'Explaining China's Recent Political Corruption', *Corruption and Reform* 1, pp. 209–233.

PALMIER, L. (1975) 'Corruption In India', *New Society* 5 June, pp. 577–579.

PALMIER, L. (1983) 'Bureaucratic Corruption and its Remedies' in Clarke, M. (ed.) pp. 207–219.

PERKIN, H. (1969) *The Origins of Modern English Society 1780–1880* (London: Routledge and Kegan Paul).

PERROW, C. (1972) *Complex Organisations; A Critical Essay* (Glenview, Illinois: Scott, Foresman and Company).

PETERS, B. G. (1978) *The Politics of Bureaucracy: A Comparative Perspective* (London: Longman).

PINTO-DUSCHINSKY, M. (1977) 'Corruption in Britain', *Political Studies* 25/2, pp. 274–284.

PITT-RIVERS, J. A. (1954) *People of the Sierra* (New York: Criterion Books).

PLUMB, J. H. (1966) *England in the Eighteenth Century 1714–1815* (Harmondsworth: Penguin).

POTTER, J. M., DIAZ, M, N., and FOSTER, G. M. (1967) *Peasant Society: A Reader* (Boston: Little, Brown).

POWELL, J. D. (1970) 'Peasant Society and Clientelist Politics', *American Political Science Review* 64, pp. 411–25.

RANDALL, V. and THEOBALD, R. (1985) *Political Change and Underdevelopment* (London: Macmillan).

REILLY, R. (1979) *William Pitt the Younger* (New York: Putnams).

REILLY, W. (1979) *Training Administrators for Development* (London: William Heinemann).

RETTIE, J. (1982) 'Where Corruption is Used as a Means of Political Control,' *Guardian Weekly*, 24 October, p. 8.

RICHARDS, P. G. (1963) *Patronage in British Government* (London: Allen and Unwin).

RIDDELL, P. (1985) *The Thatcher Government* (Oxford: Basil Blackwell).

RIDING, A. (1987) *Mexico: Inside the Volcano* (London: I. B. Tauris).

RIGGS, F. W. (1971) 'Bureaucrats and Political Development: a Paradoxical View' in LaPalombara, J. (ed.) pp. 120–167.

RILEY, S. (1983) ' "The Land of Waving Palms": Political Economy, Corruption Inquiries and Politics in Sierra Leone' in Clarke, M. (ed.) pp. 190–204.

RITTER, A. (1975) *The Economic Development of Revolutionary Cuba* (London: Praeger).

ROCHA, J. (1988) 'Life Remains in Limbo for Poor Brazilians', *Guardian Weekly* 10 July, p. 10.

ROETT, R. (1972) *Brazil: Politics in a Patrimonial Society* (New York: Praeger).

ROGOW, A. A. and LASSWELL, H. D. (1963) *Power, Corruption and Rectitude* (Englewood Cliffs, N. J.: Prentice-Hall).

ROSE-ACKERMAN, S. (1978) *Corruption: A Study in Political Economy* (London: Academic Press).

ROTH, G. (1968) 'Personal Rulership, Patrimonialism and Empire-Building in the New States', *World Politics* 20, pp. 194–206.

RUDÉ, G. (1972) *Europe in the Eighteenth Century: Aristocracy and Bourgeois Challenge* (London: Weidenfeld and Nicolson).

RUDOLPH, L. I. and RUDOLPH, S. H. (1979) 'Authority and Power in Bureaucratic and Patrimonial Administration', *World Politics* 31/1, pp. 195–227.

SAGE, C. (1988) 'Coca, Cocaine and the Subterranean "Boom": the Consequences for Development in Bolivia' in Gauhar, A. (ed.) pp. 150–160.

SAIT, E. M. (1930) 'Machine, Political', *Encyclopaedia of the Social Sciences* vol. ix, pp. 657–661.

SALAMAN, G. and THOMPSON, K. (eds) (1980) *Control and Ideology in Organisations* (Milton Keynes: Open University Press).

SAMPSON, A. (1962) *Anatomy of Britain* (London: Hodder and Stoughton).

SAMPSON, A. (1983) *The Changing Anatomy of Britain* (London: Coronet).

SANDBROOK, R. (1986) *The Politics of Africa's Economic Stagnation* (Cambridge: Cambridge University Press).

SARFATTI, M. (1966) *Spanish Bureaucratic Patrimonialism in Latin America* (Berkeley: University of California Press).

SASSOON, D. (1986) 'Italian Freemasonry: the Propaganda 2 Lodge', *Corruption and Reform* 1/1, pp. 63–68.

SCHMITTER, P. D. (1973) 'The "Portugalisation" of Brazil' in Stepan, A. (ed.) pp. 179–232.

SCHRAM, S. R. (ed.) (1973) *Authority, Participation and Cultural Change in China* (London: Cambridge University Press).

SCHWARTZ, C. A. (1979) 'Corruption and Political Development in the USSR', *Comparative Politics* 11, pp. 425–442.

SCOTT, J. C. (1969) 'Corruption, Machine Politics and Political Change', *American Political Science Review* 63/4, pp. 1142–1159.

SCOTT, J. C. (1972) *Comparative Political Corruption* (Englewood Cliffs, N. J.: Prentice Hall).

SEIBEL, M. (1981) 'Mexico's Sudden Rich Men Come Under Scrutiny', *Guardian*, 27 August, p. 7.

SENTURIA, J. J. (1931) 'Corruption, Political', *Encyclopaedia of the Social Sciences* vol. IV, pp. 448–452.

SHACKLETON, J. R. (1986) 'Privatising the Third World', *Banca Nazionale del Lavoro Quarterly Review* 159, pp. 430–439.

SHANIN, T. (ed.) (1971) *Peasants and Peasant Societies* (Harmondsworth: Penguin).

SHERIFF, P. (1976) 'Sociology of Public Bureaucracies 1965–1975', *Current Sociology* 24/2.

SILLS, D. (ed.) (1968) *International Encyclopaedia of the Social Sciences* (New York: Macmillan) 18 vols.

SISSONS, M. and FRENCH, P. (eds) (1964) *Age of Austerity 1945–1951* (Harmondsworth: Penguin).

SKIDMORE, T. E. (1973) 'Politics and Economic Policy-making in Authoritarian Brazil 1937–71' in Stepan, A. (ed.) pp. 3–46.

SMITH, A. D. (1973) *The Concept of Social Change* (London: Routledge and Kegan Paul).

SMITH, D. (1988) 'Weapon Systems That Fail the Ultimate Test', *Guardian Weekly*, 7 August, p. 17.

SMITH, H. (1988) *The Power Game: How Washington Works* (New York: Random House).

SPEAR, P. (1973) *A History of India*, vol. 2 (Harmondsworth: Penguin).

SPEED, J. G. (1978) 'The Purchase of Votes in New York City' in Heidenheimer, A. J. (ed.) pp. 422–426.

SPRINGBORG, R. (1979) 'Patrimonialism and Policy-making in Egypt: Nasser and Sadat and the Tenure Policy for Reclaimed Lands', *Middle Eastern Studies* 15/1, pp. 49–69.

STALKER, J. (1988) *Stalker* (Harmondsworth: Penguin).

STEFFENS, L. (1904) *The Shame of the Cities* (New York: McClure Phillips and Co.).

STEPAN, A. (ed.) (1973) *Authoritarian Brazil* (New Haven: Yale University Press).

STIEFEL, M. and WERTHEIM, W. F. (1983) *Production, Equality and Participation in Rural China* (London: Zed Press).

STONE, L. (1973) *The Causes of the English Revolution 1529–1642* (London: Routledge and Kegan Paul).

STONE, L. (1982) *Family, Sex and Marriage in England 1500–1800* (Harmondsworth: Penguin).

SUTHERLAND, G. (ed.) (1972) *Studies in the Growth of Nineteenth Century Government* (London: Routledge and Kegan Paul).

SWART, K. W. (1978) 'The Sale of Public Offices' in Heidenheimer, A. J. (ed.) pp. 82–90.

SZEFTEL, M. (1982) 'Political Graft and the Spoils System in Zambia – the State as a Resource in Itself', *Review of African Political Economy* 24, pp. 4–21.

THEOBALD, R. (1983) 'The Decline of Patron-Client Relations in Developed Societies', *Archives Européennes de Sociologie* 24, pp. 136–147.

TILLY, C. (ed.) (1975) *The Formation of Nation States in Europe* (Princeton: Princeton University Press).

TILMAN, R. O. (1968) 'Emergence of Black-Market Bureaucracy: Administration, Development and Corruption in the New States', *Public Administration Review* 28, pp. 437–443.

TODARO, M. P. (1977) *Economics for a Developing World* (London: Longman).

TOINET, M.-F. and GLENN, I. (1982) 'Clientelism and Corruption in the "Open" Society: The Case of the United States' in Clapham, C. (ed.) pp. 193–213.

URRY, J. and WAKEFORD, J. (eds) (1973) *Power in Britain* (London: Heinemann Educational Books).

VANDIVIER, K. (1978) 'Why Should My Conscience Bother Me?' in Ermann, M. D. and Lundman R. (eds) pp. 80–100.

VANHECKE, C. (1988) 'Brazil in Crisis – Yet Again', *Guardian Weekly*, 6 November.

VENKATAPPIAH, B. (1968) 'Office, Misuse of' in Sills, D. (ed.) vol. II, pp. 272–276.

WACHTEL, H. M. (1987) *The Politics of International Money* (Amsterdam: Transnational Institute).

WALKER, M. (1986) 'Party Patronage and Party Corruption', *Guardian Weekly*, 2 March, p. 9.

WALLERSTEIN, I. (1971) 'The Range of Choice: Constraints on the Policies of Governments of Contemporary African Independent States' in Lofchie, M. F. (ed.) pp. 19–37.

WARD, R. E. and RUSTOW, D. (1964) *Political Modernisation in Japan and Turkey* (Princeton: Princeton University Press).

WASHINGTON LOBBY (1982) (Washington D. C.: Congressional Quarterly Inc).

WATERBURY, J. (1976) 'Corruption, Political Stability and Development:

Comparative Evidence from Egypt and Morocco', *Government and Opposition* II, pp. 426–445.

WEBER, M. (1968) *Economy and Society* (New York: Bedminster Press) 3 vols.

WEINGROD, A. (1968) 'Patrons, Patronage and Political Parties', *Comparative Studies in Society and History* 10, pp. 377–400.

WERLIN, H. H. (1972) 'The Roots of Corruption – the Ghanaian Enquiry', *The Journal of Modern African Studies* 10/2, pp. 247–266.

WHITAKER, R. (1987) 'Neo-Conservatism and the State' in Miliband, R., Panitch, L. and Saville, J. (eds) pp. 1–31.

WILLAME, J.-C. (1972) *Patrimonialism and Political Change in the Congo* (Stanford: Stanford University Press).

WILLIAMS, R. (1987) *Political Corruption in Africa* (Aldershot: Gower Publishing Company).

WILSON, J. Q. (1978) 'Corruption: the Shame of the Cities' in Heidenheimer, A. J. (ed.) pp. 298–306.

WOLF, E. (1966) *Peasants* (Englewood Cliffs: Prentice-Hall).

WOLF-PHILLIPS, L. (1987) 'Why "Third World"', *Third World Quarterly* 9/4, pp. 1311–1328.

WORLD DEVELOPMENT REPORT (1983) (London: Oxford University Press).

WORLD DEVELOPMENT REPORT (1986) (London: Oxford University Press).

WORLD DEVELOPMENT REPORT (1987) (London: Oxford University Press).

WRAITH, R. and SIMPKINS, E. (1963) *Corruption in Developing Countries* (London: Allen and Unwin).

ZOLBERG, A. (1966) *Creating Political Order: The Party-States of West Africa* (Chicago: Chicago University Press).

Index